STUDY GUIDE
TO ACCOMPANY

The Power of Logic

SECOND EDITION

C. Stephen Layman

Keith Coleman
Johnson County Community College

Richard Botkin
University of Kansas

Boston   Burr Ridge, IL   Dubuque, IA   Madison, WI   New York
San Francisco   St. Louis   Bangkok   Bogotá   Caracas   Kuala Lumpur
Lisbon   London   Madrid   Mexico City   Milan   Montreal   New Delhi
Santiago   Seoul   Singapore   Sydney   Taipei   Toronto

McGraw-Hill Higher Education

*A Division of The **McGraw-Hill** Companies*

1 2 3 4 5 6 7 8 9 0 BKM/BKM 0 9 8 7 6 5 4 3 2 1

International Standard Book Number (ISBN): 0-7674-2036-5

www.mhhe.com

CONTENTS

PREFACE

Welcome to your study of logic! This Study Guide to accompany C. Stephen Layman's *The Power of Logic* will provide you with additional resources to aid you in your study of logic. Specifically, each chapter of the Study Guide is composed of four main parts: a chapter summary, a discussion of key concepts, an answers-to-exercises section, and some topics for further consideration.

This Study Guide is not designed to replace *The Power of Logic,* and you should not get into the habit of reading it instead of the text. You should attend class regularly as well as read the text and consult the Study Guide. Learning logic, particularly formal logic, requires diligence and a careful attention to details. Students who fail to master the subject typically do not take full advantage of the resources available to them.

The following is a brief synopsis of the four main sections within each chapter of the Study Guide.

CHAPTER HIGHLIGHTS

This section gives a brief overview of the corresponding chapter in *The Power of Logic.* The main points of the text are presented so that you can focus squarely on the most important material.

DISCUSSION OF KEY CONCEPTS

This section contains a subsection corresponding to each section within a chapter of *The Power of Logic.* Each subsection contains a part A that presents important reminders concerning points you may have trouble with, a part B that details answers to commonly asked questions, and a part C that provides additional exercises. Because students often benefit from having ideas explained to them in more than one way, this section of the guide may also present some material already covered in the text. However, because it would serve no purpose to re-create the text in the Study Guide, rehashes of text material are kept to a minimum.

ANSWERS TO EXERCISES

This section is divided into two subsections. The first subsection, *Answers to Selected Exercises in the Text,* contains explanations of answers given in *The Power of Logic* for cases in which elaboration might be helpful. The second subsection, *Answers to Supplemental Exercises,* gives answers to the exercises in this Study Guide.

FOR FURTHER CONSIDERATION

This section elaborates on issues raised in the text and provides additional information that may be of interest to the curious student.

CHAPTER 1

Basic Concepts

*In this chapter, you get an idea of what logic is and are introduced
to the basic terminology with which every logic student needs to be
familiar. This chapter also introduces the notion of an argument
form and explores the relation between the validity and invalidity
of arguments and the validity and invalidity of argument forms.
It also presents the names of seven famous argument forms within
a discussion of conditionals, negations, and disjunctions.*

CHAPTER HIGHLIGHTS

Logic is the study of the methods involved in the evaluation of arguments. Logicians want to know when it is true that the premises of an argument provide adequate justification or warrant accepting the argument's conclusion. An **argument** is a series of statements consisting of premises and a conclusion. The **premises** of an argument are the statements given in support of a conclusion; the **conclusion** is a statement whose truth is taken to be a consequence of the truth of the premises. A **statement** is a sentence that has a truth value, either true or false. To identify which statements in an argumentative passage are functioning as premises and which are acting as conclusions, find those statements that are not argued for but are assumed to be true within a particular inference and those statements the truth of which is being affirmed on the basis of the truth of other statements. The former will be the premises, and the latter will be the conclusions.

In a **valid** argument, the truth of all the premises ensures the truth of the conclusion. A valid argument can have one or more false premises. An argument with all true premises is not necessarily a valid argument, even if the conclusion is also true. Thus, the question of the truth of the premises is in general distinct from the question of the validity of the argument. Validity, though, preserves truth: Only a true conclusion can be validly derived from true premises. However, validity does not preserve falsehood: From false premises, it is possible to derive true conclusions validly. Thus, from premises all of which are true only a true conclusion can be validly derived, but from premises not all of which are true either a true or a false conclusion can be validly derived. If an argument is not valid, then it is invalid. In an **invalid** argument, it is not necessary that, if all the premises are true, then the conclusion is also true.

A **sound** argument is an argument that both is valid and has premises all of which are true. A sound argument will always have a true conclusion. An **unsound** argument is an argument that is not sound. An argument fails to be sound and is thus unsound whenever it is invalid (with or without true premises) or is valid and has at least one false premise. **Deductive logic** is the branch of logic that deals with tests for validity and invalidity.

An **argument form** is a pattern of reasoning. Arguments that have the same form follow the same pattern of reasoning. Some arguments involve reasoning about categories or kinds of things. Where A, B, and C are categorical terms (i.e., words or expressions that are used to designate a category or kind of thing), the following are four argument forms:

1. All A are B.
   All B are C.
   So, all A are C.

2. All A are B.
   Some C are not B.
   So, some C are not A.

3. All A are B.
   All C are B.
   So, all A are C.

4. All A are B.
   Some B are not C.
   So, some C are not A.

An argument can be generated from any one of these argument forms by uniformly replacing the schematic letters "A," "B," and "C" with actual terms. Any argument that can thus be generated from a particular argument form is said to be a **substitution instance** of the form.

If an argument form is such that there is no way to replace uniformly its contained schematic letters so that all of its premises are true statements and its conclusion is a false statement, then it is a valid argument form. If the schematic letters of an argument form can be replaced uniformly in such a way that the premises are all true statements and the conclusion is a false statement, then it is an invalid argument form. The validity of an argument is determined by form alone; the meaning of the words or expressions used to replace the schematic letters does not fix the validity of the argument.

To show that an argument is invalid, one can find an argument form of which the argument is a substitution instance and then show that the form is invalid by finding a substitution instance in which the premises are all true and the conclusion is false. The original argument can then be judged to be invalid, provided that the logical features of the argument are fully represented in the form identified. The invalidity of an argument form is often demonstrated by finding a counterexample to the form. A **counterexample** to an argument form is an argument that is a substitution instance of the form and has premises that are well-known truths and a conclusion that is a well-known falsehood.

The method of finding a counterexample to an argument form has its limitations. First, the method can only be used to show the invalidity, and not also the validity, of an argument form. Second, we cannot conclude that an argument form is valid just because we are unable to find a counterexample to that argument form. The method simply does not allow us to determine whether a particular argument form is indeed valid or has a counterexample among arguments we have not examined.

Any conclusion regarding the invalidity of an argument based on the invalidity of an argument form of which the argument is a substitution instance must be considered provisional. Every argument, whether valid or invalid, is a substitution instance of at least one invalid argument form. Every valid argument, though, is a substitution instance of at least one valid argument form, and no invalid argument is a substitution instance of any valid argument form. Thus, to show that an argument is invalid, it is not enough to show that it is a substitution instance of an invalid argument form. Rather, to show that the argument is invalid, one must show that the argument is not a substitution instance of any valid argument form. If the argument form to which we are finding a counterexample makes explicit all the logical features of the argument we are evaluating, then the invalidity of that argument form will mean that the argument in question is not a substitution instance of any valid argument form. Therefore, our concluding that an argument is invalid on the basis of the invalidity of its form is a reasonable inference, only provided that we have analyzed the correct argument form. Even though the counterexample method will not always work to show that an argument is invalid, it will always work to show that an argument form is invalid.

Some argument forms are such that their substitution instances are generated from the form by uniformly replacing the schematic letters, not by terms but by whole sentences. Some of these argument forms are so common that logicians have named them. Many of these common argument forms involve conditionals and/or disjunctions, in some cases in combination with negations.

A **conditional** is a statement of the form "If A, then B" (or a statement that is a stylistic variant of that form, such as "Given A, B"; "Assuming that A, B"; "B if A"; "B given that A"; "B assuming that A"; and "A only if B"). Notice that any statement of the form "A only if B" says the same thing as the corresponding statement of the form "If A, then B" but does not in general say the same thing as the corresponding statement of the form "If B, then A." In an if-then statement, the statement within the if-clause is the antecedent of the conditional, and the statement within the then-clause is the consequent of the conditional. When a conditional statement is asserted, neither the antecedent nor the consequent is asserted as a separate claim. The assertion of a conditional involves the making of only one (conditional) claim.

A **negation** is a statement that is the denial of a statement. A negation most often will be expressed in the form "It is not the case that A"; "It is false that A"; "It is not true that A;" or "not A." A **disjunction** is a statement of the form "Either A or B." The statements that occur on either side of the word "or" are called the **disjuncts** of the disjunction. An inclusive disjunction means the same as "Either A or B, or both A and B," while an exclusive disjunction means the same as "Either A or B, but not both A and B." For our purposes, we will always assume, unless otherwise noted, that disjunctions are to be understood in the inclusive sense.

Any argument of the form *modus ponens* has as premises a conditional together with its antecedent and has as a conclusion the consequent of the conditional. Any argument of the form *modus tollens* has as premises a conditional together with the negation of its consequent and has as a conclusion the negation of the antecedent of the conditional. Any argument that is an instance of the **fallacy of denying the antecedent** has as premises a conditional together with the negation of its antecedent and has as a conclusion the negation of the consequent of the conditional. Any argument that is an instance of the **fallacy of affirming the consequent** has as premises a conditional together with its consequent and has as a conclusion the antecedent of the conditional. Any argument of the form **hypothetical syllogism** has as premises two conditionals, the antecedent of the second conditional being the consequent of the first conditional, and has as a conclusion the conditional whose antecedent is the antecedent of the first conditional and whose consequent is the consequent of the second conditional. Any argument of the form **disjunctive syllo-gism** has as premises a disjunction together with the negation of its left disjunct and has as a conclusion the right disjunct. Any argument of the form **constructive dilemma** has as premises a disjunction together with two conditionals, the ante-cedent of one conditional being one of the disjuncts and the antecedent of the other conditional being the other disjunct, and has as a conclusion a disjunction whose disjuncts are the consequents of the two conditionals. Any argument of the form *modus ponens, modus tollens,* hypothetical syllogism, disjunctive syllogism, or con-structive dilemma is a valid argument. The fallacy of denying the antecedent and the fallacy of affirming the consequent are two invalid argument forms, even though the invalidity of some arguments that have these forms is not immediately obvious.

The valid and invalid argument forms discussed above can be represented in the following manner:

Modus ponens (valid)	*Modus tollens* (valid)	Hypothetical syllogism (valid)
If A, then B.	If A, then B.	If A, then B.
A.	Not B.	If B, then C.
So, B.	So, not A.	So, if A, then C.

Disjunctive syllogism (valid)	Constructive dilemma (valid)
Either A or B.	Either A or B.
Not A.	If A, then C.
So, B.	If B, then D.
	So, either C or D.

Fallacy of denying the antecedent (invalid)	Fallacy of affirming the consequent (invalid)
If A, then B.	If A, then B.
Not A.	B.
So, not B.	So, A.

A **strong** argument is invalid but has this feature: It is probable that if its premises are (or were) true, then its conclusion is (or would be) true. The strength of an argument, unlike the validity of an argument, is a matter of degree. Some argu-ments are slightly strong, some are moderately strong, and some are very strong. A **weak** argument has this feature: It is not probable that if its premises are (or were) true, then its conclusion is (or would be) true. Arguments from authority and argu-ments from analogy are two kinds of arguments that are sometimes strong.

Inductive logic is the branch of logic that deals with tests for the strength and weakness of arguments. A **cogent** argument is any argument that both is strong and has premises all of which are true. Unlike a sound argument, a cogent argument can have a false conclusion. An **uncogent** argument is an argument that is weak (with or without true premises) or is strong and has at least one false premise.

Given these definitions, all arguments are either sound or unsound, but no sound argument is cogent, for sound arguments are valid. Any valid argument can be sound or unsound, depending on the truth of its premises, but it can be neither cogent nor uncogent. All invalid arguments are either strong or weak and are thus either cogent or uncogent. All invalid arguments, and hence all strong and weak arguments, and thus all cogent and uncogent arguments, are unsound, since only valid arguments can be sound. A strong argument is uncogent only if it has a false premise, while a weak argument is always uncogent regardless of the truth or falsity of its premises.

Deductive and inductive logic differ fundamentally not in terms of the different kinds of arguments with which they deal but rather in terms of the different standards of argument evaluation with which they are concerned.

A premise or a conclusion, as is the case for any statement, is always either true or false but is never valid, invalid, sound, unsound, strong, weak, cogent, or uncogent. On the other hand, an argument is always valid, invalid, sound, unsound, strong, weak, cogent, or uncogent but is never either true or false.

DISCUSSION OF KEY CONCEPTS

I. Validity and Soundness

A. *Helpful Reminders*

1. Remember just what validity concerns. The validity of an argument depends on a relationship that holds between premises and conclusion. That relationship obtains or fails to obtain depending on not just the actual truth values of premises and conclusion but on all the possible truth values of premises and conclusion. So don't think that a valid—and thus a sound—argument is merely any argument with all true premises and a true conclusion. Both valid and invalid arguments can have true premises and a true conclusion. In general, knowing the actual truth values of an argument's premises and conclusion does not tell you anything about the argument's validity. *The only exception to this general rule is when you happen to know that the premises of a particular argument are all true and its conclusion is false.* In this case, you know that the argument is invalid, for this combination of true premises and false conclusion is not possible in a valid argument. For the most part, you should neglect the actual truth values of the premises and conclusion and concentrate more on their possible truth values in considering whether an argument is valid. Whether the premises are in reality true is a matter of principal concern for those who deal with the subject matter of the argument. Logicians typically are more concerned with the logical nature of an argument's statements than with what those statements are about, since validity and invalidity depend only on the former.

2. Except for the case in which you know that an argument is both valid and has either all true premises or a false conclusion, knowing the validity or invalidity of an argument does not tell you anything about the actual truth values of either premises or conclusion. A valid argument can have at least one false premise and a false conclusion, at least one false premise and a true conclusion, or all true premises and a true conclusion. The only case that is ruled out by an argument's validity is the case in which the premises are all true and the conclusion is false. (So, if you know that an argument is valid and has all true premises, you can infer that its conclusion is true; and if you know that an argument is valid and has a false conclusion, you can infer

that at least one of its premises is false.) In contrast, an invalid argument can have any combination of true and/or false premises with or without a true conclusion. An argument's invalidity does not rule out any possible combination of true or false premises and conclusion.

3. Only a sound argument can be said to have established its conclusion decisively. A valid argument with a false premise can have a conclusion that is either true or false. (An invalid argument, with or without a false premise, can have a conclusion that is either true or false.) Thus, validity guarantees only that, if all of the premises should happen to be true, then its conclusion would have to be true. However, when not all of the premises of an argument are true, we do not know for sure that its conclusion is true, even when we know the argument is valid. We can be assured that the conclusion is true only if the argument is sound. One consequence of this is that whenever someone wishes to reject the inevitability of an argument's conclusion, he or she must reject the soundness of the argument by showing either that the argument is invalid or that not all of its premises are in fact true. Consider the following argument.

If God exists, then there is no evil in the world. However, there is evil in the world. Thus, God does not exist.

Both an atheist and a theist can recognize that this argument is valid without being thus committed to the truth or falsity of the conclusion. A theist, though, would have inconsistent beliefs if he or she were to acknowledge both the validity of the argument and the truth of all its premises and yet deny the truth of its conclusion. The theist must therefore defend the uncertainty of the conclusion by arguing that the argument either is invalid or has a false premise. (Since the argument is technically valid, most theists will launch an attack against the truth of one of the premises, most likely the first premise.) In so doing, the theist in effect argues that the argument is unsound.

B. Commonly Asked Questions

1. If the truth of all the premises and the conclusion does not determine an argument's validity, then why do we define validity by making reference to the truth of an argument's premises and its conclusion?

The validity of an argument is independent of the factual truth of the premises and conclusion. The actual truth value of premises and conclusion is not what really determines validity. What does determine validity is the relationship between the possible truth values of the premises and the conclusion. In a valid argument, the combination of all true premises and a false conclusion is not possible. In a valid argument, the combination of all true premises and a false conclusion in not possible. The definition of validity thus makes essential reference to this relationship between possible truth values and not to the actual truth or falsity of premises and conclusions.

2. Why make the distinction between validity and soundness?

Keeping this distinction in mind helps us to remember that any argument we give must meet two conditions to establish its conclusion decisively. The argument must provide good support for its conclusion in the sense that, if its premises should all be true, its conclusion would also have to be true. In order for such support to provide adequate justification for saying that the conclusion is true, the argument's premises must all be true; hence the distinction between validity and soundness. Arguments that satisfy the first condition are valid, while arguments that satisfy both conditions are sound. Furthermore, when an argument fails to meet one of the conditions necessary for a conclusive argument, we can easily identify the mistake if we recognize the distinction between validity and soundness. Any argument that fails the first condition is invalid and unsound, and any argument that fails only the second condition is valid but unsound.

C. Exercises

(a) For each of the following, indicate whether it is a sentence but not a statement, both a sentence and a statement, or neither a sentence nor a statement.

1. Oh, what a beautiful morning!
2. Let's take a walk.
3. Oops!
4. Every sentence is either true or false.
5. I want to buy a sloop.
6. Abortion is immoral.
7. Abortion is not immoral.
8. Blood is thicker than water.
9. All species are monophyletic groups, but not all monophyletic groups are species.
10. This sentence is false.

(b) Indicate whether the following statements regarding truth, validity, and soundness are true or false. In each case, justify your answer.

1. If the conclusion of an argument is true, then the argument must be sound.
2. If all the premises of an argument are true, then it must be valid.
3. An argument is valid if its premises and conclusion are all true.
4. A sound argument both is valid and has all true premises.
5. A valid argument can have a false conclusion.
6. A sound argument can have a false premise.
7. If the premises of an invalid argument are all true, then its conclusion must be false.
8. A valid argument with a false premise can have a true conclusion.
9. A valid argument can have all true premises and a false conclusion.
10. A valid argument can have all false premises and a false conclusion.
11. If not all of the premises of a valid argument are true, then its conclusion must be false.
12. If a valid argument has a conclusion that is false, then at least one of its premises must also be false.
13. An argument is valid if it is impossible for all its premises to be false and its conclusion to be true.
14. All valid arguments are sound arguments.
15. All sound arguments are valid arguments.

II. Forms and Counterexamples

A. *Helpful Reminders*

1. Chapter 1 of *The Power of Logic* introduces you to argument forms and the relation between the validity of arguments and the validity of argument forms. Do not be alarmed if you are not completely clear on all the ideas presented in this chapter. The various argument forms and the reasons they are valid or invalid will be covered in more detail in the subsequent chapters on formal logic. (The goal of formal logic is to appraise arguments on the basis of their form, and because formal techniques have worked so successfully to determine validity and invalidity, formal logic is now regarded as virtually the same as deductive logic.) The primary virtue of discussing argument forms in an introductory chapter is that it gives you some idea of the patterns arguments often follow and helps you discern arguments from nonarguments, which is something you will be asked to do in Chapter 2.

2. Although the nature of the relationship between the validity/invalidity of arguments and the validity/invalidity of argument forms will become clearer when we discuss categorical and propositional arguments in greater detail, some elaboration at this time may be helpful. The only reliable fundamental principle that always holds to connect the validity of argument forms with the validity of arguments is the following: *All substitution instances of valid argument forms are valid arguments.* (There is no analogous principle in the case of invalid argument forms, for some substitution instances of invalid argument forms are invalid arguments, while others are valid arguments.) So, given that principle, how do we determine whether a certain argument form is valid or invalid and then use our knowledge of valid and invalid argument forms to assess whether any particular argument is valid? Since any argument form potentially has an infinite number of arguments that are its substitution instances, we cannot determine whether an argument form is valid simply by examining all of its substitution instances. Instead, what we try to do is determine whether there can be substitution instances of the form that have all true premises and a false conclusion. If there can be no such substitution instances, then it will be impossible for any argument of the form to have all true premises and a false conclusion, which means that all substitution instances of the form are valid arguments, and the form is thus a valid argument form. The determination of an argument form's invalidity is a simpler matter. For a given argument form, as long as we can find at least one invalid substitution instance of that argument form, we know that the argument form is invalid. Often, we find a substitution instance of the form that is an argument having all true premises and a false conclusion, such a substitution instance being a counterexample to the form. We know that such an argument is invalid directly from the definition of validity. (Since the argument has all true premises and a false conclusion, it is possible for all of its premises to be true when its conclusion is false and is thus an invalid argument.)

3. Once we know the valid and invalid argument forms, we can use this information to assess the validity or invalidity of a given argument. It is a simple matter in the case of a valid argument, for all we have to do is find at least one valid argument form of which the argument is a substitution instance. In the case of an invalid argument, the situation is a bit trickier (unless, of course, the argument has all true premises and a false conclusion). An argument, in general, can be a substitution instance of many different argument forms. In order to conclude that an argument is

invalid, we must be sure that it is not a substitution instance of any valid argument form. We can be confident that an argument is not a substitution instance of any valid argument form only if a particular argument form of which the argument is a substitution instance is an invalid argument form. This particular argument form makes explicit all of the logical structure of the argument. The problem with merely using any one of the argument forms of which an argument is a substitution instance in order to determine the argument's invalidity is that the argument may have some logical structure that is not made explicit by the argument form considered. This hidden logical structure could make the argument valid. Only by determining that the precise form of an argument is invalid will we always know that the argument is invalid, because only then will we always know that the argument does not have any logical structure, which could make it valid.

B. Commonly Asked Questions

1. What exactly is an argument form?

Arguments contain words or expressions the meaning of which do not fix the validity of arguments. These words or expressions are the nonlogical words of an argument. The nonlogical words in a statement determine the subject matter of the statement but do not in virtue of their meanings determine the inferential relations between the statement and other statements. Arguments often contain words or expressions the meanings of which *do* fix the validity of arguments. These words or expressions are the logical words of an argument. The logical words in a statement do not determine the subject matter of the statement but do in virtue of their meanings determine the inferential relations between the statement and other statements. In an attempt to make explicit the logical form of an argument, a logician will often use special symbols (such as letters) that are devoid of any particular meaning to represent the nonlogical words of an argument. When all the nonlogical words of an argument have been replaced by these symbols, the result is an argument form. Which expressions are being regarded as logical and which as nonlogical will depend on what type of arguments one is attempting to analyze. Arguments that involve reasoning about classes or kinds (the concern of categorical and predicate logic) contain categorical terms that are understood to be nonlogical. Arguments that involve reasoning about the relations among propositions or sentences (the concern of statement logic) contain simple statements that are understood to be nonlogical. Thus, the argument forms corresponding to categorical arguments are different from the argument forms corresponding to propositional arguments. All the valid and invalid argument forms given special names as discussed in Chapter 1 of *The Power of Logic* are argument forms of propositional arguments.

2. What does it mean to say that an argument form is valid?

An argument form is valid if and only if it has no substitution instances with all true premises and a false conclusion. All substitution instances of a valid argument form will also be valid arguments. In contrast, an argument form is invalid if and only if it has a substitution instance with all true premises and a false conclusion. Not all substitution instances of an invalid argument form are invalid arguments; most will be invalid, but some will be valid.

3. Why study the counterexample method?

The counterexample method, despite its limitations, is a powerful practical way of demonstrating to someone that an argument's logic is at least suspect. People often try to refute someone's argument by responding, "That's just like arguing that . . ." If the argument that is produced is obviously invalid and has the same form as that of the original, then this strategy of refutation is often successful in assessing the validity of someone's argument. Unfortunately, there is no mechanical procedure you can follow that will always enable you to construct a counterexample to a given argument form. When asked to find a counterexample, start by finding substitutions that will make the conclusion false, and then use those substitutions, together with others, to make all the premises true. However, sometimes ingenuity and insight are required in order to construct a counterexample.

C. Exercises

(a) For each of the following statements, indicate whether it is true or false.

1. All substitution instances of valid argument forms are valid arguments.
2. An argument form is valid if all of its substitution instances are valid.
3. All substitution instances of invalid argument forms are invalid arguments.
4. Any argument having the same form as an invalid argument is an invalid argument.
5. Any argument having the same form as a valid argument is a valid argument.

(b) Construct counterexamples to show that each of the following arguments is flawed.

1. All people who love music are artists. No house painter is a person who loves music. Hence, no house painter is an artist.
2. If beer is dangerous, then so is wine. Beer is not dangerous. Therefore, wine is not dangerous either.
3. Some mammals are flying animals. All flying animals are winged animals. Thus, some winged animals are not mammals.
4. One should smoke. The longer you smoke, the longer you live.
5. All preschool teachers are people who help raise children. Some people who help raise children are not kind. So, some preschool teachers are not kind.

(c) Rewrite each of the following conditionals in standard "If A, then B" form.

1. It will snow only if it turns colder.
2. Given that Mark will attend the class, he is enrolled in the course.
3. Oxygen is present if there is a fire in the room.
4. I will go assuming that Larry stays home.
5. Susan will stay home given that there is no class tomorrow.
6. You pass the course only if you pass the final.
7. We choose a different route if the road is closed ahead.
8. Harry will buy a new car assuming that he has enough money.
9. Given that you buy the book, you own it.
10. We live here only if we pay the rent each month.

III. Some Famous Forms

A. Helpful Reminders

1. The ability to recognize an argument quickly as a substitution instance of one of the famous forms requires one to know the seven famous forms discussed in this chapter. Thus, you need to memorize them. In addition, the valid forms of argument will be introduced as inference rules in chapter 8, so the time spent memorizing them now will be time well spent.

2. Note the differences between *modus ponens, modus tollens,* the fallacy of affirming the consequent, and the fallacy of denying the antecedent. These forms are often confused with one another. Note especially the difference between *modus ponens* and the fallacy of affirming the consequent, and the difference between *modus tollens* and the fallacy of denying the antecedent.

B. Commonly Asked Questions

1. Why are the so-called "famous forms" of valid and invalid arguments famous?

The argument forms recognized as famous forms are frequently occurring patterns of argumentation. Many actual arguments are explicitly in one of these forms, can be rewritten so as to be explicitly in one of these forms, or can be resolved into a series of arguments, each of which is an instance, explicitly or implicitly, of these forms. The names of many of these forms are standard and stem from the descriptions given these forms by logicians in the Middle Ages.

2. Why know the famous forms?

If you know the famous forms and know which are valid and which are invalid, then you can easily recognize a valid argument when you are presented with a substitution instance of a valid form. When presented with a substitution instance of an invalid form, you can at least be immediately skeptical, provided you know your valid and invalid forms. This ability is of practical significance, since many real-world arguments display these famous forms.

3. Are all substitution instances of the fallacies of affirming the consequent and denying the antecedent fallacies and thus invalid arguments?

Unlike the case with valid argument forms, not all substitution instances of an invalid argument form are invalid arguments. Most such substitution instances will be invalid arguments, but it is always possible to construct an odd substitution instance of an invalid form that is nonetheless a valid argument. So not all instances of the two invalid argument forms called fallacies are fallacious (in the sense of invalid) arguments. (By the way, the notion of fallacy that will be discussed in Chapter 4 is a notion distinct from the notion of an invalid instance of one of these two famous invalid argument forms.)

C. Exercises

Name the form of each of the following arguments and indicate whether the argument is valid or invalid. (If you can't determine the form by inspection, then follow the procedure of assigning capital letters to each of the simple statements, as outlined in section 1.3 of *The Power of Logic.*)

1. If the weather is hot, then the air pressure is high. The air pressure is high. Hence, the weather is hot.
2. If it is compatible with God's goodness that I sometimes be deceived, then it is also compatible with God's goodness that I always be deceived. If it is compatible with God's goodness that I always be deceived, then no knowledge is possible. So, if it is compatible with God's goodness that I sometimes be deceived, then no knowledge is possible.
3. If Jim laughed, then Susan wept. Susan did not weep. Thus, Jim did not laugh.
4. If it turns colder, then it will snow. It will snow. Thus, it does turn colder.
5. If it is raining outside, then the sidewalks are wet. It is not raining outside. So, the sidewalks are not wet.
6. If Tom drives a Ford, then he drives an automobile. Tom does not drive a Ford. So, Tom does not drive an automobile.
7. Either a politician holds steadfastly to his beliefs regardless of the evidence, or he changes his beliefs according to the evidence. If a politician holds steadfastly to his beliefs regardless of the evidence, then he is charged with having a closed mind. If a politician changes his beliefs according to the evidence, then he is charged with being inconsistent. Therefore, a politician is charged either with having a closed mind or with being inconsistent.
8. Either what happened was an accident, or it was a case of murder. What happened was not an accident. So, what happened was a case of murder.
9. If something can be viewed as in motion from one vantage point and as motionless from another vantage point, then all motion is relative. Something can be viewed as in motion from one vantage point and as motionless from another vantage point. Thus, all motion is relative.
10. If the moon is a perfect sphere, then it is nearly always invisible. The moon is not nearly always invisible. Therefore, the moon is not a perfect sphere.
11. If Camus is right, then there is no fate that cannot be surmounted with scorn. Camus is right. Hence, there is no fate that cannot be surmounted with scorn.
12. If a meteorite hit Earth 65 million years ago, then traces of iridium can be found in the soil. Traces of iridium can be found in the soil. Thus, we can conclude that a meteorite hit Earth 65 million years ago.
13. The hurricane in the Gulf will swerve either to the left or to the right. If the hurricane in the Gulf swerves to the left, then it will hit Louisiana. If the hurricane in the Gulf swerves to the right, then it will hit Florida. It follows that the hurricane in the Gulf will hit either Louisiana or Florida.
14. The convention will be held in either New York or San Francisco. The convention will not be held in New York. Hence, the convention will be held in San Francisco.
15. If Susan owns a dog, then she has a pet. Susan does not own a dog. Therefore, Susan does not have a pet.
16. If Bill caught a cold, then he did not take the final examination. If Bill did not take the final examination, then he will fail the course. Consequently, if Bill caught a cold, then he will fail the course.
17. If the weather will turn nasty, then the game will be canceled. The game will not be canceled. So, the weather will not turn nasty.

18. The solution to the problem is either greater than ten or less than ten. The solution to the problem is not greater than ten. Therefore, the solution to the problem is less than ten.
19. If we will not get rain soon, then the grass will die. We will not get rain soon. So, the grass will die.
20. If today is Friday, then we are in Seattle. But we are not in Seattle. Hence, today is not Friday.

IV. Strength and Cogency

A. Helpful Reminders

1. Note the connection between valid/invalid arguments and strong/weak arguments and the difference between soundness and cogency. Some invalid arguments, even though the truth of other premises does not ensure the truth of their conclusions, are nevertheless of a nature such that the truth of all their premises does make their conclusions probable. Such arguments are strong arguments, and, even though they are not valid, they are sometimes significant arguments that need to be taken seriously. The other sort of invalid arguments, those that are of a nature such that the truth of all their premises does not confer a high probability of truth on their conclusions, are weak arguments. A cogent argument is a *strong* argument all of whose premises are true. An uncogent argument is an *invalid* argument that either is weak or has at least one false premise. Some important clarifications, though, need to be made.

2. Note the distinction between an argument from authority and an argument from analogy. In an argument from authority, the words, beliefs, or view of an expert or authoritative source is cited in support of some claim. Here is an example:

Plato considered knowledge to be a kind of justified true belief. Therefore, knowledge probably is a sort of justified true belief.

In an argument from analogy, a comparison is made between two or more items in a number of respects. All the items except one in the comparison are observed to have a certain additional feature, and the conclusion is then made that the remaining item in the comparison has that additional feature. Here is an example:

Both the fruit of the tomato plant and the fruit of the nightshade plant are brightly colored berries that are produced on plants that are members of the same plant family. The fruit of the nightshade plant is poisonous. Therefore, the fruit of the tomato plant is poisonous.

There are, of course, other kinds of arguments that can be strong. We will examine more of these in chapter 10.

B. Commonly Asked Questions

1. Are cogent arguments actually good arguments?

Cogent arguments are good arguments in the sense that their premises are all true and the truth of their premises means that their conclusions are very likely true. Granted, the conclusion of a cogent argument isn't established with certitude (since a cogent argument is unsound), but a cogent argument is often recognized in practice as a reasonable argument. In fact, some cogent arguments provide such good support for their conclusions that they place their conclusions beyond any reasonable doubt. We can't always demand that our arguments be sound, and we lack an indubitable basis for believing many of the factual statements about the world that we have come to believe.

2. Are there strong argument forms analogous to valid argument forms?

Unfortunately, in the case of invalid arguments, we can only identify the kind of argument it is and not its degree of strength. The strength of an argument is not determined by its form; other factors have to be brought into consideration. Some of these factors are discussed in *The Power of Logic* in Chapters 10 and 11.

C. Exercises

(a) Indicate whether the following statements regarding truth, soundness, and cogency are true or false. In each case, justify your answer.

  1. All sound arguments are also cogent arguments.
  2. All cogent arguments are also sound arguments.
  3. Every argument with a false conclusion is either unsound or uncogent.
  4. Every argument with a false premise is either unsound or uncogent.
  5. The conclusion of any cogent argument must be true.
  6. If an argument is cogent, then the truth of its conclusion is highly probable.
  7. The terms "strong" and "weak" are, when applied to arguments, absolute terms.
  8. If an argument has a false conclusion, then the argument either has a false premise or is a cogent or an uncogent argument.
  9. If an argument has a true conclusion, then the argument either has a false premise or is a cogent or an uncogent argument.
  10. Sound arguments provide conclusive grounds for the truth of their conclusions, while cogent arguments provide only some justification or reasons for accepting the truth of their conclusions.

(b) Indicate whether the following arguments are either valid, invalid, sound, unsound, strong, weak, cogent, or uncogent. Say as much as you can about each argument.

  1. All rectangles are parallelograms. All squares are rectangles. Hence, all squares are parallelograms.
  2. Oprah Winfrey says that mad cow disease is serious enough for us to stop eating beef. Therefore, mad cow disease is serious enough for us to stop eating beef.
  3. About 10 percent of the people born in California are Asian American. Nixon was born in California. Therefore, Nixon was Asian American.
  4. All species of birds known to science are egg layers. Thus, all species of birds are egg layers.
  5. Hitler once supposedly argued: The elephant is the strongest animal, and it is a vegetarian. I am a vegetarian, so I will remain strong.

6. Any number greater than four is greater than three. Five is greater than four. Thus, five is greater than three.
7. Every marine animal is a fish. Whales are marine animals. So, whales are fish.
8. Ethyl alcohol and water are both liquids at room temperature, and they are both transparent fluids. Since water is not flammable, ethyl alcohol is not flammable either.
9. All reptiles are vertebrates. No reptiles are insects. Thus, no insects are vertebrates.
10. A bat is either a bird or a mammal. Since a bat is not a bird, it must be a mammal.
11. Astronomer Jack Horkheimer says that there will be a meteor shower next week. Thus, there will be a meteor shower next week.
12. Both Richard Nixon and Ronald Reagan were Republican presidents from California. So, all Republican presidents are from California.
13. All prime numbers are odd numbers. No odd numbers are perfect numbers. Hence, no perfect numbers are prime numbers.
14. Over 90 percent of the people who have eaten pickles at least once will someday die. Bill Gates has eaten pickles at least once. So, Bill Gates will someday die.
15. The number of books on the table is three, and the number of books on the desk is four. None of the books on the table are books on the desk. Therefore, the number of books either on the table or on the desk is seven.

ANSWERS TO EXERCISES

Answers to Selected Exercises in the Text

Exercise 1.1
Part A

1. The sentence makes a claim and thus is a statement.
4. The sentence makes a claim and thus is a statement.
7. This is a sentence fragment and makes no claim and thus is not a statement.
14. The sentence expresses a proposal (something that is neither true nor false) and is thus not a statement.
19. The sentence makes a claim about what General Bradley ordered and is thus a statement.

Part B

1. False. There is no requirement that a valid argument have a false premise. If valid arguments always had a false premise, then there would be no sound arguments. The following argument is an example of a valid argument with no false premises:

> All integers are rational numbers. All rational numbers are real numbers. Thus, all integers are real numbers.

4. True. Logic as a discipline of study is characterized in the text this way.
7. False. If an argument is sound, then it is valid and all of its premises are true. If an argument is valid, then, if its premises are all true, its conclusion is also true. Thus, a sound argument will always have a true conclusion.
10. False. Truth is a property of sentences, not a property of arguments.
13. True. Every sound argument both is valid and has premises all of which are true.
16. False. A valid argument with a false premise is unsound. The following argument, for instance, is unsound but is not an invalid argument:

> All snakes are reptiles. All reptiles are limbless vertebrates. Thus, all snakes are limbless vertebrates.

19. True. This is the one case in which a knowledge of the actual truth values of the premises and conclusion of an argument tells you something about the argument's validity. Any argument that has all true premises and a false conclusion is an argument in which it is possible for all its premises to be true at the same time its conclusion is false and is thus an invalid argument.
22. False. Soundness is a property of arguments, not a property of statements.
25. False. Falsity is a property of statements, not a property of arguments.

Part C

1. This is a valid argument. It has the form: If A, then B. A. Therefore, B.
4. This is a valid argument. It has the form: If A, then B. Not B. Therefore, not A.
7. This is an invalid argument. You may as well argue: All Fords are automobiles. No Toyotas are Fords. Thus, no Toyotas are automobiles.
10. This is an invalid argument. Just because A likes B and B likes C, it doesn't follow that A likes C.
13. This is an invalid argument. Just because each of two events is possible, it doesn't follow that the event of both happening is possible.

Part D

1. This is a sound argument. It is valid, and all of its premises are true.
4. This is an unsound argument (with, nonetheless, a true conclusion). Since, according to the first premise, "Let's party" could be both a sentence and a statement, it does not follow that "Let's party" is not a statement because it is a sentence. The argument is thus invalid.
7. This is a sound argument. It has the same form as the argument in problem 4 from part C: If A, then B. Not B. Therefore, not A.
10. This is an unsound argument. It is a valid argument, but its first premise is false.
13. This is an unsound argument. It is a valid argument, but its second premise is false.

Exercise 1.3
Part D

modus ponens
If Tabby is a cat, then Tabby is a mammal. Tabby is a cat. So, Tabby is a mammal.

modus tollens
If Smith is the murderer, then he knows the password. Smith does not know the password. Therefore, Smith is not the murderer.

hypothetical syllogism
If it turns colder, then it will rain. If it will rain, then the game will be canceled. Thus, if it turns colder, then the game will be canceled.

disjunctive syllogism
Either unemployment will increase, or the rate of inflation will decline. It's not true that unemployment will increase. So, the rate of inflation will decline.

constructive dilemma
Either the chef put too much sugar in the dough, or the chef put too little sugar in the dough. If the chef put too much sugar in the dough, then it will taste too sweet. If the chef put too little sugar in the dough, then it will not rise properly. Hence, either the dough will taste too sweet, or it will not rise properly.

denying the antecedent
If whales are marine fishes, then whales live in the sea. Whales are not marine fishes. Thus, whales do not live in the sea.

affirming the consequent
If five is greater than ten, then five is greater than two. Five is greater than two. Thus, five is greater than ten.

Exercise 1.4
Part B

1. False. A sound argument has only true premises but (since it is valid) is not cogent.
4. False. A valid argument with a false premise is not uncogent.
7. False. Truth is a property of statements, not a property of arguments.
10. False. A weak argument having only true premises is uncogent but is not an argument with a false premise.
13. False. The argument is an argument from analogy.

Part C

1. This is an invalid argument. Since, given the truth of its premises, its conclusion is just as likely to be false as true, it is also a weak argument.
4. This is an invalid argument. Provided that the number of frogs dissected is large and various kinds of frogs have been dissected, the premise alone (i.e., independent of some rather obvious reasons why frogs must have hearts) gives us good reason to believe the conclusion, and the argument is thus strong.
7. This is an invalid and weak argument (from analogy). The premises, even though they are all true, do not make the conclusion probable.
10. This is a valid argument.

13. This is an invalid but strong argument (from authority).
16. This is an invalid and weak argument. The argument is clearly invalid, since its premises are all true but its conclusion is false.
19. This is an invalid and weak argument (from analogy). The truth of the premises does not give us good reason to believe the conclusion to be true, since there are some obvious differences between humans and computers that make the conclusion rather unlikely.

Part D

4. This is a strong argument, but, since its premise is not true, it is uncogent.
7. This argument is valid and is thus neither a cogent nor an uncogent argument.
10. This argument is weak and hence uncogent.

Answers to Supplemental Exercises

I(a)

1. neither a sentence nor a statement
2. a sentence but not a statement
3. neither a sentence nor a statement
4. both a sentence and a statement
5. both a sentence and a statement
6. both a sentence and a statement
7. both a sentence and a statement
8. both a sentence and a statement
9. both a sentence and a statement
10. a sentence but not a statement (The antecedent of the pronoun "This" can't without contradiction refer to the sentence itself. The expression "This sentence" thus does not succeed in referring, and the sentence thereby does not say anything either true or false.)

I(b)

1. False. When an argument is sound, it is always the case that its conclusion is true. However, it would be incorrect to say that the truth of an argument's conclusion ensures that the argument is sound. Consider the following argument:

   All birds lay eggs. All mammals are warm-blooded animals. Therefore, no birds are mammals.

   This argument has a true conclusion. Nevertheless, it is an invalid, and hence not a sound, argument.
2. False. An argument's validity is something that is in general independent of the truth of the argument's premises. Some valid and some invalid arguments have true premises. For instance, all the premises of the following argument are true:

All cats are mammals. France is a European country. Therefore, there are no unicorns.

Despite the fact that all the premises are in fact true, the argument is obviously invalid.

3. False. Notice that, in the preceding argument, each premise is true, as is the conclusion. The argument is, nonetheless, invalid. Thus, the truth of all the premises and the conclusion does not ensure that the argument is valid.

4. True. This statement is true in virtue of the definition of a sound argument.

5. True. A valid argument that has at least one false premise can have a false conclusion. The following argument, for instance, is certainly valid but has a false conclusion:

If Napoleon was English, then he was not French. Napoleon was English. Therefore, Napoleon was not French.

Notice, though, that the only way this argument can have a false conclusion is for it to have at least one false premise. It is clearly a valid argument, but if it didn't have a false premise, it couldn't be valid, since a valid argument cannot have all true premises and a false conclusion.

6. False. According to the definition of soundness, an argument must both be valid and have all true premises in order to be sound.

7. False. Even if all the premises of an invalid argument are true, it is still possible for the conclusion to be false, but it is not necessary for it to be false in order for the argument to be invalid. Some invalid arguments with all true premises have a true conclusion, while others have a false conclusion.

8. True. The validity of an argument with a false premise does not guarantee that the conclusion will be true. Neither does it guarantee that the conclusion will be false. Consider the following example:

All Asians are French. Napoleon was Asian. Therefore, Napoleon was French.

This argument is valid, and both of its premises are false, but it has a true conclusion nonetheless. Both true and false conclusions can be validly derived from premises not all of which are true.

9. False. In virtue of the definition of validity, the combination of all true premises and a false conclusion is not possible in the case of a valid argument.

10. True. A false conclusion can be validly derived from premises all of which are false. The following argument is valid, but each premise is false, as is the conclusion:

All mammals lay shelled eggs. All lizards are mammals. Therefore, all lizards lay shelled eggs.

11. False. The crucial word in this statement is "must." If the premises of a valid argument are not all true, the conclusion can be false, but the conclusion does not have to be false in order for the argument to be valid.

12. True. If a valid argument with a false conclusion did not have at least one false premise, then it would be an argument with all true premises and a false conclusion. However, such an argument cannot be valid.
13. False. The definition of validity only declares that a valid argument cannot have premises all of which are true and a conclusion that is false.
14. False. A valid argument with a false premise is a valid argument that is not sound.
15. True. The notion of soundness includes the notion of validity. If an argument is sound, then it is a valid argument, and all of its premises are true.

II(a)

1. True. Any substitution instance of a valid argument form cannot have all true premises and a false conclusion and must therefore be a valid argument.
2. True. If all the substitution instances of an argument form are valid arguments, then it will be impossible for there to be a substitution instance of the form with all true premises and a false conclusion. Such an argument form will thus be a valid argument form.
3. False. Some substitution instances of an invalid argument form are valid arguments, and others are invalid arguments.
4. False. Two arguments could both be substitution instances of the same form with one argument invalid and the other valid. Take this form: A. B. So, C. Any instance of *modus ponens,* for example, has this form, but many arguments having this form are invalid, such as "Red is a color. Dogs exist. So, there is a Santa Claus."
5. False. An invalid argument and a valid argument could both be substitution instances of some invalid argument form. See the answer to item 4.

II(b)

1. All people who were born in Arkansas are U.S. citizens. No naturalized citizen is a person who was born in Arkansas. Hence, no naturalized citizen is a citizen.
2. If Kansas is greater in size than Alaska, then it is also greater in size than Rhode Island. Kansas is not greater in size than Alaska. Therefore, Kansas is not greater in size than Rhode Island.
3. Some automobiles are Ford Rangers. All Ford Rangers are Fords. Thus, some Fords are not automobiles.
4. One should play Russian roulette. The longer you play, the longer you live.
5. All oak trees are plants. Some plants are not trees. So, some oak trees are not trees.

II(c)

1. If it will snow, then it turns colder.
2. If Mark will attend the class, then he is enrolled in the course.
3. If there is a fire in the room, then oxygen is present.
4. If Larry stays home, then I will go.
5. If there is no class tomorrow, then Susan will stay home.

6. If you pass the course, then you pass the final.
7. If the road is closed ahead, then we choose a different route.
8. If Harry has enough money, then he will buy a new car.
9. If you buy the book, then you own it.
10. If we live here, then we pay the rent each month.

III

1. fallacy of affirming the consequent; invalid
2. hypothetical syllogism; valid
3. *modus tollens;* valid
4. fallacy of affirming the consequent; invalid
5. fallacy of denying the antecedent; invalid
6. fallacy of denying the antecedent; invalid
7. constructive dilemma; valid
8. disjunctive syllogism; valid
9. *modus ponens;* valid
10. *modus tollens;* valid
11. *modus ponens;* valid
12. fallacy of affirming the consequent; invalid
13. constructive dilemma; valid
14. disjunctive syllogism; valid
15. fallacy of denying the antecedent; invalid
16. hypothetical syllogism; valid
17. *modus tollens;* valid
18. disjunctive syllogism; valid
19. *modus ponens;* valid
20. *modus tollens;* valid

IV(a)

1. False. No cogent arguments are valid arguments. All sound arguments are valid arguments. Hence, no sound arguments are cogent arguments.
2. False. No sound arguments are invalid arguments. All cogent arguments are invalid arguments. Hence, no cogent arguments are sound arguments.
3. False. It is true that an argument with a false conclusion cannot be sound, but it is possible for an argument to have a false conclusion and yet be cogent. Any inductive argument, regardless of how strong it is and regardless of the truth of all its premises, can still have a conclusion that is false.
4. True. An argument with a false premise cannot be sound, nor can it be cogent, for both sound and cogent arguments must have premises all of which are true. If an argument with a false premise is valid, then it is unsound but not uncogent. If an argument with a false premise is invalid, then it is both unsound and uncogent.
5. False. Granted, it is unlikely for the conclusion of a cogent argument to be false, but it is always possible for it to be false.
6. True. This is true in virtue of the notion of a cogent argument.

7. False. Unlike arguments that are "valid" and "invalid" (which are absolute terms), arguments can vary in their degree of strength or weakness from very weak to moderately weak to moderately strong to very strong.
8. True. An argument with a false conclusion cannot be a sound argument. Such an argument is always unsound. Any unsound argument either has a false premise or is an invalid argument, and any invalid argument is either cogent or uncogent.
9. False. One possibility has been left out of consideration. If an argument has a true conclusion, then it could be a sound argument. If an argument is sound, then it does not have a false premise and is neither cogent nor uncogent.
10. True. The conclusion of a sound argument must be true, so such an argument conclusively establishes its conclusion. An invalid argument, regardless of how strong it is, always provides us with less than conclusive grounds for accepting the truth of its conclusion. Thus, any inductively strong argument will only provide us with some reasons for accepting the truth of its conclusion.

IV(b)

1. This is a valid and sound argument.
2. This is an invalid, weak, unsound, and uncogent argument. (It is also an argument from authority.)
3. This is an invalid, weak, unsound, and uncogent argument.
4. This is an invalid, unsound, strong, and cogent argument.
5. This is an invalid, weak, unsound, and uncogent argument. (It is also an argument from analogy.)
6. This is a valid and sound argument.
7. This is a valid but unsound argument.
8. This is an invalid, weak, unsound, and uncogent argument. (It is also an argument from analogy.)
9. This is an invalid, weak, unsound, and uncogent argument.
10. This is a valid and sound argument.
11. This is an invalid and unsound but strong argument. (It is also an argument from authority.)
12. This is an invalid, weak, unsound, and uncogent argument.
13. This a valid but unsound argument.
14. This is an invalid and unsound argument. Whether this argument is strong is not immediately obvious. There is plenty of good evidence, having nothing to do with what is talked about in the premises of the argument, indicating that the conclusion is true. The premises thus seem to be irrelevant to establishing the conclusion. However, the truth of all the premises does, by itself, given certain statistical considerations as background assumptions, give us good reason to believe that the conclusion is true. The argument should thus be regarded as strong.
15. This one is controversial. The argument certainly appears to be valid, but demonstrating its validity is no simple, straightforward matter. Some logicians would argue that the argument is indeed valid but that its validity cannot be shown without supplementation from set theory.

FOR FURTHER CONSIDERATION

Formal deductive logic is based on the idea that the form of an argument determines its validity or invalidity. When an argument is valid, it is impossible, just from the meanings of the logical words involved in the argument, for its conclusion to be false if its premises should all be true. The conclusion follows from the premises with logical necessity in a valid argument.

Some, however, have challenged the notion that argument form fixes validity. Some claim that the necessary connection between the truth of the premises and the truth of the conclusion is not always logical necessity but is sometimes some other sort of necessity, such as conceptual or metaphysical necessity. These other kinds of necessity are not determined, they claim, just by argument form or by the meanings of words. Instead, whether the other forms of necessary connection obtain is thought to be determined by the nature of our concepts or the nature of the world. Thus, if this view is correct, then validity is not always just a matter of argument form.

Such a contention seems to be not altogether implausible. For example, consider the following simple argument:

Argument A: John is a bachelor. Thus, John is an unmarried man.

Certainly, the conclusion must be true if the premise is true, but how is this necessary connection revealed in the logical form of the argument? Some claim that it is not and that the necessity is derived from, in this case, the nature of our notion of a bachelor. Since the concept of a bachelor includes the concept of an unmarried male, the necessary relation between premise and conclusion obtains. Furthermore, since "bachelor" is not a logical word (and thus does not appear in any representation of the logical form of the argument), the validity of argument A is not fixed by its logical form. In a similar vein, it is thought that the nature of the world, rather than the nature of our concepts, accounts for the validity of other arguments.

The defenders of the formal notion of validity often respond to their critics by claiming that the only notion of necessity that is needed—and indeed the only notion of necessity that makes sense ultimately—is the notion of logical necessity. The validity of any argument can be shown, they claim, to depend on form alone. This is done, they argue, by considering such arguments as containing unstated but assumed premises regarding the nature of our concepts or of the world. To illustrate, some might suggest adding a premise to argument A to get a complete argument:

Argument B: John is a bachelor. All bachelors are unmarried men. Thus, John is an unmarried man.

With the additional (second) premise, the argument has a valid form. Hence, if argument A is best regarded as an abbreviated version of argument B, then it seems reasonable to maintain that argument A is valid by virtue of its form.

Identifying Arguments

Before an argument can be adequately appraised with regard to its soundness or cogency, it often needs to be clarified and restated in a complete but concise fashion. Chapter 2 of The Power of Logic *discusses how to distinguish arguments from nonarguments, how to pick out premises and conclusions from other statements in an argumentative passage, and how to identify the structure of an argument.*

CHAPTER HIGHLIGHTS

In an argument, one statement (the conclusion) is affirmed on the basis of at least one other statement (the premise or premises). Thus, an unsupported assertion is not an argument. Nevertheless, some types of unsupported assertions, such as **reports, illustrations, explanations**, and **conditional statements**, are often confused with arguments.

Rewriting an argument as a **well-crafted argument** involves identifying the argument's premises and conclusion; recognizing the proper order of premises, intermediate conclusions, and final conclusion; and rewriting the argument so as to make its structure explicit and to eliminate all unnecessary verbiage. In a **well-crafted version** of an argument, the final conclusion will occur last, and the premises and intermediate conclusions used to reach the final conclusion will occur in order. Five principles govern the process of constructing a well-crafted version of an argument. According to **principle 1**, the premises and conclusions of an argument must be identified. It is often helpful to identify the final conclusion first. The presence of certain words or expressions that commonly are used to signal a premise (premise indicators) or a conclusion (conclusion indicators) is often helpful in picking out the premises and conclusions in an argumentative passage. According to **principle 2**, the argument proper should be extracted from the excess verbiage in a passage. Rhetorical elements, those elements that are used to make an argument more psychologically persuasive without affecting its validity, strength, or soundness, should be eliminated. Common rhetorical elements include discounts (which often occur with discount indicators), assurances, and hedges. The repetition of premises or conclusions is another type of excess verbiage that needs to be eliminated. **Principle 3** requires that uniform language be employed in restating an argument. The structure of an argument is sometimes obscured when the same statements or terms occur more than once in the argument but are expressed differently. According to **principle 4**, one must be fair and charitable in interpreting an argument. Fairness requires us to interpret an argument in a manner consistent with the author's intentions. Charity involves putting an unclearly stated argument in the best possible light. Finally, **principle 5** encourages us not to confuse subconclusions with the final conclusion of an argument. Such confusion will usually lead to the misrepresentation of an argument's structure.

Arguments can be diagrammed in order to make explicit their exact inferential structure. To diagram an argument, one first places brackets around each sentence, or part of a sentence, that states a premise, a subconclusion, or the final conclusion (these three kinds of statements being the **steps** of an argument). The steps of the argument are then numbered consecutively. When premises provide *independent support* for a conclusion (or subconclusion), an arrow is drawn *from* (a) the number assigned to each such premise *to* (b) the number assigned to the conclusion (or subconclusion).

DISCUSSION OF KEY CONCEPTS

I. Arguments and Nonarguments

A. Helpful Reminders

1. Conditionals and other unsupported statements are not complexes of statements and thus are not, by themselves, arguments. Conditionals (in isolation from accompanying statements) are frequently mistaken for arguments, it being erroneously supposed that the antecedent is a premise and the consequent is a conclusion. However, a conditional statement is either a premise or a conclusion when it occurs as part of an argument. A conditional by itself is not an argument, even though a conditional has components that may be either a premise or a conclusion in an argument. Whenever someone makes a conditional claim, neither the antecedent nor the consequent is being asserted in uttering the conditional statement. For instance, consider the weather forecaster who says, "If the cold front arrives while the humidity is high, then we will have rain tomorrow." The forecaster is neither predicting the arrival of the cold front while the humidity is high nor predicting rain for tomorrow. The forecaster's claim is only that, *if* the cold front arrives while the humidity is high, *then* it will rain tomorrow. In any argument, both the premises and the conclusions are being asserted. Since neither the antecedent nor the consequent is being asserted in the utterance of any conditional claim, a conditional in itself is not an argument.

2. In general, a complex of statements can constitute an argument, an explanation, an illustration, or a report. In a report, one presents factual information to inform an audience rather than to convince them of something. Reports typically describe or give a narrative account of the features of something or the way things are, or were, in the world. Reports are thus usually either descriptions or narratives. When an author gives an illustration, he or she usually presents one or more instances of a generalization (that is, applications of a generalization to one or more particular cases) as a means of helping the audience to understand the generalization or to appreciate its significance. The purpose of an explanation is to show why or how something is, was, or will be the case. In an explanation, as opposed to an argument, one statement is not being justified on the basis of another, but rather one statement is being explained on the basis of another. In addition, as is the case with both arguments and explanations, there is often a point to an illustration, description, or

narrative, and this represents another respect in which explanations, illustrations, descriptions, and narratives resemble arguments.

3. Explanations are the complexes of statements that are most frequently confused with arguments. As a means of distinguishing between the two, be aware of the different purposes that arguments and explanations serve. In an explanation, the truth of the statement that gets explained (the *explanandum*) is not called into question, for it is not the purpose of an explanation to argue that something is the case. In many explanations, the explanandum statement is better known than are the statements that do the explaining (the *explanans*). Indeed, in most explanations, the statements of the explanans would never convince anyone of the truth of the explanandum if it were called into question. This situation is in contrast to what occurs in an argument. In an argument, the conclusion is the point of contention, and the premises are not argued for (within a single inference, anyway) so that the premises are better known than the conclusion. In an argument, the truth of the premises is used to convince an audience to accept a conclusion, a statement whose truth is called into question. In order to distinguish arguments from explanations, it may also help to know something about the different kinds of explanations. In a causal or mechanistic explanation, a phenomenon is explained in terms of causes or mechanisms. Such explanations occur in the physical sciences. In an action explanation, the behavior of an agent is explained in terms of the behavior being motivated by the agent's desires and/or the agent's beliefs about what constitutes a means of achieving what is desired. Explanations in psychology and history tend to be action explanations. In a functional explanation, the attributes of a thing or the elements of a process are explained in terms of the function or purpose those attributes or elements serve. Explanations in the biological sciences tend to be functional explanations.

B. Commonly Asked Questions

1. When interpreting a passage, how do you figure out the author's intentions with regard to arguing, reporting, illustrating, or explaining?

There are two important factors to bear in mind when assessing the intentions of a speaker or writer. First of all, you should look for certain contextual clues that may give away the author's intentions. Arguments often occur within a discussion of controversial matters, and the parts of an argument are often signaled by premise and conclusion indicators. Illustrations tend to occur in a passage immediately after a generalization and are often introduced by such phrases as "for example" and "for instance." Explanations frequently occur within a discussion that is descriptive, not argumentative, in character and are often foreshadowed by the mention of an issue or a question that is in need of an explanation. Such words or expressions as "because" and "the reason for" may be used to signal the explanans of an explanation. Please note, however, that these contextual elements occasionally are misleading. It is particularly important to note that the words and expressions that often signal the parts of an argument or an explanation have other uses. For instance, the word "because" may signal a premise of an argument or the explanans of an explanation, or the word may occur simply as a component of a causal statement. So, in general, do not rely on these contextual features exclusively, but also take into consideration the other important factor that helps one determine an author's intentions. This other factor concerns the plausibility of interpreting a passage one way as opposed to another. If the interpretation of a passage as an argument results in an argument that is so incredibly poor that few people would even consider it, then chances are the author is not presenting an argument. Many illustrations, for instance, would be really bad arguments if they were to be interpreted as such. Similarly, if the interpretation of a passage as a report or an illustration results in losing the author's point of contention, then chances are the author is giving an argument. Granted, people do present bad arguments and reports and illustrations that go astray, and thus in general this latter factor should not be relied upon exclusively.

2. Can a passage contain both an argument and a nonargument?

Yes, just as a passage can contain more than one separate argument, a passage can contain a combination of an argument together with a report, an illustration, or an explanation. A philosopher, for instance, may defend a particular thesis by first reporting how people have in the past defended or argued against the thesis and then presenting an original defense of the thesis. Alternatively, an arguer may entertain as a premise a generalization that is clarified by an illustration or may offer an explanation for something that has been argued must be the case.

C. Exercises

For each of the following passages, indicate whether an argument is present.

1. The first rule of coping with anyone aggressive, hostile or not, is that you stand up to that person, for if you let yourself be pushed around by aggressive people, you simply fade into the scenery for them. That is, they will not see you as someone to whom attention need be paid. —Robert M. Bramson, *Coping with Difficult People* (New York: Ballantine Books, 1981), p. 12. [This quotation is slightly altered for use as an exercise.]

2. There is grandeur in this view of life, with its several powers, having been originally breathed by the Creator into a few forms or into one, and that, whilst this planet has gone cycling on according to the fixed law of gravity, from so simple a beginning endless forms most beautiful and most wonderful have been and are being evolved. —Charles Darwin, *The Origin of Species*

3. If species were natural kinds, then the binomials and other expressions that are used to refer to particular species could be eliminated in favor of predicates. However, the binomials and other expressions used to refer to particular species cannot be eliminated in favor of predicates. It follows that species are not natural kinds.

4. Good sense is of all things in the world the most equally distributed, for everybody considers himself so abundantly provided with it that even those most difficult to please in all other matters do not commonly desire more of it than they already possess. —René Descartes, *A Discourse on Method*

5. Male ornate box turtles have a lower shell (plastron) that is slightly concave in order to allow the male to balance himself on the female's back during mating.

6. Tornadoes, one of nature's most violent storms, are produced along the edge of quickly advancing cold fronts when cold, dry air overrides warm, moist air. The air masses in such situations are very unstable, as currents of warm air spiral upward, displacing the heavier cold air, which sinks. Prevailing air currents in the upper atmosphere then constrict the spiraling

column of warm and cold air, and condensation occurs, so that a funnel-shaped cloud is formed.

7. Why do the stars appear to twinkle regardless of how far they are from the horizon, while both the stars and the distant planets appear to twinkle when they are close to the horizon? All starlight is very weak and is always distorted due to reflection off dust particles as light rays travel through the atmosphere. Light from a distant planet may also be weak enough and may encounter sufficient dust particles, as it travels through more layers of the earth's atmosphere when near the horizon, so that its light, too, is distorted by such reflection.

8. When General George McClellan commanded the Union forces encamped along the Potomac in 1862, he steadfastly refused to cross the river and attack General Lee's Army of Northern Virginia. Had he attacked Lee's army, he most likely would have defeated Lee and possibly brought a quick end to the war. McClellan felt that he was insufficiently supplied, and he mistakenly believed that he was outnumbered by Lee's army. McClellan believed in committing troops to a battle only when an easy and decisive victory could be assured, as he desired to minimize his casualties. It was for these reasons that McClellan unfortunately hesitated and did not engage the enemy.

9. The power set of any set (i.e., the set of all subsets of a given set) must be larger than the original set. The universal set is, by definition, the set of everything. Consequently, the universal set must not be possible, since its power set would have to contain more members than there are things in the universe.

10. The valve located at this junction in the pipe was designed in the odd spiral shape in order to allow for widely varying rates of flow without the development of significant backup pressure.

11. Seaworthy vessels are not all made of a material that floats in water. As is well known, modern-day ships are made with tons of steel, yet they can traverse the oceans without sinking. Such a ship is able to do this because it is large enough and has enough empty space so that with its volume it is actually less dense than seawater. Since any object suspended in water will sink until it displaces a volume of water equal to the weight of the object, the lower portion of the ship sinks below the waterline until the ship is buoyed up by a force that is equal to the weight of the ship and to the weight of the water the ship displaces. Since the ship is less dense than seawater, the entire volume of the ship will not be submerged, and the ship will thus float and not sink.

12. Digital audiotape (DAT) decks are being built with special internal processing chips that allow only a single good copy of a cassette to be made in order to prevent extensive pirating of copyrighted material.

13. For several reasons, we humans must remain ignorant on many important matters if we refuse to accept testimony (that is, the reports of others). First, since an individual can access only a minuscule portion of the past through his or her own memory, most of one's beliefs about the past rest on testimony. Second, most of one's beliefs about distant places must depend on the reports of others simply because an individual cannot be in two places

at once. Third, although many people associate scientific knowledge with direct observation, most of what a given individual knows about science is, in fact, based on testimony. After all, most of us learn science by reading books on science. And books on science are full of testimony, for they contain reports of observations and experiments conducted by others.

14. In the coastal regions throughout the world, high tides arrive at regular twelve-hour intervals; however, these high tides are sometimes not as high as at other times, for there are low high tides and high high tides. The reason for this has to do with the alignment of the sun and the moon. The gravitational pull of each of these bodies has an effect on the tides, but sometimes these effects are opposed. When the moon is in line with the sun and the earth, the pull of the sun and the pull of the moon combine to produce high high tides. When the moon is situated at a right angle to the earth–sun axis, the pull of the sun is canceled out by the pull of the moon so that low high tides are produced.

15. When an electrolyte is dissolved in water, the resulting solution conducts electricity. Saltwater made from common table salt, for example, conducts electricity quite well.

16. The conclusion that has been reached by some contemporary paleontologists is now unavoidable: The dinosaurs could not have been cold-blooded reptiles. Unlike modern reptiles and more like warm-blooded birds and mammals, some dinosaurs roamed the continental interiors in large migratory herds. In addition, the large carnivorous dinosaurs would have been too active and mobile had they been cold-blooded reptiles. As is indicated by the estimated predator-to-prey ratios, they also would have consumed too much for their body weight had they been cold-blooded animals.

17. In order for something to move, it must go from a place where it is to a place where it is not. However, since a thing is always where it is and is never where it is not, motion must not be possible.

18. Mental states cannot be brain events. This is so because all brain events are physical events, and no physical events can be adequately accounted for in intensional terms, and it is only in terms of intensions that mental states can be adequately described.

19. Reptiles were the first vertebrates to evolve a cleidoic egg, an egg with a shell that could be laid on land. Reptiles thus became much less dependent upon the bodies of freshwater that had limited the distribution of their amphibian ancestors, which had to return to the water to lay their eggs. As a result, reptiles colonized the dry interior regions of the supercontinents and developed into myriad different forms.

20. Susan drove to the bank this afternoon to use the automatic teller to get some cash. When she got to the bank, she realized she had forgotten to bring her bank card. She then decided to go to the grocery store to buy a few items and get a check cashed. However, while she was shopping, she inadvertently dropped her checkbook and lost it. After leaving the store with neither cash nor groceries, she ran out of gas driving home and had to walk the rest of the way. Susan has not had a very good day.

II. Well-Crafted Arguments

A. Helpful Reminders

1. The conclusion is always the result of an inference drawn from the premises. So, the conclusion in an argument is always what is argued for, while the premises are taken for granted or assumed to be true. We say that the conclusion is *inferred* from the premises. The conclusion is the single sentence in the argument requiring justification. When you examine an argumentative passage, you should always first find the sentence whose truth is not taken for granted but whose truth is the whole point of the passage. That sentence will be the conclusion, and by finding it first you will probably be able to locate the premises more easily. Once you have identified the premises and the conclusion of an argument, you can construct a well-crafted version of the argument. Remember that your well-crafted version of the argument should be as close in content to the original argument as practically possible. Don't leave out premises or the conclusion, and don't simplify or abbreviate sentences in such a way as to change their meaning.

2. Premises and conclusions are always relative to a single inference. What is taken as a premise in one part of an argument may be the conclusion of a prior part of the argument. Thus, arguments in long passages may consist of a series or a network of interconnected inferences.

3. The statements in an argument often will be in the form of declarative sentences. However, this is not always the case. Sometimes questions, particularly rhetorical questions, and commands will occur as premises. This will happen only when such sentences can be thought of as making a claim even though they are not in the form of declarations. Any sentence (regardless of the mood of its verb) that can be interpreted as making a claim can be a premise or a conclusion.

4. More than one premise, or a premise and a conclusion, may be conjoined in a single sentence. The single sentence may be grammatically compound or complex. Alternatively, the sentence may contain a noun phrase that itself expresses a proposition even though it does not contain both a subject and a verb. In other words, a premise or a conclusion may occur as a sentence fragment contained within a complete sentence that makes more than one assertion. For example, consider the following argument:

> If numbers were symbols, then there would be just as many numbers as there are symbols. However, there are only a finite number of symbols and an infinite number of numbers. Hence, numbers are not mere symbols.

You will notice that the second sentence is not a grammatically compound sentence, even though there are two assertions being made by the sentence. It is saying both that there are only a finite number of symbols and that there are an infinite number of numbers. In analyzing an argument, we want to restate it in such a fashion that we know exactly what the premises and conclusion are and each is stated in a single declarative sentence. Thus, the preceding argument may be rewritten as a well-crafted argument in the following manner:

1. If numbers are symbols, then there are just as many numbers as there are symbols.
2. There are only a finite number of symbols.
3. There are an infinite number of numbers.

So, 4. Numbers are not mere symbols.

5. In the logical analysis of arguments, we prefer to state the premises and conclusion in such a fashion that the assertion made by each sentence is explicit. This presents problems because a sentence's meaning is quite often dependent upon its context. So, in order to understand what assertion is being made by a sentence, you often need to rely on the information provided by its context. The context (such as the accompanying sentences or the time or place at which the sentence is uttered or written) may determine the exact claim made. Pronouns occurring in a sentence sometimes have their antecedents outside the sentence. Take, for instance, the sentence "It is a citrus fruit." This sentence would be true if the pronoun "It" referred to a lemon but false if "It" referred to a muskmelon. Sentences may also contain certain time indexicals. Consider the sentence "The current president of the United States is a Republican." This sentence would be true if uttered in 1991 and false in 1998 and then true again in 2001. In the logical analysis of arguments, we prefer to have sentences that are dependent on context as little as possible. So, for example, the preceding sentences need to be restated in a manner such as "A lemon is a citrus fruit" and "The president of the United States in March 2001 is a Republican." Thus, when we reconstruct an argument by restating its premises and/or its conclusion, we favor declarative sentences that contain no pronouns that have an antecedent outside the sentence and no time indexicals such as "current," "present," "past," "recent," and "future."

6. For a variety of reasons, an argumentative passage may contain information that is not part of the argument proper. Consider the following passage:

Bertrand Russell made the following case against naive realism. Naive realism, he claimed, leads to physics, and if physics is true, then naive realism is false. Hence, naive realism is false.

The first sentence is not really needed, for its content does not help establish the conclusion. It only tells us that what follows is an argument. This argument, properly speaking, begins with the second sentence. We can construct a well-crafted version of the argument as follows:

1. Naive realism leads to physics.
2. If physics is true, then naive realism is false.

So, 3. Naive realism is false.

Certain rhetorical devices that are not part of the argument proper may be present in a passage. Discount indicators may be used to reject some suggestion. Various kinds of assurances may be used to indicate an author's high degree of confidence in the truth of a premise or conclusion. Assurances may also be used to suggest that there is good evidence for a claim even though the author does not provide that evidence. An arguer may use a hedge so as to withhold, in an inconspicuous fashion, his or her total commitment to a premise or conclusion in order to strengthen an argument. In addition, in some argumentative passages, a premise or the conclusion is repeated either for emphasis or as a reminder for the reader or listener. The premise or conclusion may be expressed each time in the same words or in different words. As is the case with sentences and rhetorical elements that are not part of the argument, the second occurrence of a premise or a conclusion is ignored when the argument is recast as a well-crafted argument.

7. While some reconstructions of an argument are of course better than others, there can be more than one way to reconstruct an argument in a plausible manner. The amount of detail revealed in a reconstruction will often depend on how much of the argument's logical structure needs to be made explicit.

B. *Commonly Asked Questions*

1. Why produce a well-crafted version of an argument?

You can evaluate an argument legitimately only if you adequately understand it. By rewriting an argument as a well-crafted argument, you lay out the inferences made in the argument so that the argumentative moves the arguer makes are explicit. That is why it is important, when attempting to analyze and appraise the soundness or cogency of a real-world argument, to isolate the argument from its surrounding context and reformulate (reconstruct) it as a well-crafted argument.

2. What is one aiming for in constructing a well-crafted version of an argument?

The basic goal in reconstruction is to write the argument in a manner wherein each premise and conclusion is a single declarative sentence that can be understood independently of the other sentences in the argument. Unfortunately, since arguments occurring in written or verbal passages are sometimes obscure and are frequently not neatly structured to allow for easy reconstruction, one needs to acquire certain skills of interpretation in order to figure out what is being argued for and from what assumptions.

3. What words and expressions can I omit when writing a well-crafted version of an argument?

Generally speaking, one should discard all premise indicators and all other words, phrases, and whole sentences that are not required in order to state the argument accurately. A note of caution regarding assurances and hedges: Expressions that in some contexts are used merely to assure or to hedge may not serve that purpose in other contexts and should not be eliminated as excess verbiage. Watch out for probability phrases (such as "it is certain that," "it is likely that," and "it is probably true that") and expressions that describe the arguer's cognitive state (such as "I believe that" and "I know that"). When the point of the argument is to justify a conclusion about the relative probability of something being the case or a conclusion about the arguer's beliefs or state of knowledge, these expressions should not be dropped when they occur as part of the argument's premises or a conclusion.

C. *Exercises*

For each of the passages that contains an argument in the previous set of exercises (at the end of subsection I), rewrite the argument as a well-crafted argument.

Appendix to Chapter 2: Argument Diagrams

A. Helpful Reminders

1. An argument diagram is like a road map of the course of an argument. The arrows drawn from the designations of single statements or of complexes of statements to the designations of single statements depict the inferential flow from premises to conclusions. The pattern of inference present in an argument is thus made apparent in the diagram. The argument diagrams we construct are similar to debaters' flowcharts in this respect.

2. Don't fret at this stage if you do not automatically see the structure of all arguments as they occur in argumentative passages. The explication of the logical structure of arguments is one of the main tasks of the logician, and a great deal of your study in a logic course will be aimed at achieving this goal. As you proceed through the course, your ability to look at argumentative passages and understand the inferential connections among the various statements should improve.

B. Commonly Asked Questions

1. Why construct an argument diagram?

An argument diagram is a visual representation of the logical interconnections between the steps in an argument. The diagram reveals the inferential moves an arguer makes by showing what premises or combinations of premises lead to what conclusions. The purpose of argument diagramming is to make the pattern of inference in an argument explicit so that the precise logical structure of the argument is well understood.

2. How do you go about constructing an argument diagram?

Always begin by making sure that each step of the argument you wish to diagram is clearly identified and numbered. A series of consecutive numbers should be assigned the initial premises, the subsequent premises, the intermediate conclusions, and the final conclusion. To construct the diagram, determine what intermediate conclusions the initial premises support, and depict this support by drawing a figure consisting of the line numbers of the premises with arrows pointing to the line numbers of the intermediate conclusions. If a single premise provides its own support for a conclusion independent of other premises, then draw an arrow from the line number of the premise to the line number of its conclusion. If more than one premise work together to support a conclusion, then connect the line numbers of the premises with the plus sign (+), underline the resulting series of numbers, and draw a single arrow from the series to the line number of the conclusion. Continue in this fashion, adding to the diagram the line numbers of subsequent premises with arrows pointing to the line numbers of the conclusions they support. Also draw arrows from the line numbers of the intermediate conclusions to the line numbers of other intermediate conclusions and ultimately to the line number of the final conclusion.

C. Exercises

Construct an argument diagram for each of the arguments reconstructed in the previous exercise (at the end of subsection II).

ANSWERS TO EXERCISES

Answers to Selected Exercises in the Text

Exercise 2.1
Part A

1. This is a nonargument. Although it is entirely plausible to interpret this as a brief explanation, it is possible that the word "because" is used here just to assert a causal relationship between Americans being exposed to more advertising than any other people on Earth and Americans being materialistic.
10. This is a nonargument. The statement in this passage does resemble the sort of statement found in problem 1, but in this case the word "because" is not being used to assert a cause-and-effect relationship. Rather, the observation that humans desire to control other humans is offered as the reason for (but not necessarily the cause of) wars, and thus the statement in the passage is a brief explanation.

Exercise 2.2
Part A

10. This is not an argument. This passage contains a report, which in this case is a description.
19. This is not an argument. This passage contains a report, which in this case contains both descriptive and narrative components.

Part B

1. This is not an argument. The passage contains a causal explanation.
10. This is not an argument, since no conclusions are drawn. This passage contains a report, which in this case is a description.
19. This is not an argument. This passage contains a report, which in this case is a description.

Exercise : Appendix to Chapter 2
Part B

7. Sometimes an author's intentions are somewhat unclear, and when this is so (as it is in this case), alternative diagrams can be equally correct. Accordingly, this argument could also be diagrammed as follows:

$$
\begin{array}{c}
\underline{1 + 2 + 3} \\
\downarrow \\
4 \\
\downarrow \\
5 \\
\downarrow \\
6
\end{array}
$$

Answers to Supplemental Exercises

I

1. argument
2. nonargument (description)
3. argument
4. argument
5. nonargument (functional explanation)
6. nonargument (causal explanation)
7. nonargument (causal explanation)
8. nonargument (action explanation)
9. argument
10. nonargument (functional explanation)
11. nonargument (causal explanation)
12. nonargument (functional explanation)
13. argument
14. nonargument (causal explanation)
15. nonargument (illustration)
16. argument
17. argument
18. argument
19. nonargument (description)
20. nonargument (narrative)

II

1.
  1. If you let yourself be pushed around by aggressive people, they will not see you as someone to whom attention needs to be paid.
  So, 2. The first rule of coping with anyone aggressive, hostile or not, is that you stand up to that person.

3.
  1. If species were natural kinds, then the binomials and other expressions that are used to refer to particular species could be eliminated in favor of predicates.
  2. The binomials and other expressions used to refer to particular species cannot be eliminated in favor of predicates.
  So, 3. Species are not natural kinds.

4.
  1. Virtually everybody considers himself to be so abundantly provided with good sense that even those most difficult to please in all other matters do not commonly desire more good sense than they already possess.
  So, 2. Most people believe that they possess enough good sense.

9.
  1. The power set of any set (i.e., the set of all subsets of a given set) is always larger than the original set.
  2. The universal set is, by definition, the set of everything.
  So, 3. The power set of the universal set would have to contain more members than there are things in the universe.
  So, 4. The universal set is not a possible set.

13.
  1. An individual can access only a minuscule portion of the past through his or her own memory.
  So, 2. Most of one's beliefs about the past rest on testimony (i.e., the reports of others).

3. An individual cannot be in two places at once.
So, 4. Most of one's beliefs about distant places must depend on testimony.
   5. Books on science contain reports of observations and experiments conducted by others.
So, 6. Books on science are full of testimony.
   7. Most of us learn science by reading books on science.
So, 8. Most of what a given individual knows about science is, in fact, based on testimony.
So, 9. If we refuse to accept testimony, we humans must remain ignorant on many important matters.

Note: The clause "although many people associate scientific knowledge with direct observation" is a discount. Also note that "testimony" replaces "reports of others" in step 4 to secure uniform language.

16.   1. Unlike modern reptiles and more like warm-blooded birds and mammals, some dinosaurs roamed the continental interiors in large migratory herds.
   2. The large carnivorous dinosaurs would have been too active and mobile had they been cold-blooded reptiles.
   3. The estimated predator-to-prey ratios indicate they would have consumed too much for their body weight had they been cold-blooded animals.
So, 4. The dinosaurs were not cold-blooded reptiles.

17.   1. In order for something to move, it must go from a place where it is to a place where it is not.
   2. A thing is always where it is and is never where it is not.
So, 3. Motion is not possible.

18.   1. All brain events are physical events.
   2. No physical events can be adequately accounted for in intensional terms.
   3. It is only in terms of intensions that mental states can be adequately described.
So, 4. Mental states are not brain events.

Appendix to Chapter 2

Note: These diagrams are constructed according to the reconstructions in subsection II.

1. 1
   ↓
   2

3. $\underline{1 + 2}$
     ↓
     3

4. 1
$\downarrow$
2

9. $\underline{1 + 2}$
$\downarrow$
3
$\downarrow$
4

13.   5
$\downarrow$
1   3 $\underline{6 + 7}$
$\downarrow$ $\downarrow$ $\downarrow$
2   4   8
$\searrow$ $\downarrow$ $\swarrow$
9

16. 1   2   3
$\searrow$ $\downarrow$ $\swarrow$
4

17. $\underline{1 + 2}$
$\downarrow$
3

18. $\underline{1 + 2 + 3}$
$\downarrow$
4

FOR FURTHER CONSIDERATION

Reconstructing an argument can sometimes be a very difficult task, particularly when the claims made are vague or ambiguous or the arguer does not make clear the parts of his or her argument. Arguers will sometimes even omit the explicit mention of a key premise. (Such incompletely stated arguments, enthymemes, will be discussed in Chapter 6.) Besides criticizing an argument by exposing its failure to be sound or cogent, one can also criticize an argument by disclosing its lack of clarity. Unfortunately, real-world arguments frequently lack such clarity, and the muddled nature of an argument is often revealed when one has trouble reconstructing the argument. So, when you find it difficult or impossible to reconstruct an argument, the trouble *may* be due to flaws in the way the argument has been stated. Furthermore, when you discover such flaws in the way an argument is stated, you have a legitimate basis for either rejecting the argument or requiring the arguer to clarify his or her position.

Logic and Language

*Occasionally, the invalidity or weakness of an argument is concealed
by the language in which the argument is expressed. Many mistakes
in reasoning that lead to fallacious argumentation (the subject of
Chapter 4) are due to a careless or manipulative use of language.
Chapter 3 discusses some of the features of language that give rise to
problems with arguments and looks at the nature of definitions,
which are often given in order to avoid linguistic confusions.*

CHAPTER HIGHLIGHTS

Logic deals with the inferential connections among statements. Because the meanings of words change over time and because statements are sentences, it would seem that logic is merely a matter of linguistics and that the nature of what logicians study changes over time. However, this is not the case, since the logical relations among truths and falsehoods do not change with changes in language and meaning, and such relations are what logicians study. To avoid unwanted suggestions, some logicians define arguments as complexes of propositions. Any sentence that can be interpreted as stating a truth or falsehood is said to express a proposition. The truth or falsehood asserted is said to be the proposition expressed. Alternatively, a proposition can be considered what any two synonymous sentences express, whether they be in the same language or in different languages. However, an account of arguments in terms of propositions is not needed in order to understand the nature of logic.

Statements often have emotive force as well as cognitive meaning. A statement has **cognitive meaning** to the extent that it conveys information. A statement has **emotive force** to the extent that it expresses or elicits emotions. Since the logical connections among complexes of statements are part of the informational content of statements, logic is primarily concerned with cognitive meaning, not emotive force. One needs, though, to distinguish between the two because emotionally loaded language often interferes with a recognition of the presence or absence of logical relationships. This interference can happen in two ways: (a) Highly emotive language can compel us to misunderstand the cognitive content of statements, and (b) emotionally charged language can cause us to overlook the need for arguments and evidence.

Even though emotionally charged language can interfere with logical insight, it is neither possible nor desirable to eliminate all emotive force from the language in which arguments are presented. The point to remember is that emotively charged language should never be used as a substitute for argumentation.

Ambiguous or vague language often interferes with clear thinking. A word is **ambiguous** if it has more than one meaning in the context in which it is used.

A word is **vague** if it admits of too many borderline cases in which it is uncertain whether the term applies. Definitions are important because they can be used to avoid or eliminate ambiguity or vagueness.

The word "term" is defined in this chapter as *any word or phrase that refers to a single individual or to a category or kind of individual.* Such words or phrases can occur as the grammatical subject of a sentence. The **extension of a term** is the nonempty set of things to which the term applies. The **intension of a term** consists of the properties something must possess for it to be a member of the term's extension. **Extensional definitions** serve to specify the meaning of a word by delimiting the term's extension. **Intensional definitions** serve to specify the meaning of a term by revealing the term's intension.

Extensional definitions are either verbal or nonverbal. An **ostensive definition** is a nonverbal extensional definition in which the extension of a term is indicated (and, if successful, the meaning of the term is conveyed) by pointing to some or all of the members of the term's extension. An **enumerative definition** is a verbal extensional definition in which a term is defined by mentioning or listing members of the term's extension. A partial enumerative definition names one or more, but not all, members of the term's extension. A complete enumerative definition names all the members of the term's extension. A **definition by subclass** is a verbal extensional definition in which the extension of a term is specified by referring to the groups or subclasses the union of which comprises the term's extension. Definitions by subclass are either partial (if not all subclasses are mentioned) or complete (if all subclasses are mentioned). Although extensional definitions are useful, they have their drawbacks. Terms that are empty (that is, have no extension) cannot be defined extensionally. Also, the purposes of argumentation often cannot be served by merely specifying the things to which a term applies, since what is needed for careful analysis is an account of the concept that lies behind the use of the term. Hence, in argumentation there is often a need for intensional definitions instead of extensional definitions.

Lexical definitions are intensional definitions that report on the customary or conventional intension of a term. Lexical definitions are either true or false and are best exemplified by dictionary definitions. **Stipulative definitions** specify the intension of the term independently of convention or established use. Stipulative definitions are neither true nor false, since they represent only recommendations or proposals to use a term in a certain way. **Precising definitions** are intensional definitions used to reduce the vagueness of a term by modifying the term's conventional meaning in such a way as to make the term's range of applicability more precise. **Theoretical definitions** are intensional definitions given in an attempt to provide a deep understanding of the thing defined.

One method of constructing a definition for a term involves (a) specifying a general category (a genus) in which is included the thing or things to which the term applies and (b) distinguishing the proper subclass (the species) in which is included only the thing or things to which the term applies by mentioning the attribute (the difference) that separates that proper subclass from other proper subclasses within the general category. A definition constructed by this technique is a **definition by genus and difference**. The method of definition by genus and difference is often useful in constructing lexical, stipulative, precising, and theoretical definitions.

A definition by genus and difference may be inadequate if it fails to meet any of these six criteria:

1. A definition should not be obscure, ambiguous, or figurative.
2. A definition should not be circular (i.e., it should not contain a form of the definiendum in the definiens).
3. A definition should not be negative if it can be affirmative (i.e., it should not, if at all possible, define a term only by specifying the items to which the term does not apply).
4. A definition should not be too wide or too broad (i.e., it should not apply to any object outside the extension of the definiendum).
5. A definition should not to be too narrow (i.e., it should not fail to apply to any object in the extension of the definiendum).
6. A definition is flawed if it specifies the term's correct extension via mention of attributes that are unsuitable relative to the context or purpose.

When no adequate intensional definitions are available, two negative consequences may be the result: equivocation and merely verbal disputes. **Equivocation** occurs when an expression appears more than once in an argument, but the meaning of the expression is not kept constant, so the argument is invalid. A **merely verbal dispute** occurs when disputants who appear to be, but in fact are not, in disagreement talk past each other because they both use a particular word or phrase to which each party attaches a different meaning.

The improper use of a persuasive definition is sometimes confused with a merely verbal dispute. A **persuasive definition** is a definition that is biased in favor of some conclusion or point of view. Persuasive definitions should be avoided when a term needs to be defined in as neutral a manner as possible in order to have a fair and rational discussion. The use of persuasive definitions is distinct from a merely verbal dispute, since definitions are provided in the former but not in the latter. The use of persuasive definitions does not always constitute an error in reasoning—only when they are used as a substitute for sound argumentation.

DISCUSSION OF KEY CONCEPTS

I. Logic, Meaning, and Emotive Force

A. Helpful Reminders

1. The emotive force of statements can sometimes overwhelm an audience so that the cognitive meaning of and the lack of inferential support among statements is obscured. Slanting is a form of discourse in which a speaker or writer puts something in an emotively good or bad light within a context in which doing so is either inappropriate or accomplished without adequate justification. Through the use of slanted discourse, a speaker may present a case that is so emotively biased in favor of his position or biased against his opponent's position that the audience is led to accept his position with little evidence or in spite of much evidence to the contrary. In this manner, emotionally charged language can be used to cover up the logical shortcomings of an argument or to conceal information from an audience.

2. Slanting can be accomplished through the use of euphemisms and dysphemisms. A euphemism is a word or phrase that is emotively positive or emotively neutral and is used instead of a word or phrase that has a less favorable emotive

force. A dysphemism is a word or phrase that is emotively neutral or negative and is used instead of a word or phrase with a more favorable emotive force. Through the careful and crafty use of euphemisms and dysphemisms, a speaker can avoid mention, and thus conceal positive or negative aspects of his or her position or that of an opponent. Thus, a politician may refer to a proposed tax hike as an "additional revenue enhancement" or to a bill to increase funding as a "budget buster."

B. Commonly Asked Questions

1. What is the relationship between cognitive content and emotive force?

The cognitive content (i.e., the descriptive factual content) of a word or statement is distinct from the emotive force (i.e., the evaluative content) of a word or statement. This is made apparent by the fact that two people can be in total agreement about the facts of the matter but in complete disagreement with regard to their attitudes toward those facts. Nevertheless, expressions often have both a cognitive content and an emotive force. Both the cognitive content and the emotive force of a particular expression may vary according to its context of use. For instance, calling someone a "liberal" may well have a different signification when done among a group of liberal Democrats than when done among a group of conservative Republicans.

2. When is the presence of emotive language in an argument unacceptable?

In general, the rule of thumb is this: If an argument containing emotively charged language no longer seems compelling when the argument is restated using emotively neutral language with the same cognitive content, then the emotionally charged language is a substitute for good reasons and is thus unacceptable. However, it is often neither possible nor desirable to remove all the emotive force from the language in which an argument is stated. Many words carry some sort of emotive force due to their literal or implied meanings. Furthermore, one's emotional response to something can function as a legitimate reason in a justification for a particular course of action. For example, a person who has feelings of compassion for the poor and knows that she can help may well justify her decision to aid the poor in terms of both her compassion and her knowledge. (See the discussion of the appeal to pity in Chapter 4 of *The Power of Logic*.) The problem with emotionally charged language arises only when the persuasive force of an argument resides *solely* in the emotive force of the language used to state the argument.

C. Exercises

Rewrite each of the following sentences in two ways: (a) so as to make the sentence as emotively neutral as possible, and (b) so as to reverse the emotive force from emotively negative to emotively positive or from emotively positive to emotively negative.

1. Bill is a lazy bum.
2. Linda is vivacious.
3. Sam is a natural born leader.
4. Tony is a methodical worker.
5. Sally is a snob.
6. Barry is a clown.
7. John is a do-gooder.

8. Cindy is a blabbermouth.
9. George is a wimp.
10. Gloria is a liberated woman.
11. Kelly is sensitive.
12. Tim is a fierce competitor.
13. Brad is a cool guy.
14. Susan is imaginative.
15. Bob is a loser.

II. Definitions

A. Helpful Reminders

1. The distinction between ambiguity and vagueness is important. An expression is ambiguous if it can be interpreted in more than one way and the speaker or writer's intended meaning cannot be determined from the context. An expression is vague if it is imprecise in that its range of application is not made clear from the context of its use. Both ambiguity and vagueness are context dependent: a word or phrase that is ambiguous or vague in one context may not be so in another. When a word is ambiguous, you don't know which of its possible meanings is the intended one. In contrast, when a word is vague, you know what its meaning is but not exactly how the word is being applied (i.e., to what cases the term applies and to what cases the term does not apply). Thus, if a tourist says, "I know a little Italian," he is being ambiguous. If a politician says, "The new tax increase will not affect the middle class," she is being vague unless she specifies what sort of income one must have in order to be in the "middle class."

2. The six criteria for a good intensional definition constructed by genus and difference are important to remember. Such a definition should not be vague or ambiguous, circular, negative when it can be positive, too broad, or too narrow, or define something in terms of its nonessential or inappropriate features. Some definitions that fail the sixth criterion are improper definitions in a rhetorically interesting way. Occasionally, in the course of argumentation a speaker may define a term in such a fashion as to assume as unproblematic some view that is actually a component of the very position the speaker wishes to defend. In the course of a debate on the morality of abortion, for instance, a person defending the view that abortion is immoral may define abortion as the deliberate killing of an unborn child. The view of the fetus as an unborn child is accepted by the person who takes abortion to be immoral but is almost invariably rejected by the person who believes abortion to be morally permissible. Thus, the definition is improper because it defines "abortion" in terms of a feature, the killing of an unborn child, that is inappropriate given the nature of the debate. A speaker who gives such a definition tries, in effect, to win an argument by definition.

B. Commonly Asked Questions

1. Why study definitions when we are primarily concerned with arguments?

A good understanding of the various types of definitions provides us with some helpful tools for dealing with the problems that arise from ambiguity and vagueness in argumentative contexts. After all, arguers often attempt to avoid or eliminate such problems by introducing definitions.

2. Can a stipulative definition be a precising definition?

No, a stipulative definition is always different from a precising definition. A stipulative definition is an intensional definition that is used either to assign a meaning to a new expression or to give a new meaning to a familiar expression. Such a definition makes no use of an established meaning, as the meaning stipulated for a term is always novel. In contrast, a precising definition is an intensional definition that is used to make the standard meaning of an expression more precise. Such a definition does not supplant the standard meaning of a term but merely sharpens its conventional meaning by making clear the term's exact range of application.

C. Exercises

(a) Each of the following passages contains an ambiguous word or phrase. Identify the word or phrase and briefly describe its two meanings.

1. While serving the iced tea, Laura dropped the tray and broke her glasses and then couldn't see to clean up the mess.
2. There was something funny about the way she smiled.
3. The young lady approached Groucho and said, "I'm having lunch in the ballroom. Will you please join me?" Groucho responded, "Join you? Why, whatever for? Are you coming apart?"
4. The headline in the newspaper read, "Prostitutes Appeal to the Bishop."
5. Rick picked up his pet pigeon from the vet and took it with him downtown to make a deposit on a new car.

(b) Identify each of the following definitions as an ostensive, enumerative, lexical, stipulative, precising, or theoretical definition or a definition by subclass.

1. "Clarion," adjective, means "clear and shrill," and "clarion," noun, refers to (a) an ancient trumpet with a curved shape, (b) the sound of this ancient trumpet, and (c) any sound similar to the sound of this ancient trumpet.
2. By the word "blurp," we mean "any declarative sentence that is not a statement."
3. The seven deadly sins are the sins of pride, covetousness, lust, anger, gluttony, envy, and sloth.
4. By a "conservative politician," I mean to refer to anyone such as George W. Bush, John McCain, or Jack Kemp.
5. A book, as opposed to a booklet, is any bound publication that contains 100 or more pages.
6. Reptiles include snakes and lizards.
7. In physics, the measure of a moving object's kinetic energy is defined as one half the product of the measure of the object's mass and the measure of the object's velocity squared.
8. An alcoholic beverage, in contrast to a medication containing alcohol, is any liquid normally consumed as a beverage that contains at least 2 percent ethyl alcohol by volume and contains no other officially recognized drug.
9. To be a member of a major political party in the United States means being either a Democrat or a Republican.
10. The following symbol is the symbol for "if and only if": ↔

(c) By appealing to the six criteria for a good intentional definition, critique each of the following definitions constructed by genus and difference. Assume that the definitions are meant to be good lexical definitions.

1. A hammer is a hand tool primarily used for driving nails.
2. Inflation is the economic situation that results when too much money is chasing too few goods.
3. A virtue is a quality of a person that enables him or her to act virtuously.
4. A whale is a mammal that lives in the ocean.
5. A Republican is a person who is not a Democrat.
6. A book is a publication like Thomas Paine's *Common Sense*.
7. A copulative verb is a verb that functions as a copula.
8. To be (to exist) is to be the value of a bound variable.
9. The imaginary numbers are the numbers that are not real numbers.
10. A snake is a reptile that lays soft, leathery eggs.

III. Using Definitions to Evaluate Arguments

A. Helpful Reminders

1. The notion of equivocation is an important one. A speaker equivocates on a term when he or she uses the term more than once but does not mean the same thing each time. When an arguer's equivocation on a term leads to a conclusion not actually being supported by premises, an unsound or uncogent argument is the result. Under such circumstances, we say the speaker has committed the fallacy of equivocation (which will be discussed in Chapter 4).

2. Note the difference between equivocation and a merely verbal dispute and the difference between a merely verbal dispute and the use of a persuasive definition. Equivocation always involves a speaker or writer using the same word or phrase more than once in the course of an argument that is faulty due to the word or phrase undergoing a shift in meaning. In a merely verbal dispute, both parties in the dispute use the same expression in their separate discussions, but each of them uses the expression in a different sense so that they appear to be in disagreement but in fact are not. The use of a persuasive definition always involves a speaker or writer in a discussion or debate offering what amounts to an emotionally charged definition of a key term.

B. Commonly Asked Questions

1. Why is it important to recognize a disagreement as a merely verbal dispute?
Merely verbal disputes are not really uncommon. When the parties to a disagreement wind up in a merely verbal dispute, often none of the participants in the dispute realizes that each is talking about a completely different thing. Confusion and much misunderstanding of one another's positions and defenses of those positions are the results. Consequently, an adequate understanding of the arguments offered by each of the disputants requires a clarification of the exact nature of the disagreement. Unraveling the disagreement will involve showing that the participants are actually talking past one another and that the disagreement is not substantive but only a verbal disagreement.

2. What are persuasive definitions, and how are they used unfairly in arguments?

A persuasive definition is a definition that typically has little in the way of cognitive content but much in the way of emotive force. The primary purpose of persuasive definitions is to convey not information about a subject but an attitude about a subject. Persuasive definitions can be used to slant discourse. A speaker will sometimes try to gain an unfair rhetorical advantage over his or her opponent by introducing a persuasive definition as a means of emotionally compelling the audience to think favorably of his or her position or to think disparagingly of the opponent's position. However, fair argumentation often requires all parties to state their positions and define the necessary terms in as emotively neutral a manner as possible to facilitate honest discussion and debate.

C. Exercises

Choose the letter below that corresponds to the best way of completing each of the following sentences.

A. ostensive definition
B. precising definition
C. definition by genus and difference
D. lexical definition
E. theoretical definition
F. enumerative definition
G. stipulative definition
H. definition by subclass
I. persuasive definition
J. equivocation
K. a merely verbal dispute

1. A definition that specifies the standard meaning of a term as that term is customarily used by speakers of the language in which the term occurs is a _____.
2. A definition that is used to make clear the exact meaning of a term and thus avoid or eliminate vagueness is a(n) _____.
3. A definition that attempts to provide an adequate understanding of the thing(s) to which the term applies is a(n) _____.
4. When an author specifies that a term is to have a special meaning for only his or her particular use, the author gives a(n) _____.
5. When one defines a term by specifying a general category and the special distinguishing features of the things to which the term applies, one constructs a(n) _____.
6. To define a term by pointing at or displaying one or more representative items in the term's extension is to give a(n) _____ of the term.
7. When one defines a term by naming some or all of the members of the term's extension, one gives the term a _____.
8. When one characterizes a kind of thing by naming some or all of the more specific kinds of thing that are within the kind thus defined, one gives a _____.
9. A case of _____ occurs when two disputants who are in apparent but not real disagreement talk at cross purposes because they are using the same language to talk about two different things.
10. A case of _____ occurs when the same word or phrase appears more than once in the course of an argument but the meaning of the word or phrase is not kept constant throughout the argument.

ANSWERS TO EXERCISES

Answers to Selected Exercises in the Text

Exercise 3.1

1.   The argument in this passage can be stated in even more neutral language, as revealed by the following slightly different alternative reconstruction:
  1. The activity of various insurgent groups in the Middle East who attempt to coerce governments to conform to their wishes is the most likely cause of instability in the world today.
  So, 2. We should remove the leadership of the main insurgent groups in the Middle East who attempt to coerce governments to conform to their wishes.

Exercise 3.2
Part A

1. This definition is used to assign a meaning to a new word and is thus a stipulative definition.
4. This is a precising definition because it in effect tells you where to draw the line between what is a tall man and what is not a tall man.
7. This is the sort of definition a dictionary would give for this word. Thus, the definition is a lexical definition.
10. This is a precising definition in that it makes the notion of a sound argument much more precise. It could also be considered a theoretical definition in that it is used to inform logic students about the nature of sound arguments.
13. Although this definition appears to be rather simplistic, it is nevertheless a theoretical definition, at least as it has occurred in Western thought. The ancient Greeks considered the essential nature of mankind to reside in man's being a rational animal. The definition of man as a rational animal did constitute a theoretical account of mankind and was therefore a theoretical definition.

Part E

1. B		6. I	
2. H		7. A	
3. G		8. J	
4. E		9. D	
5. C		10. F	

Answers to Supplemental Exercises

I

1. Bill is a person who occasionally is motivationally challenged.
   Bill is a person who is careful not to overexert himself.
2. Linda has an overall optimistic outlook on life and tends to do a lot.
   Linda is hopelessly optimistic and hyperactive.

3. Sam is a person who is inclined to suggest to others what to do, not a person to whom others suggest what to do.
   Sam is bossy.
4. Tony characteristically tends to work by following a preset order deemed necessary to accomplish the task.
   Tony is an inflexible worker who tends to do all things according to a pre-conceived pattern.
5. Sally is a person who tends to avoid people with whom she does not wish to associate.
   Sally chooses her associates very carefully.
6. Barry is a person who compensates for his lack of ability by amusing others with his humor.
   Barry is quite a comedian.
7. John is a person who takes seriously his perceived duty to others.
   John is a decent, upright person who is dedicated to helping others.
8. Cindy is often loquacious.
   Cindy is quite communicative and is always willing to talk.
9. George is a person who does not often respond to challenges and tends not to make or be faithful to commitments.
   George is prudent when it comes to making commitments and accepting the challenges people put to him.
10. Gloria is a person who rejects most of the restrictions she perceives have been placed upon her because of her sex.
    Gloria is a flaming feminist.
11. Kelly often finds offensive the manner in which people around her look at her and talk to and about her.
    Kelly is inordinately sensitive.
12. Tim is a person who takes seriously the competitive challenge.
    Tim is a ruthless, aggressive competitor.
13. Brad is a man who desires to be popular and to keep up with the current trends.
    Brad is an ostentatious stud who is a slave to the latest fads.
14. Susan often exercises her imagination.
    Susan is a dreamer.
15. Bob has little talent or motivation.
    Bob is comfortable with himself; he doesn't need to prove his worth to others.

II(a)

1. glasses: eyeglasses, drinking glasses
2. funny: humorous, strange
3. join you: accompany you, put you together
4. appeal to: plead for help, elicit a favorable response from
5. deposit: financial deposit, fecal deposit

II(b)

1. lexical definition
2. stipulative definition
3. (complete) enumerative definition
4. (partial) enumerative definition
5. precising definition
6. (partial) definition by subclass
7. theoretical definition
8. precising definition
9. (complete) definition by subclass
10. ostensive definition

II(c)

1. The definition is too narrow, since there are hammers that are not hand tools (such as jackhammers) and there are hammers that are not primarily used to drive nails (such as ball peen hammers and sledgehammers).
2. The main fault of this definition is that it is too figurative and vague. Because money does not actually chase goods, one can't interpret the definiens literally. The definition may also be too narrow.
3. The definition is circular. If you don't know what a virtue is, then you are not likely to know what it means to act virtuously.
4. The definition is too broad. Dolphins and seals are marine mammals that are not whales.
5. The definition is unnecessarily negative and too broad. Most people in the world do not belong to either party, so you can't characterize the membership of one party as the people who don't belong to the other party.
6. The definition is too obscure and defines the word in terms of an inessential property. Just what it is about *Common Sense* that makes similar publications books is not clear, and being similar to *Common Sense* is not an essential or meaningful property of books.
7. The definition is circular. If you don't know what a copulative verb is, you are unlikely to know what a copula is.
8. The definition is too obscure and is circular. Existence seems to be a clearer notion than being the value of a bound variable, and so, if you don't understand the former, you aren't likely to comprehend the latter. The definition is also figurative in the sense that it is not intended to be taken literally.
9. The definition is unnecessarily negative. While it is true that the imaginary numbers are not real numbers, a positive characterization of the former can be given and would be more helpful.
10. The definition is too broad and too narrow. It is too broad, since lizards and turtles are reptiles and many of them lay soft, leathery eggs. It is too narrow, since some snakes do not lay soft, leathery eggs.

III

1. D
2. B
3. E
4. G
5. C
6. A
7. F
8. H
9. K
10. J

FOR FURTHER CONSIDERATION

Any emotively charged, confusing, or misleading discourse designed to conceal something from an audience is sometimes referred to as *doublespeak*. In addition to slanted discourse, there are other forms of doublespeak. *Puffery* is doublespeak designed to impress or dazzle an audience through the use of big words and sophisticated-sounding expressions. *Gobbledygook* is any convoluted discourse that is almost incomprehensible and is designed to confuse an audience. A *pacifier* is discourse replete with nice-sounding but empty words and phrases that is designed to lull an audience into a false sense of satisfaction. *Hyperbole* is a form of discourse in which exaggeration is used to bias (often by the misrepresentation of a position) a discussion in favor of or against a particular view. A study of the various forms of doublespeak can be useful as a means of understanding how the features of language discussed in this chapter can contribute to misleading argumentation.

The six criteria for good intensional definitions given in this text are essentially the time-honored criteria for a good definition originally discussed by Aristotle. For an excellent alternative perspective on the nature of good definitions, see Chapter 8 of Patrick Suppes' *Introduction to Logic* (1957, Van Nostrand).

CHAPTER 4

Informal Fallacies

Chapter 4 of The Power of Logic *focuses on what is perhaps the most important topic dealt with by informal logic, the informal fallacies. By studying the informal fallacies you will gain insight into the common ways in which argumentation can go awry. Also, a knowledge of the many ways people can be "tricked" into believing something will provide you with a means of both recognizing and avoiding bad arguments.*

CHAPTER HIGHLIGHTS

The **informal fallacies** are errors in reasoning that are nevertheless often psychologically persuasive. In contrast to a formal fallacy, such as the fallacy of denying the antecedent or the fallacy of the undistributed middle (discussed in Chapter 6), an informal fallacy does not involve the explicit use of an invalid argument form. The faulty nature of an informal fallacy is revealed by looking at the content of what is said rather than the form of argument employed.

There are many ways of categorizing the informal fallacies, and there is no common agreement among logicians as to the best way to classify them. In *The Power of Logic*, the informal fallacies are divided into three groups: (a) the fallacies involving irrelevant premises, (b) the fallacies involving ambiguity, and (b) the fallacies involving unwarranted assumptions.

The **fallacies involving irrelevant premises** are the argument against the person (the *ad hominem* fallacy), the straw man fallacy, the appeal to force (the *ad baculum* fallacy), the appeal to the people (the *ad populum* fallacy), the appeal to pity (the *ad misericordiam* fallacy), and the appeal to ignorance (the *ad ignorantiam* fallacy).

1. When the speaker, instead of addressing the issues at hand, chooses to discuss the personal nature of her opponent and thereby encourages her audience to reject the claims of her opponent, the speaker is said to have presented an *ad hominem* **argument**. The **abusive *ad hominem* fallacy** involves the speaker's making an obvious character assassination of her opponent. The approach can be more subtle, though. A speaker can offer an *ad hominem* argument by fallaciously arguing that her opponent's special circumstances (such as his having something to gain if his conclusion is accepted) prevent him from presenting an objective, reasoned account of why his position is correct. The speaker then concludes that, because of this situation, there is little reason to believe what her opponent says in defense of his views. This form of the *ad hominem* fallacy is called the **circumstantial *ad hominem***. Alternatively, in the *tu quoque* version of this fallacy, the speaker, on the basis of the claim that her opponent is a hypocrite, urges her audience to reject her opponent's claims.

2. In the **straw man fallacy**, the speaker mischaracterizes the position or the argument of his opponent and then proceeds to attack his own mischaracterization. The speaker then urges his audience to reject his opponent's actual position or argument on the basis of the rejection of his misrepresentation. The mischaracterization may sometimes be accomplished by falsely charging that the opponent's position involves problematic assumptions when it does not. The mischaracterization of the opponent's view can also result from a persuasive definition offered by the speaker.

3. When the speaker tries to convince her audience by issuing threats, the speaker makes an **appeal to force**. Such threats may be rather blatant or veiled behind talk of factual matters merely suggestive of a threat. The threat may involve the possibility of either psychological or physical harm.

4. An **appeal to the people** is made whenever the speaker appeals to the desire of his audience to be accepted or valued by others in an attempt to compel his audience to accept what he is advocating. Such an *ad populum* appeal does not always involve addressing a large group of people.

5. Rather than presenting reasons and evidence in support of some contention, the speaker may try to gain the sympathy of her audience in order to promote the acceptance of her claims. Under such circumstances, the speaker is said to have made an **appeal to pity**.

6. A speaker commits the fallacy of the **appeal to ignorance** when he either argues for his position by claiming that it has never been disproven or urges his audience to reject his opponent's position by claiming that it has never been proven. In other words, the speaker attempts to convince his audience either (1) that, since his conclusion has not been proven false, it is true, or (2) that, since his opponent's conclusion has not been proven true, it is false.

The **fallacies involving ambiguity** are the fallacies of equivocation, amphiboly, composition, and division.

7. The speaker commits the **fallacy of equivocation** when, in the course of her argumentation, she uses a word or phrase in more than one sense, but the plausible inference from premises to conclusion requires that the word or phrase be understood in the same sense throughout the argument.

8. An amphibolous statement is one that is ambiguous due to faulty sentence structure. The speaker commits the **fallacy of amphiboly** when he argues in such a way that an inference he makes using an amphibolous premise is plausible only if that premise is interpreted in a manner inconsistent with its intended meaning.

9. The speaker commits the **fallacy of composition** when she presents a bad argument that involves either arguing from what is true of the parts of a whole to what is true of the whole, or arguing from what is true of a population distributively to what is true of the population collectively.

10. The speaker commits the **fallacy of division** when he presents a bad argument that involves either arguing from what is true of a whole to what is true of the parts of the whole, or arguing from what is true of a population collectively to what is true of the population distributively.

The **fallacies involving unwarranted assumptions** are the fallacies of begging the question (*petitio principii*), the false dilemma, the appeal to unreliable authority (the *ad verecundiam* fallacy), the false cause, and the complex question.

11. The speaker is said to **beg the question** when she argues in such a fashion that she assumes (takes for granted) the truth of the very proposition she is trying to

prove. A question-begging argument either will contain a conclusion that is identical to or a paraphrase of one of the premises or will have a premise that can be believed to be true only if the truth of the conclusion has already been granted.

12. In the **fallacy of the false dilemma**, the speaker employs a premise that unjustifiably limits the number of possibilities to be considered. The speaker then may reach his conclusion by ruling out as false or implausible all but one of these options or may infer that his conclusion follows regardless of which option is taken.

13. The speaker makes an **appeal to unreliable authority** when she urges her audience to accept her position, or to reject her opponent's position, on the basis of the testimony of an authority whose reliability may reasonably be doubted. The speaker who commits this fallacy assumes, though, that the authority cited is reliable. This fallacy often involves the speaker's appealing to a person who is an authority in one area (such as physical science), although the conclusion of the argument concerns another area that is outside the authority's special competence (such as morality).

14. The **false cause fallacy** is committed whenever the speaker unjustifiably assumes that one possible cause of a phenomenon is a (or the) cause, even though other causes are possible given the available information. The most common form of this fallacy is the *post hoc, ergo propter hoc* **fallacy**. The post hoc fallacy is committed when the speaker concludes, or suggests to his audience, that, because one event follows another, the first event is the cause of the second. This is a fallacious inference, since causal connections between events are in fact more difficult to establish and require of separate events more than mere temporal succession. A speaker will sometimes contend, without good evidence, that the occurrence of one event will result in the occurrence of a series of events that will ultimately lead to disaster. This variety of the false cause fallacy is the **slippery slope fallacy**.

15. A speaker commits the **fallacy of complex question** when she poses a misleading or loaded question and illicitly draws a conclusion from an answer to the question. The particular question posed is misleading because it can be appropriately asked (and answered) only if a falsehood or an unsettled issue is taken for granted.

DISCUSSION OF KEY CONCEPTS

I. Fallacies Involving Irrelevant Premises

A. Helpful Reminders

1. A fallacy involving irrelevant premises occurs when an arguer introduces into his argument one or more premises the truth of which, although it may seem relevant, is actually irrelevant to the conclusion he wishes to establish. A speaker, then, commits a fallacy involving irrelevant premises when he fails to argue in a straightforward manner for his claim but instead brings up issues that aren't directly related or pertinent to justifying the conclusion he desires.

2. Be especially careful in identifying *ad hominem* fallacies that involve the charge of hypocrisy (*tu quoque* fallacies). Note that, in an *ad hominem* in which the speaker charges his opponent with hypocrisy, the speaker, on the basis of the claim that his

opponent is a hypocrite, is urging his audience to reject his opponent's claims. However, people who are accused of some wrongdoing often respond by arguing that their accusers have no right or are in no position to level accusations at them, since the accusers are themselves guilty of the same sort of wrongdoing. The point of such a response is to argue not that the charges are wrong but that the accusers are acting in an inappropriate manner. Such a line of argument may be reasonable; after all, most of us endorse the old saying, "People who live in glass houses shouldn't throw stones." So, as long as people accused of wrongdoing merely argue that their accusers have committed this sort of impropriety, the accused do not engage in *ad hominem* argumentation. However, if those accused go on to argue that, because of this inappropriate behavior on the part of their accusers, the accusations of the latter can be dismissed, then the accused do pursue *ad hominem* argumentation.

3. A speaker or writer often commits an appeal to the people (an *ad populum* argument) by arguing that, when it comes to the issue at hand, the beliefs of most people are in agreement with what he advocates. This kind of argument would be reasonable only if it were reasonable to assume that the majority is always right (that is, that whatever is believed by the majority of people is always correct). This assumption, of course, cannot be made. The automobile dealer who encourages potential customers to buy a particular car he sells because it is the number one import in America uses this kind of *ad populum*. Presumably, the fact that it is the number one import car in the United States, if true, means that most people believe it to be the best imported car. The conclusion that one should buy the automobile then only follows if it is taken for granted that most people cannot be wrong in their beliefs about this car. An *ad populum* argument is fallacious, since it does not follow that, because a belief is popular or makes one feel good, it must be true.

B. Commonly Asked Questions

1. Since discrediting a witness typically means casting doubt upon what the person says, what exactly is wrong with an *ad hominem* argument?

In an *ad hominem* argument, the speaker or writer always urges her audience to reject her opponent's claims solely on the basis of the opponent's personal characteristics, position, biases, or hypocrisy. Such an argument is fallacious, since these factors are irrelevant to the truth or falsity of what the opponent is claiming. People who have character defects, who have ulterior motives for saying what they say, who are biased in favor of a certain view, or who are guilty of hypocrisy may nevertheless be saying things that are true. Thus, the presence of these attributes in a person does not automatically mean that what the person says is false. When a witness is discredited, say, in a court of law, what is shown is the unreliability of the witness as a source of accurate information. In many cases, this is sufficient to show only that the veracity of the testimony of the witness can be doubted, particularly if others do not corroborate that testimony—not that the testimony should be accepted as false.

2. Aren't there times when the attributes of a person are relevant to arguing that what the person says is likely false?

Special background assumptions will sometimes exonerate an argument that occurs in the course of what looks like *ad hominem* argumentation. If, for example, John were to argue that Bill probably will not repay money loaned him because Bill is dishonest, then John might appear to be engaging in *ad hominem* argumentation. Nevertheless, John's argument might be a good one, for in this case Bill's dishonesty is a character trait that is relevant to determining whether he is likely to repay a loan. Bill's dishonesty is relevant, since dishonest people frequently fail to keep important agreements. In a similar vein, a disgruntled taxpayer may argue that a politician's promise to lower taxes will not be kept in the future because the politician has in the past not kept her promises to lower taxes. Since we generally assume that, unless there is evidence to the contrary, a person's future behavior will be similar to her past behavior, the taxpayer's conclusion that the politician will not keep her current promise is not without warrant. (The conclusion is not completely certain, though, and would be less certain if there were conditions no longer present that had prevented the politician in the past from keeping her promises.)

C. Exercises

Identify the fallacy involving irrelevant premises in the following passages.

1. Officer, I realize that just now I ran a red light, but you simply cannot give me a ticket. If I should be delayed here, I most certainly would not make it to the hospital in time to visit my poor Aunt Nidia after her recent brain surgery, and I most assuredly would miss my plane to Geneva. In Geneva, I intend to present to the world my foolproof plan for world peace and an end to those obnoxious Eveready battery commercials.
2. Those people who say that it is society's fault that there are criminals on our city streets are claiming that we should turn loose all of the convicted killers, give them all a pension for life, and shoot the rest of the city. Such nonsense obviously should not be believed.
3. Religious people are people who are very insecure and dissatisfied with life. That is why they feel the need to believe in God. Their firm belief is just a ploy to hide their insecurity. Therefore, there is really no reason for the normal, healthy individual to believe in God.
4. The church is the final authority in all matters pertaining to the affairs of men, for many a heretic has denied this and has lost his life on the pyre.
5. There must be a God, for men throughout the ages have always believed in and sought after a Divine Being.
6. In spite of the current scientific examination of the Shroud of Turin, its authenticity still has never been completely discredited. Therefore, we must protect and honor this relic as the genuine burial shroud of Christ.

II. Fallacies Involving Ambiguity

A. Helpful Reminders

1. A fallacy involving ambiguity is committed when an arguer couches his argument in language that is ambiguous or misleading or involves a shift in meaning.

2. The kind of confusion involved in making the fallacious inferences of the composition and division fallacies is all too often present in discussions of matters dealing with statistics. A statistic is a number that represents information only about a whole population, in spite of the fact that the number is derived from numerical data about individual elements of the population. To make a statistical claim about the nature of a population on the basis of an examination of one or a few of its members (part of the population) is often to commit the fallacy of composition, particularly if

the research has not been properly done. Likewise, to draw a conclusion about one or a few particular members of a population (part of the population) on the basis of statistical data is often to misinterpret the data and to commit the fallacy of division. Consider the following silly argument:

An American couple has, on average, 2.5 children.
John and Mary are an American couple.
Therefore, John and Mary have an average of 2.5 children.

Clearly, John and Mary, whoever they are, have a discrete whole number of children, not an average of 2.5, at any time even if both of the premises are true. The mistake one would make in inferring this conclusion from those premises would be a division fallacy resulting from a misunderstanding of the nature of the first premise. The first premise is a statistical statement about the population of American couples. The statement claims that the average or mean number of children of couples for the population (of American couples) as a whole is 2.5, so the statement is a claim about a whole population. This is true in spite of the fact that only individual couples have children, not the population as a whole, and the number 2.5 is in part calculated by counting the number of children of each particular couple. The number 2.5 is assigned to the population as a statistical whole on the basis of the nature of the individual members (or parts) of the whole population, but that number represents information about the whole population and does not give one knowledge about any particular elements of that population. Hence, the inference involved in the foregoing argument is a movement from what is true of a population as a collective whole to what is true of an element of that population. The argument is, therefore, an instance of the fallacy of division.

B. Commonly Asked Questions

1. What exactly is the difference between the fallacy of equivocation and the fallacy of amphiboly?

What is crucial to distinguishing these two fallacies is the type of ambiguity that is involved. The fallacy of equivocation involves an argument that is faulty due to an ambiguous *word* or *phrase*. The fallacy of amphiboly involves an unjustified inference from a *statement* that is ambiguous due to a structural (i.e., syntactical) flaw. Note that equivocation can easily occur when a speaker or writer uses relative terms (such as "large," "small," "fast," "slow," "heavy," "light," etc.), since such terms have a more definite meaning only in the context in which they occur. Consider the following argument:

All juvenile elephants are small elephants, and all elephants are animals.
Hence, all juvenile elephants are small animals.

The equivocation in the above argument is on the word "small"; however, this word is not an equivocation in isolation but rather in combination with the noun it modifies. The expressions "small elephants" and "small animals" refer to two entirely different kinds of small things even though the word "small" occurs in each expression. Because nothing that is a small elephant could be considered a small animal, the inference is flawed.

2. Aren't there perfectly reasonable arguments in which a speaker reaches a conclusion about what is true of the whole or the parts from what is true of, respectively, the parts or the whole?

Not every inference from what is true of the parts to what is true of the whole is an instance of the fallacy of composition. Similarly, not every inference from what is true of the whole to what is true of the parts is an instance of the fallacy of division. Some properties can be possessed by both a whole and its parts. For instance, to argue that a machine weighs more than two pounds because each of its parts weighs more than two pounds is not to commit the fallacy of composition. Neither is it a fallacy of division to argue that the parts of a machine are made of nothing but metal since the machine is made of nothing but metal. A fallacious inference is made only when what is asserted to be true of the whole can diverge from what is asserted to be true of its parts.

C. Exercises

Identify the fallacy involving ambiguity in the following passages:

1. Elephants are not found in Great Britain. Therefore, when visiting your friend in London, you should remember not to lose your elephant there, for it will never be found.
2. Every part of the universe is organized and regulated by strict causal laws. Everything in the universe that we know of has a cause. Therefore, the universe as a whole must likewise have a cause.
3. Diane said that, ever since she was a child, she has always wanted to dance so badly. After viewing the videotape of her attempt at ballet, the critics were not impressed. So, it would appear, then, that Diane got her wish.
4. Reptiles have been on the earth for over 250 million years. Human beings have been around for only about 1 million years. Therefore, Bob's pet snake is about 250 times older than he is.

III. Fallacies Involving Unwarranted Assumptions

A. Helpful Reminders

1. When a speaker presents an argument that is plausible only if certain problematic assumptions are taken for granted, the speaker commits a fallacy involving unwarranted assumptions. The presumptions involved in such an argument are problematic because the conclusion depends on them and they are in need of proof, and yet the arguer merely presupposes that they are true.

2. There is a regrettable tendency in ordinary parlance to misapply the term "begging the question." When used properly, "to beg the question" means "to take for granted beforehand the truth of the very conclusion that is being defended." Unfortunately, given the manner in which some commentators sometimes talk about begging the question, "to beg the question" may mean either "to invite the question" or "to ignore a challenge to a key assumption an arguer has made."

3. Occasionally, a speaker will subtly introduce into an argument a premise that unjustifiably limits the number of options to just two and will thereby commit the fallacy of the false dilemma. This is accomplished by maintaining that one has to choose either one of two options, since they cannot both be accepted. For example,

some creationists have maintained that, since one cannot be both an evolutionist and a creationist, one must be either an evolutionist or a creationist. However, even if the two options are indeed incompatible, it does not follow that they are the only options available.

4. Note that, when a speaker commits the fallacy of the appeal to unreliable authority, the appeal made to the authority can be fallacious for a number of different reasons. The authority's area of expertise may be lacking or outside the subject he comments on, or the precise identity of the authority referred to may be unknown. Alternatively, when authorities disagree, it may not be reasonable to believe that the question the authority is called upon to settle can be settled just by citing an authority.

B. Commonly Asked Questions

1. Since anyone who argues for a conclusion already accepts the truth of the conclusion, how does any arguer avoid begging the question?

Granted, an arguer already believes her conclusion to be true (otherwise there is no point to argue), but an arguer will avoid begging the question by presenting grounds for believing the conclusion that are independent of a prior belief in the conclusion. An argument will be successful at convincing an audience only if the audience is led to accept the conclusion on the basis of a prior belief not in the conclusion but in the premises. Thus, the conclusion of a good argument does not need to be accepted as true prior to accepting the truth of all the premises.

2. Why aren't we engaging in *ad hominem* argumentation when we criticize an argument from authority by pointing out that the authority cited is unreliable?

In legitimately rejecting an argument as a case of the fallacious appeal to unreliable authority, we do not commit the *ad hominem* fallacy for two reasons. First, the features having to do with the reliability of the authority cited are relevant to whether a conclusion should be accepted solely on the basis of the testimony of that authority. A critique of the alleged expertise of the authority cited is thus relevant to the evaluation of an argument from authority. Second, in rejecting as fallacious an argument from authority, we are not arguing that its conclusion is false but only that the argument does not provide us with sufficient reason to accept its conclusion as true. If we were to argue that a conclusion of an argument from authority is false merely because of the unreliability of the authority cited, then we would be engaging in *ad hominem* argumentation.

C. Exercises

(a) Identify the fallacy involving unwarranted assumptions in the following passages:

1. Certainly some people have ESP! After all, there are human beings who have perceptual faculties other than sight, hearing, taste, smell, and touch.
2. Darwin's theory of evolution is the root cause of many evils with which the world must now cope. The curses of communism, secular humanism, and rock 'n' roll did not emerge until after the publication of *The Origin of Species*.
3. The President has clearly stated his position on this issue and unequivocally is in favor of the measure we are now considering. We senators and representatives here in Congress should therefore support our President and pass this vital piece of legislation.

4. You never should start smoking cigarettes. Even if you start out smoking one or two cigarettes a day, your smoking will soon cause you to smoke at least a pack of cigarettes a day. A year or two later, you will then be smoking so frequently that you will be spending all your money on cigarettes. Once your money is exhausted, you will then either starve to death or become a ward of the state.

5. When it comes to the issue of race relations, either you're part of the solution or you're part of the problem. Those who argue against the political correctness movement are not helping to solve such matters. Thus, the critics of the PC movement are themselves part of the problem of race relations.

6. Do you suppose that Reagan knew about arms being sold to Iran before or after he lied to Congress about the Iran–Contra scandal? If he lied to Congress before knowing about it, then his lying was somewhat excusable, but it was still deception. If he lied to Congress after he had learned about what was happening, then his deception was even more flagrant than it initially appeared. Either way, it is clear that Reagan deliberately attempted to deceive Congress.

In order to master the material on fallacies, you need to work on acquiring two skills: (a) a knowledge of the general argumentative strategies associated with each of the fallacies and (b) the ability to recognize a stretch of argumentation as an instance of one of the fallacies. The following two sets of exercises should help you in developing these skills.

(b) Choose the letter below that corresponds to the best way of completing each of the following sentences.

A. *ad hominem* fallacy	G. equivocation	L. false dilemma
B. straw man fallacy	H. amphiboly	M. appeal to unreliable
C. appeal to force	I. composition	authority
D. appeal to the people	J. division	N. false cause fallacy
E. appeal to pity	K. begging the	O. slippery slope fallacy
F. appeal to ignorance	question	P. complex question

1. When a speaker assigns an improbable meaning to a statement that is ambiguous due to flawed sentence structure and draws an illicit inference from his interpretation of the statement, the speaker commits the fallacy of _____.

2. When a speaker attempts to convince an audience that, because one event followed another, the first event was the cause of the second event, the speaker commits the _____.

3. A person commits the informal fallacy of _____ when she takes for granted the truth of the very proposition she is attempting to prove.

4. When a speaker reaches an unwarranted conclusion about what is true of the whole from a premise about what is true of the parts of the whole, he commits the fallacy of _____.

5. When a speaker discredits what is a misinterpretation of her opponent's position and thereby urges the audience to reject her opponent's actual position, the speaker commits the _____.

6. When a speaker attempts to discredit an opponent's claim by pointing out that his opponent cannot be trusted because he is biased, the speaker commits the _____.

7. When a speaker tries to get her audience to feel sorry for her so that the audience will then agree with what she is saying, the speaker commits the fallacy of the _____.

8. When a speaker compels the audience to accept his position by threatening the audience, the speaker commits the fallacy of the _____.

9. When a speaker conducts a character assassination of her opponent and thereby urges her audience to reject her opponent's position, the speaker commits the _____.

10. To defend a conclusion with premises that could only be accepted by someone who already accepts the truth of the conclusion is to commit the fallacy of _____.

11. When a speaker oversimplifies a situation and presents to his audience only a limited number of options from which his audience must choose, and then proceeds to rule out all but one of these options in order to encourage the audience to accept a conclusion, the speaker commits the fallacy of the _____.

12. A speaker commits the informal fallacy of _____ when she reaches an illicit conclusion from premises containing a term that is used in two different senses.

13. When a speaker argues that what he is saying is true merely because a well-known person says it is true, the speaker is likely to commit the fallacy of the _____.

14. When a speaker argues that her opponent's claim should be dismissed because her opponent is a hypocrite, the speaker commits the _____.

15. When a speaker urges his audience either to accept his position because it has never been disproven or to reject his opponent's position because it has never been proven, the speaker commits the fallacy of the _____.

16. The speaker commits the fallacy of the _____ when she reaches an unwarranted conclusion by assuming that what most people believe to be the case is the case.

17. When a speaker reaches an unwarranted conclusion about what is true of the parts of a whole from a premise about what is true of the whole, he commits the fallacy of _____.

18. When a speaker urges her audience not to perform some action because its performance will cause the subsequent occurrence of a series of events that will ultimately lead to disaster, the speaker commits the _____ fallacy if there is insufficient evidence that some of the events are causally related to others.

19. When a speaker draws an illicit conclusion from the response given to a misleading question, the speaker is said to have committed the fallacy of _____.

20. When a speaker urges his audience to accept some conclusion so that the beliefs of the audience will be in conformity with those of the majority, the speaker commits the fallacy of the _____.

(c) Identify any fallacy committed in the following passages.

1. Certain vocal members of the NRA say that handguns should not be outlawed because "if guns are outlawed, only outlaws will have guns." These fanatics are arguing that the American people will never be safe from criminals until every man, woman, and child over the age of three months owns a pistol and a submachine gun. Their position on this issue thus is clearly wrong.

2. Now, Professor, I must have done well on this exam; otherwise, I may have to drop the class and change my major. If this should happen, I would fail to inherit my father's business, and this would cause me and my descendents to roam the earth in utter poverty and despair, living on the handouts of people more fortunate than myself.

3. The war against Iraq in the Persian Gulf was evidently justified. The vast majority of Americans supported George Bush's handling of the situation and believed that there was no alternative course of action the United States could have taken.

4. A recent study supposedly has shown that the gap between the upper class and the middle and lower classes has widened in the past 15 years. Liberals are always claiming that there is a problem with the income distribution in this country. But income is not distributed. It is earned. There is no income distribution in this country. There is thus no problem with the income distribution in this country. (attributed to Rush Limbaugh)

5. Only those who have faith in God know that there is a God, for only through faith do we become cognizant that God exists.

6. Mr. Osawa is always talking about the rudeness of American businessmen toward Japanese businessmen in this country, but we really should not let this bother us. Mr. Osawa fails to keep in mind that, in his native Japan, Korean nationals are regarded as second-class citizens and are treated as such.

7. The total mass of iron in the earth's crust is greater than the total mass of gold in the earth's crust. Therefore, a chunk of iron must have a mass greater than that of a chunk of gold.

8. Each manufacturer is perfectly free to set his own prices on the products he produces, so there can be nothing wrong with all manufacturers getting together to fix the prices of the commodities made by all of them.

9. When a team competes in football, it either wins or loses. So, since the Bulldogs did not win, they must have lost the game.

10. Pat belongs to an ethnic group that has been discriminated against in the past. Therefore, Pat has been discriminated against in the past.

11. It has never been conclusively proved that FDC yellow #5 dye is a carcinogen. Therefore, the Food and Drug Administration's failure to ban this product must be deemed reasonable, since it evidently poses no danger to the public health.

12. This liniment is good for anything like the pain of arthritis. However, nothing is anything like the pain of arthritis. Thus, this liniment must be good for nothing.

13. The Reverend Graham once argued, "Yes, we can know God exists, and not only exists but also loves us and wants us to know him personally. We know this because God has come down in the person of his son, Jesus Christ."
14. Mr. Brandon says that offshore drilling platforms pose very little risk of damage to the marine environment. However, what Mr. Brandon says is probably false, since he works for Exxon, an oil company that has invested heavily in offshore drilling.
15. They put fences around cemeteries because people are dying to get in.

ANSWERS TO EXERCISES

Answers to Selected Exercises in the Text

Exercise 4.1
Part B

10. This is not a fallacious appeal to pity. The sympathy or pity wealthy Americans may have for poor people in Third World countries is a relevant reason for these Americans providing aid. It is also not the only reason suggested in the passage for giving this aid.

Exercise 4.2
Part A

20. Note that this is still a case of equivocation, even though the ambiguous phrase "created equal" does not occur more than once in the argument proper in this passage.

Exercise 4.3
Part B

7. A psychology professor may well be an expert on the origins of certain common beliefs and experiences and thus may be able to give an account of how it is that people often acquire the belief in God. However, this expertise does not make one an authority on the question of God's existence. Furthermore, note that, even if it is true that people have religious experiences and come to believe in God because of the need for a father figure, it does not follow that their beliefs are false.
25. Just as not knowing that a hypothesis is true is not equivalent to knowing that the hypothesis is not true, not believing that a hypothesis is true is not equivalent to believing that the hypothesis is not true. Hence, it is not the case that either you believe that the doctrine of reincarnation is true or you believe that it is false, even though it is the case that either you believe that the doctrine of reincarnation is true or you do not believe that it is true. The argument in this passage is consequently an instance of the fallacy of the false dilemma.

Answers to Supplemental Exercises

I

1. the appeal to pity
2. the straw man fallacy
3. the (abusive) *ad hominem* fallacy
4. the appeal to force
5. the appeal to the people
6. the appeal to ignorance

II

1. equivocation
2. the fallacy of composition
3. amphiboly
4. the fallacy of division

III(a)

1. begging the question
2. the false cause
3. the appeal to unreliable authority
4. the slippery slope fallacy
5. the false dilemma
6. the complex question

III(b)

1. H	2. N	3. K	4. I	5. B
6. A	7. E	8. C	9. A	10. K
11. L	12. G	13. M	14. A	15. F
16. D	17. J	18. O	19. P	20. D

III(c)

1. the straw man fallacy
2. the appeal to pity and the slippery slope fallacy
3. the appeal to the people
4. equivocation
5. begging the question
6. the *ad hominem* fallacy (the *tu quoque* version)
7. the fallacy of division
8. the fallacy of composition
9. the false dilemma
10. the fallacy of division
11. the appeal to ignorance
12. equivocation
13. begging the question
14. the (circumstantial) *ad hominem* fallacy
15. equivocation

FOR FURTHER CONSIDERATION

Authors of introductory logic textbooks do not always define "fallacy" in the same way, and there is disagreement about how a fallacy can be best characterized. Logicians generally agree on what the particular fallacies are, but there is no uniform recognition of what a fallacy is in general. One way to characterize a fallacy is to say that it is an argument that purports to establish decisively its conclusion but in fact fails to do so. A fallacy under this interpretation is just an unsound or uncogent argument. However, if we view a fallacy as merely an argument that lacks soundness or cogency, then we run into troubles of a technical nature. In spite of the fact that most fallacious arguments are indeed unsound or uncogent, some (such as some circular arguments in which a conclusion is also a premise) are actually sound arguments. The reason such arguments are without merit has to be accounted for in terms of something other than their lack of soundness.

Perhaps the most plausible way to think about the fallacies is to regard them as patterns of argumentation that may be psychologically persuasive but do not represent totally reliable means of establishing a conclusion. Fallacious argumentation can then be regarded as any argumentation, fitting the pattern of a fallacy, in which a bad argument is given. Such argumentation is specious in the sense that it may seem plausible on the surface; however, a careful examination of the reasons presented in a stretch of fallacious argumentation should reveal their inadequacy for warranting the acceptance of a particular conclusion.

Although attempts have sometimes been made to define the various fallacies in such a way that any instance of the named fallacy will be a bad argument, it is perhaps better to think of each fallacy as a specific manner of arguing in which an objectionable argument may, but not necessarily will, occur. Any argument, occurring within argumentation that fits the pattern of a fallacy, that has premises that are not all true or that inadequately or inappropriately support the conclusion can then be said to be a fallacious argument. Whenever you recognize that a stretch of argumentation appears fallacious, you should be on the lookout for the sort of fallacious argument associated with that fallacy. The fallacious argument may or may not be present, but you should always be watchful for it and maintain a healthy skepticism toward any argument presented to you in a logically suspect manner.

CHAPTER 5

Categorical Logic: Statements

*The validity of some arguments turns on the way in which the state-
ments that make them up are used to assert relationships between categories of things. In Chapter 5, the nature of categorical statements,
the logical relations that obtain between categorical statements, and
the valid immediate inferences that can be made from the truth or
falsity of categorical statements are examined.*

CHAPTER HIGHLIGHTS

A **categorical statement** is a statement that expresses a relationship between two
classes or categories of things. A **categorical term** is any term that designates a class
or category of things. Every categorical statement has two categorical terms in it: a
subject term and a predicate term. The **subject term** is the categorical term that occurs in the statement's grammatical subject position. The **predicate term** is the categorical term that occurs in the statement's grammatical predicate position.

A categorical statement is said to be **in standard form** (or is a **standard-form categorical statement**) when it is an instance of one of the **standard forms**, "All S are P,"
"No S are P," "Some S are P," or "Some S are not P." Any statement that is an instance
of the first of these forms is an **A** statement; any statement that is an instance of the
second form is an **E** statement; any statement that is an instance of the third form
is an **I** statement; and any statement that is an instance of the fourth form is an
O statement.

The subject and/or predicate terms of categorical statements are not always simple and are occasionally quite complex. Any expressions that can replace the "S" and
the "P" in one of the standard forms to form a standard-form categorical statement
can be a subject and a predicate term. Categorical statements are sometimes not in
standard form because they contain a predicate adjective instead of an adjective together with a noun. In addition, a statement can fail to be a categorical statement because it contains a proper name instead of a categorical term.

Every categorical statement is either universal or particular in **quantity** and either affirmative or negative in **quality**. A **universal affirmative** statement asserts
that all the members of one class are included in the membership of another class.
Every universal affirmative statement is an instance of the form or can be restated as
an instance of the form "All S are P." A **universal negative** statement asserts that all
of the members of one class are excluded from the membership of another class.
Every universal negative statement is an instance of the form or can be restated as an
instance of the form "No S are P." A **particular affirmative** statement asserts that at
least one of the members of one class is included in the membership of another class.
Every particular affirmative statement is an instance of the form or can be restated as

an instance of the form "Some S are P." A **particular negative** statement asserts that at least one member of one class is excluded from the membership of another class. Every particular negative statement is an instance of the form or can be restated as an instance of the form "Some S are not P."

A categorical statement can fail to be in standard form for a number of reasons. Some categorical statements contain a predicate adjective instead of a noun phrase and can be put into standard form by supplying them with a noun in the predicate position. Some statements have all the components of a standard-form categorical statement but do not have them in the right order. Such statements can be put into standard form by rearranging their elements. A categorical statement can also fail to be in standard form because it lacks the standard copula (a form of the verb "to be") that occurs between the subject and predicate terms. Such a statement is put into standard form by adding the standard copula and replacing the grammatical predicate with a noun and a modifying adjective clause containing the predicate. Other categorical statements fail to be in standard form because they are stylistic variants of standard-form categorical statements. Any such nonstandard-form categorical statement easily can be restated as an instance of one of the standard forms.

When the truth or falsity of one statement is inferred from the truth or falsity of just one other statement, the inference made is said to be an **immediate inference**. According to traditional categorical logic, a number of logical relations hold between two related categorical statements of various forms (provided that the categorical statements are neither necessarily true nor necessarily false). Two categorical statements having the same subject and predicate terms are called **corresponding statements**. Corresponding **A** and **O** categorical statements, as well as corresponding **E** and **I** categorical statements, are **contradictory** statements, meaning that they cannot both be true and cannot both be false. Corresponding **A** and **E** categorical statements are **contrary** statements, which means that they cannot both be true but can both be false. Corresponding **I** and **O** categorical statements are **subcontrary** statements, meaning that they cannot both be false but can both be true. The logical relation between **A** and **I** categorical statements, as well as between **E** and **O** categorical statements, is **subalternation**, which means that **A** statements (the superaltern) imply their corresponding **I** statements (the subaltern), and **E** statements (the superaltern) imply their corresponding **O** statements (the subaltern). Thus, if an **A** statement is true, then its corresponding **I** statement is also true, and if an **E** statement is true, then its corresponding **O** statement is also true. All of these relations between corresponding statements are depicted in a diagram called the **traditional square of opposition**.

Given the logical relations between corresponding categorical statements as represented in the traditional square of opposition, the following inferences can be made:

1. If an **A** statement is true, then its corresponding **I** statement is true, and its corresponding **E** and **O** statements are both false.
2. If an **A** statement is false, then its corresponding **O** statement is true.
3. If an **E** statement is true, then its corresponding **O** statement is true, and its corresponding **A** and **I** statements are both false.
4. If an **E** statement is false, then its corresponding **I** statement is true.
5. If an **I** statement is true, then its corresponding **E** statement is false.

6. If an **I** statement is false, then its corresponding **A** statement is false, and its corresponding **E** and **O** statements are both true.
7. If an **O** statement is true, then its corresponding **A** statement is false.
8. If an **O** statement is false, then its corresponding **E** statement is false, and its corresponding **A** and **I** statements are both true.

There are other forms of immediate inference recognized by traditional categorical logic. These other inferences do not involve relations between corresponding statements. The **converse** of a standard-form categorical statement is formed by interchanging its subject and predicate terms. **Conversion** (the inference from a categorical statement to its converse) is a valid form of inference for only **I** and **E** categorical statements. The **converse by limitation** of an **A** statement is formed by interchanging its subject and predicate terms and converting the **A** statement to an **I** statement. **Conversion by limitation** (the inference from an **A** statement to its converse by limitation) is valid for all **A** statements. The **obverse** of a standard-form categorical statement is formed by replacing its predicate term with its term-complement and changing the quality of the categorical statement. (The **term-complement** of a term T is the term that designates the class of all things not included in the class designated by T.) **Obversion** (the inference from a categorical statement to its obverse) is a valid form of inference for all four forms of categorical statements. The **contrapositive** of a standard-form categorical statement is formed by replacing its subject term with the term-complement of its predicate term and replacing its predicate term with the term-complement of its subject term. **Contraposition** (the inference from a categorical statement to its contrapositive) is a valid form of inference for only **A** and **O** categorical statements. The **contrapositive by limitation** of an **E** statement is formed by replacing its subject term with the term-complement of its predicate term, replacing its predicate term with the term-complement of its subject term, and converting the **E** statement to an **O** statement. **Contraposition by limitation** (the inference from an **E** statement to its contrapositive by limitation) is valid for all **E** statements.

Two statements are **equivalent** if and only if each statement implies the other, which means that two equivalent statements must always agree in truth value. Any **I** or **E** categorical statement is equivalent to its converse. Any **A**, **E**, **I**, or **O** categorical statement is equivalent to its obverse. Any **A** or **O** categorical statement is equivalent to its contrapositive. An **A** statement will imply its converse by limitation, but the two statements are not equivalent. Similarly, an **E** statement will imply its contrapositive by limitation, but the two statements are not equivalent.

DISCUSSION OF KEY CONCEPTS

I. Standard Forms of Categorical Statements

A. Helpful Reminders

1. The information concerning the four standard forms and the quantity and quality of the four kinds of categorical statements is summarized in the following chart.

		Quality	
		Affirmative	Negative
Quantity	Universal	**A** All S are P.	**E** No S are P.
	Particular	**I** Some S are P.	**O** Some S are not P.

2. Note the difference between a standard form of a categorical statement and a standard-form categorical statement. A standard form of a categorical statement is one of the four standard categorical statement forms (containing the letters "S" and "P"). A categorical statement is in standard form if and only if it can be generated from one of the four standard forms by replacing the "S" and "P" with categorical terms. To put a categorical statement in standard form means to write it so that it is a standard-form categorical statement.

3. Remember that you have correctly identified the subject and predicate terms of a categorical statement if you can can substitute what you have identified as the subject and predicate terms for, respectively, the letters "S" and "P" in one of the standard forms "All S are P," "No S are P," "Some S are P," or "Some S are not P" and generate the categorical statement by that substitution.

4. The quantifier "some" is always understood to mean "at least one," regardless of whether the subject and verb of the statement are singular or plural. Thus, "Some place is a quiet place" is understood to be the same statement as "Some places are quiet places." Notice, though, that the present-tense plural "are" is always what occurs in standard-form categorical statements.

5. Unfortunately, many English statements that are used to assert a relation between two classes are not in standard form. In addition to what is discussed explicitly in *The Power of Logic*, other common ways in which categorical statements can fail to be in standard form can be recognized, and helpful strategies can be given for translating these nonstandard-form categorical statements into standard form. Remember that, because a statement can fail to be a standard-form categorical statement for more than one reason, more than one of the techniques presented below may need to be applied.

a. A categorical statement may not be in standard form because it is the negation of a categorical statement. To put such a statement into standard form, translate the statement as the contradictory of the statement negated. Any statement of the form "Not all S are P" is translated as a statement of the form "Some S are not P," and any statement of the form "It is not the case that no S are P" is translated as a statement of the form "Some S are P." Any statement of the form "It is false that some S are P" is translated as a statement of the form "No S are P," and any statement of the form "It is false that some S are not P" is translated as a statement of the form "All S are P."

b. Often a quantifier (a word indicating the quantity of a statement) is joined to a word that is actually part of the subject and predicate terms. This word is called a parameter, and typically it first must be separated from the quantifier to get the statement that contains it into standard form. Once the separation is achieved, the quantifier is replaced by an equivalent standard quantifier, and both the subject and predicate terms are rendered as noun substantives containing the translation of the parameter. Most often, the parameter will be translated as "people," "persons," "things," "places," or "times." The words "everyone," "everybody," "anyone," "anybody," "whoever" and "whosoever" are translated as "all people" or "all persons." The word "nobody" is translated as "no people" or "no persons." The words "someone" and "somebody" are both translated as "some people" or "some persons." The words "everything" and "anything" are both translated as "all things," and the word "nothing" is translated as "no things." The word "something" is translated as "some things." The words "everywhere," "anywhere," and "wherever" are translated as "all places." The word "nowhere" is translated as "no places," and the word "somewhere" is translated as "some places." The words "anytime" and "whenever" are translated as "all times." The word "always" is translated as either "all" or "all times." The word "never" is translated as either "no" or "no times." The word "sometime" is translated as "some times," and the word "sometimes" is translated as either "some" or "some times." Thus, "Nobody knew the answer" is translated as "No people are people who knew the answer," and "Somebody is a farmer" is translated as "Some people are people who are farmers" (or "Some people are farmers"). "Anything is possible" is translated as "All things are possible things," and "Something is wrong here" is translated as "Some things are things wrong here." "Somewhere there is peace" is translated as "Some places are places where there is peace," and "Joe never studies before an examination" is translated as "No times before an examination are times Joe studies."

c. The word "none" or the words "there are no" may be present instead of the standard quantifier "no." The expressions "there is (are)," "there is at least one," and "one" may occur instead of the standard quantifier "some." Thus, "There are no free lunches" is translated as "No lunches are free lunches." "None of the tires we have are Goodyear tires" is translated as "No tires we have are Goodyear tires." "There are free lunches" is translated as "Some lunches are free lunches," and "There is at least one bird in the yard that is a robin" is translated as "Some birds in the yard are robins." "One animal that inhabits Africa is an elephant" is translated as "Some animals that inhabit Africa are elephants." Certain adverbs or adverbial expressions may also be used instead of the standard quantifiers. Thus, "Salesmen are not ever trustworthy people" is translated as "No salesmen are trustworthy people," and "Politicians are occasionally big spenders" is translated as "Some politicians are big spenders." Be careful when the words "none but" (or the word "only") or the expression "the only" occurs instead of the quantifier "all." Any statement of the form "None but S are P" is put into standard form as "All P are S," and any statement of the form "The only S are P" is rendered into standard form as "All S are P." Thus, "None but the wealthy are executives" is translated as "All executives are wealthy people," and "The only people who eat tofu are vegetarians" is translated as "All people who eat tofu are vegetarians."

d. A quantifier may not occur in a statement, even though it is a categorical statement. Generalizations are sometimes made without the use of a quantifier when the context is such that it is apparent how the generalization is to be understood (as either a universal or a particular categorical statement). Thus, "Bats are mammals" is translated as "All bats are mammals," and "American troops are stationed in Korea" is translated as "Some American troops are troops stationed in

Korea." The indefinite article ("a," "an") or the definite article ("the") may occur instead of a quantifier. The context should tell you whether the quantification is universal or particular. "A horse is a herbivore" is translated as "All horses are herbivores," and "A bat is not a bird" is translated as "No bats are birds." "An alligator escaped from the zoo" is translated as "Some alligator is an alligator that escaped from the zoo," and "A student in Sam's algebra class is a person Sam does not care to be around" is translated as "Some student in Sam's algebra class is not a person Sam cares to be around." "The adult grizzly bear is a large and powerful animal" is translated as "All adult grizzly bears are large and powerful animals," and "The termite is not an insect you want to have in your house" is translated as "No termites are insects you want to have in your house."

e. A quantifier together with what is actually a subject term may occur in a statement but not be the first words of the statement. In such a case, the quantifier and the categorical term appearing after it need to be moved together to the beginning of the statement. Thus, "Sales are lost all times customers complain" is translated as "All times customers complain are times sales are lost."

f. A statement may contain a mass term rather than a sortal term. A mass term is any term to which it does not make sense to apply a strictly numerical concept. A sortal term, by contrast, is used to refer to things that can be counted. For example, terms designating substances such as "water," "salt," and "gold" are typically mass terms, whereas words designating particular kinds of things such as "table," "automobile," and "person" are typically sortal terms. To obtain a standard-form categorical statement from a statement containing a mass term, add a sortal term to the statement and put the resulting statement into one of the standard categorical forms. Thus, "Military insubordination is a serious matter" can be translated as "All cases of military insubordination are cases involving serious matters," and "Humor is not an argument" is translated as "No humorous remarks are arguments."

B. Commonly Asked Questions

1. Aren't there categorical statements that express a more complex relationship between more than two classes or categories of things?

There are indeed other categorical statements that do express more complex class relationships, but these other kinds of statements were treated by traditional logic as cases of the four recognized kinds of categorical statements. The theory of traditional categorical logic was based on the idea that any categorical statement asserts one of four class relationships that can hold between just two classes or categories of things. Nevertheless, the theory has proven to be very powerful in revealing the validity and the invalidity of categorical arguments. Admittedly, however, there are more complicated categorical arguments the validity or invalidity of which is more easily shown by appealing to modern predicate logic (the subject of Chapter 9).

2. Why isn't the standard form for an E statement "All S are not P" instead of "No S are P"?

The form "All S are not P" is ambiguous in English in that some English statements having that form are equivalent to corresponding statements of the form "No S are P," while other statements having that form are equivalent to corresponding statements of the form "Not all S are P." Thus, "All S are not P" may mean either "No S are P" or "Some S are not P." For instance, "All cats are not dogs" and "No cats are dogs" are synonymous, while "All that glitters is not gold" and "Some things that glitter are not gold things" are synonymous.

C. Exercises

(a) For each of the following categorical statements, identify its subject and predicate terms, its quantity and quality, and its form (**A, E, I,** or **O**):

    1. Some great novels are not books that are easy to read.
    2. All lipid molecules are organic molecules formed from a glycerin molecule and three fatty acids.
    3. No things that are easy to accomplish are things worth accomplishing.
    4. Some important discoveries are discoveries that were made accidentally.
    5. No meaningful counterfactual statements are statements that describe things in terms of their nonessential, or accidental, features.

(b) Rewrite each of the following statements as a categorical statement in standard form:

    1. A salamander is not a lizard.
    2. Not every reptile is a lizard.
    3. None but pacifists are Quakers.
    4. Some aquatic snakes are poisonous.
    5. Wherever there are aquatic snakes, there are frogs.
    6. The bird population decreases whenever the deer population increases.
    7. A caecilian is a limbless amphibian.
    8. If it is a lizard, then it is a reptile.
    9. Somewhere over the rainbow troubles melt like lemon drops.
  10. Everyone at the party became intoxicated.
  11. If it doesn't say "Amana," then it's not a Radarange.
  12. There is at least one Republican who is not a conservative.
  13. Nobody who wasn't there yesterday knew the answer.
  14. Some war heroes ran for office but were defeated.
  15. The only words spoken there were whispered.
  16. There is a politician who works awfully hard.
  17. Home movies sometimes can be quite boring.
  18. Whosoever shall be born after us shall be a part of a higher history.
  19. Something there is that doesn't love a wall, that wants it down.
  20. Lying under oath is always perjury.

II. The Traditional Square of Opposition

A. Helpful Reminders

    1. Two statements are corresponding statements if they differ in form but have the same subject and predicate terms. Notice that the statements "All salts are electrolytes" and "Some electrolytes are salts" are not corresponding statements. Even though they both contain the terms "salts" and "electrolytes," these terms do not occupy the same positions in the two statements.
    2. If a statement A implies a statement B, then the combination of A being true and B being false is not possible. A true statement cannot imply a false statement,

even though a true statement can imply another true statement. Thus, if A implies B, then B will be true when A is true, and A will be false when B is false. As a result, since **A** statements imply their corresponding **I** statements, an **I** statement will be true whenever its corresponding **A** statement is true, and an **A** statement will be false whenever its corresponding **I** statement is false. The same goes for **E** statements and their corresponding **O** statements.

3. If statement A is contrary to statement B, then B is contrary to A. If A is subcontrary to B, then B is subcontrary to A. If A is contradictory to B, then B is contradictory to A. If A is equivalent to B, then B is equivalent to A. However, if A implies B, then it does not automatically follow that B implies A. So, the superaltern implies its corresponding subaltern, but the subaltern does not in general imply its corresponding superaltern.

B. Commonly Asked Questions

1. If we know that an **I** statement is true, then don't we also know that its corresponding **O** statement is true, and vice versa?

No; from a logical perspective, there is no guarantee that, if an **I** statement is true, then its corresponding **O** statement must also be true and that, if an **O** statement is true, then its corresponding **I** statement must also be true. When speakers utter an **I** or **O** categorical statement, they often do suggest that the corresponding **O** or **I** categorical statement, respectively, is true. Thus, for instance, if a legislator tells her constituents, "Some bills passed this session were actually meaningful pieces of legislation," she seems to suggest to her audience that she believes that some bills passed this session were *not* actually meaningful pieces of legislation. This suggestion is due to the fact that an audience would normally expect a speaker to assert the more informative universal (**A** or **E**) categorical statement if the speaker believed the universal to be true. So, when speakers refrain from uttering the universal statement and only assert the particular (**I** or **O**) categorical statement, they suggest that the universal statement is—or at least they believe it to be—false. Thus, the assertion of an **I** statement instead of its corresponding **A** and the assertion of an **O** statement instead of its corresponding **E** both lead to the suggestion that the corresponding **I** and **O** categorical statements are both true. However, this is only a suggestion and is a case of what has been called "conversational implication." What is said literally in asserting an **I** statement or an **O** statement does not mean that its corresponding **O** statement or **I** statement, respectively, must be true as well. An **I** statement does not logically imply its corresponding **O** statement, and an **O** statement does not logically imply its corresponding **I** statement.

2. If we know the truth value of one categorical statement, can we always figure out the truth values of all its corresponding statements, given all the logical relations as depicted in the square of opposition?

Given the traditional square of opposition, a knowledge of the truth or falsity of one categorical statement may or may not lead to a knowledge of the truth or falsity of all its corresponding statements. For instance, if an **A** statement is true, then its corresponding **I** statement must be true (since **A** statements imply their corresponding **I** statements), its corresponding **E** statement must be false (since corresponding **A** and **E** categorical statements are contrary and thus cannot both be true), and its corresponding **O** statement must be false (since corresponding **A** and **O** categorical statements are contradictory). However, if an **A** statement is false, then its corresponding **O** statement must be true, but the truth values of its corresponding **E** and **I** statements are not guaranteed).

C. *Exercises*

For each of the following categorical statements, what can be inferred about the truth or falsity of all corresponding statements if we assume the given statement to be (a) true and (b) false?

1. All roses are red roses.
2. No whales are fishes.
3. Some fats are water-soluble substances.
4. Some birds are not flightless animals.

III. Further Immediate Inferences

A. *Helpful Reminders*

1. With regard to the immediate inferences of conversion, conversion by limitation, obversion, contraposition, and contraposition by limitation, it is very important to remember three things: (a) what the conclusion of each of these inferences is supposed to look like, (b) for what forms of categorical statements each of these inferences is valid, and (c) when these inferences yield a conclusion equivalent to the original statement. The tables at the end of section 5.3 in *The Power of Logic* should prove helpful in committing these three things to memory.

2. Strictly speaking, two categorical terms are complementary if and only if everything in the universe falls under one of them, but nothing in the universe falls under both of them. For many terms, we form the term-complement by adding the prefix "non-" to the term. Some term-complements, though, are not so easily formed. As an example, consider how we would write the contrapositive of the following statement:

All suitable boat anchors are metallic objects that weigh in excess of fifty pounds.

The term-complement of "suitable boat anchors" is not "nonsuitable boat anchors," since some things are not boat anchors at all (and are thus neither suitable nor unsuitable boat anchors). The term-complement of "metallic objects that weigh in excess of fifty pounds" is not "nonmetallic objects that weigh in excess of fifty pounds," nor is it "metallic objects that weigh no more than fifty pounds," since neither one of these proposed terms together with the original term partitions the universe into two mutually exclusive and jointly exhaustive classes. To form the term-complement of such troublesome terms, add the phrase "things that are not" to the term. By doing this to the terms in the above statement, we obtain the following statement as the contrapositive:

All things that are not metallic objects that weigh in excess of fifty pounds are things that are not suitable boat anchors.

3. The inference from an **A** statement to its converse by limitation can be justified in traditional categorical logic in the following manner:

Step 1.   All S are P.
Step 2.   Some S are P. (From Step 1 by subalternation from **A** to **I**)
Step 3.   Some P are S. (Conversion of Step 2)

The inference from an **E** statement to its contrapositive by limitation can be justified in traditional categorical logic in an analogous manner:

Step 1.   No S are P.
Step 2.   Some S are not P. (From Step 1 by subalternation from **E** to **O**)
Step 3.   Some non-P are not non-S. (Contraposition of Step 2)

What this means is that conversion by limitation and contraposition by limitation are reducible to, and their validity depends on, the other immediate inferences involving corresponding or noncorresponding categorical statements.

B. *Commonly Asked Questions*

1. Since a conclusion obtained from a statement by obversion or contraposition seems to be more complicated than the original and sounds unnatural, why are these forms of immediate inference of any importance to us?

Actually, a conclusion reached by obversion or contraposition is sometimes less complicated and sounds more natural than the original statement. Any categorical term is the term-complement of its term-complement, so that, when you form the term-complement of a term-complement, you get back the original term. As a consequence, the inference to a statement's obverse or its contrapositive may result in the elimination of awkward-sounding term-complements. Furthermore, by replacing a premise in an argument with its obverse or contrapositive, we may reduce the number of terms if some of the terms in the argument are the term-complements of other terms. As we shall discuss in the next chapter, this reduction of terms may enable a categorical argument to be put into proper syllogistic form.

2. When you are told to assume that a particular statement is true, and you are asked what is implied regarding the truth or falsehood of other given statements, what is the best way to proceed?

The key to doing this sort of exercise successfully is to look carefully at the original statement and the given statement and draw valid conclusions from either or both statements by conversion, obversion, or contraposition so that you end up with two statements that stand in a known relationship to one another. Let us illustrate this strategy by working an example:

Assuming that "All radicals are insurgents" is true, what is implied regarding the truth or falsehood of each of the following statements?

1. Some noninsurgents are not nonradicals.
2. No noninsurgents are radicals.
3. All nonradicals are noninsurgents.
4. No radicals are noninsurgents.

5. No nonradicals are noninsurgents.
6. All insurgents are radicals.
7. All noninsurgents are nonradicals.
8. No insurgents are nonradicals.
9. Some insurgents are not nonradicals.
10. Some noninsurgents are radicals.

Statement 1 is false, since the contrapositive of "All radicals are insurgents" and statement 1 are contradictory. Statement 2 is true, since it is the converse of the obverse of "All radicals are insurgents." The truth value of statement 3 is not guaranteed, since the contrapositive of statement 3 is the converse of "All radicals are insurgents." Statement 4 is the obverse of "All radicals are insurgents" and is therefore true. Statement 5 must be false, since the contrapositive of "All radicals are insurgents" is the contrary of the converse of statement 5. The truth value of statement 6 is not guaranteed, since statement 6 is the converse of "All radicals are insurgents." Statement 7 is true, since it is the contrapositive of "All radicals are insurgents." The truth value of statement 8 is not guaranteed, since the obverse of statement 8 is the converse of "All radicals are insurgents." Statement 9 is true, since the converse of the obverse of statement 9 is the subaltern of "All radicals are insurgents." Statement 10 is false, since "All radicals are insurgents" and the obverse of the converse of statement 10 are contradictory.

C. Exercises

(a) What can be validly inferred (in a single step) from the following statements, given all the forms of immediate inference recognized as valid by the traditional (Aristotelian) logician?

1. All humans are primates.
2. No apples are drupes.
3. Some metals are ores.
4. Some flowers are not perennials.

(b) Assuming that "No patriots are traitors" is true, what is implied regarding the truth or falsehood of each of the following statements?

1. Some patriots are not traitors.
2. All nontraitors are nonpatriots.
3. Some nontraitors are patriots.
4. Some nonpatriots are not traitors.
5. No traitors are patriots.
6. All nonpatriots are traitors.
7. Some patriots are not nontraitors.
8. All traitors are nonpatriots.
9. Some nonpatriots are traitors.
10. No nonpatriots are traitors.

(c) Assuming that "Some plants are flowers" is true, what is implied regarding the truth or falsehood of each of the following statements?

  1. Some nonflowers are nonplants.
  2. Some plants are not flowers.
  3. All nonflowers are nonplants.
  4. Some nonplants are nonflowers.
  5. Some flowers are not nonplants.
  6. No flowers are nonplants.
  7. Some nonflowers are plants.
  8. No plants are nonflowers.
  9. Some flowers are nonplants.
  10. All nonplants are nonflowers.

(d) Assuming that "Some students are not workers" is true, what is implied regarding the truth or falsehood of each of the following statements?

  1. Some nonworkers are students.
  2. Some students are nonworkers.
  3. Some nonworkers are nonstudents.
  4. All students are workers.
  5. Some nonworkers are not nonstudents.
  6. Some nonstudents are not workers.
  7. No nonworkers are students.
  8. All nonstudents are workers.
  9. Some workers are not nonstudents.
  10. No nonstudents are nonworkers.

ANSWERS TO EXERCISES

Answers to Selected Exercises in the Text

Exercise 5.3
Part A

  4. Since the term-complement of "unhappy entities" is not "happy entities" or "entities that are happy" but is "entities that are not unhappy," the answer given ("Some entities that are not unhappy are not nonpeople") cannot be made simpler.

Part E

  1. Statement 1 is the converse of "All ideologues are fools." (Not guaranteed)
  4. Statement 4 is the contrapositive of "All ideologues are fools." (True)
  7. The converse of the obverse of statement 7 is "All ideologues are fools." (Not guaranteed)
  10. The obverse of statement 10 is the subaltern of "All ideologues are fools." (True)
  13. Statement 13 is the subaltern of the contrapositive of "All ideologues are fools." (True)

Part F

1. Statement 1 is the obverse of "No psychiatrists are optimists." (True)
4. The obverse of the converse of statement 4 is the converse of the obverse of the converse of "No psychiatrists are optimists." (Not guaranteed)
7. Statement 7 is the contrary of "No psychiatrists are optimists." (False)
10. The contrapositive of statement 10 is the subaltern of "No psychiatrists are optimists." (True)
13. The converse of statement 13 is the contrary of the obverse of "No psychiatrists are optimists." (False)

Part G

1. Statement 1 is the converse of "Some chemicals are poisons." (True)
4. Statement 4 is the contrapositive of the converse of "Some chemicals are poisons." (Not guaranteed)
7. Statement 7 is the contrapositive of "Some chemicals are poisons." (Not guaranteed)
10. Statement 10 is the contrapositive of the subcontrary of the converse of "Some chemicals are poisons." (Not guaranteed)
13. The obverse of the converse of statement 13 is the subcontrary of the converse of "Some chemicals are poisons." (Not guaranteed)

Part H

1. Statement 1 is the superaltern of "Some celebrities are not saints." (Not guaranteed)
4. Statement 4 is the converse of "Some celebrities are not saints." (Not guaranteed)
7. Statement 7 is the converse of the obverse of "Some celebrities are not saints." (True)
10. Statement 10 is the converse of the contrapositive of "Some celebrities are not saints." (Not guaranteed)
13. Statement 13 is the subcontrary of the obverse of "Some celebrities are not saints." (Not guaranteed)

Answers to Supplemental Exercises

I(a)

1. The subject term is "great novels"; the predicate term is "books that are easy to read." It is a particular negative, **O**, categorical statement.
2. The subject term is "lipid molecules"; the predicate term is "organic molecules formed from a glycerin molecule and three fatty acids." It is a universal affirmative, **A**, categorical statement.
3. The subject term is "things that are easy to accomplish"; the predicate term is "things worth accomplishing." It is a universal negative, **E**, categorical statement.
4. The subject term is "important discoveries"; the predicate term is "discoveries that were made accidentally." It is a particular affirmative, **I**, categorical statement.

5. The subject term is "meaningful counterfactual statements"; the predicate term is "statements that describe things in terms of their nonessential, or accidental, features." It is a universal negative, **E**, categorical statement.

I(b)

1. No salamanders are lizards.
2. Some reptiles are not lizards.
3. All Quakers are pacifists.
4. Some aquatic snakes are poisonous snakes.
5. All places there are aquatic snakes are places there are frogs.
6. All times the deer population increases are times the bird population decreases.
7. All caecilians are limbless amphibians.
8. All lizards are reptiles.
9. Some places over the rainbow are places where troubles melt like lemon drops.
10. All people at the party are people who became intoxicated.
11. No things that don't say "Amana" are Radaranges.
12. Some Republicans are conservatives.
13. No people who were not there yesterday are people who knew the answer.
14. Some war heroes are war heroes who ran for office but were defeated.
15. All words spoken there are words that were whispered.
16. Some politicians are politicians who work awfully hard.
17. Some home movies are quite boring movies.
18. All people who shall be born after us are people who shall be a part of a higher history.
19. Some things are things that don't love a wall and want it down.
20. All cases of lying under oath are cases of perjury.

II

1. (a) If "All roses are red roses" is true, then "Some roses are red roses" is true, and both "No roses are red roses" and "Some roses are not red roses" are false. (b) If "All roses are red roses" is false, then "Some roses are not red roses" is true, and the truth values of "No roses are red roses" and "Some roses are red roses" are not guaranteed.
2. (a) If "No whales are fishes" is true, then "Some whales are not fishes" is true, and both "All whales are fishes" and "Some whales are fishes" are false. (b) If "No whales are fishes" is false, then "Some whales are fishes is true," and the truth values of "All whales are fishes" and "Some whales are not fishes" are not guaranteed.
3. (a) If "Some fats are water-soluble substances" is true, then "No fats are water-soluble substances" is false, and the truth values of "All fats are water-soluble substances" and "Some fats are not water-soluble substances" are not guaranteed. (b) If "Some fats are water-soluble substances" is false, then "All fats are water-soluble substances" is false, and both "No fats are water-soluble substances" and "Some fats are not water-soluble substances" are true.

4. (a) If "Some birds are not flightless animals" is true, then "All birds are flightless animals" is false, and the truth values of "No birds are flightless animals" and "Some birds are flightless animals" are not guaranteed. (b) If "Some birds are not flightless animals" is false, then "No birds are flightless animals" is false, and both "All birds are flightless animals" and "Some birds are flightless animals" are true.

III(a)

1. From "All humans are primates," it can be validly inferred that:
   1. Some humans are primates. (By subalternation)
   2. It is not the case that no humans are primates. (By the contrary relation)
   3. It's false that some humans are not primates. (By the contradictory relation)
   4. No humans are nonprimates. (By obversion)
   5. All nonprimates are nonhumans. (By contraposition)
   6. Some primates are humans. (By conversion by limitation)
2. From "No apples are drupes," it can be validly inferred that:
   1. Some apples are not drupes. (By subalternation)
   2. Not all apples are drupes. (By the contrary relation)
   3. It is not the case that some apples are drupes (By the contradictory relation)
   4. No drupes are apples. (By conversion)
   5. All apples are nondrupes. (By obversion)
   6. Some nondrupes are not nonapples. (By contraposition by limitation)
3. From "Some metals are ores," it can be validly inferred that:
   1. It is false that no metals are ores. (By the contradictory relation)
   2. Some ores are metals. (By conversion)
   3. Some metals are not non-ores. (By obversion)
4. From "Some flowers are not perennials," it can be validly inferred that:
   1. Not all flowers are perennials. (By the contradictory relation)
   2. Some flowers are nonperennials. (By obversion)
   3. Some nonperennials are not nonflowers. (By contraposition)

III(b)

1. True	2. False
3. True	4. Truth value not guaranteed
5. True	6. Truth value not guaranteed
7. False	8. True
9. True	10. False

III(c)

1. Truth value not guaranteed	2. Truth value not guaranteed
3. Truth value not guaranteed	4. Truth value not guaranteed
5. True	6. Truth value not guaranteed
7. Truth value not guaranteed	8. Truth value not guaranteed
9. Truth value not guaranteed	10. Truth value not guaranteed

1. True	2. True
3. Truth value not guaranteed	4. False
5. True	6. Truth value not guaranteed
7. False	8. Truth value not guaranteed
9. Truth value not guaranteed	10. Truth value not guaranteed

FOR FURTHER CONSIDERATION

Although syllogistic logic was originally developed to handle arguments that contained only categorical statements, the logical theory was later extended to arguments that contained singular statements. A singular statement asserts that a certain individual thing is or is not a member of a class. A statement that asserts that a certain individual is a member of a class is an affirmative singular statement. A statement that asserts that a certain individual is not a member of a class is a negative singular statement. A singular statement always has a singular term as its subject term and a categorical term as its predicate term. A singular term is a term that refers to one and only one individual thing, while a categorical term designates a category or kind of thing. An affirmative singular statement is in standard form when it is an instance of the statement form "a is P," and a negative singular statement is in standard form when it is an instance of the statement form "a is not P." (The letter "a" represents the singular term and the letter "P" the categorical term.) Thus, the statement "George is a banker" is an affirmative singular statement, and the statement "Terry is not a conscientious journalist" is a negative singular statement. The subject term of the first statement is the singular term "George," and the predicate term is "a banker." The subject term of the second statement is "Terry," and the predicate term is "a conscientious journalist."

Categorical Logic: Syllogisms

In Chapter 6, the nature of the arguments composed of categorical statements is examined from the perspective of syllogistic logic. The account of the logic of the syllogism is the oldest complete formal account of validity. The modern interpretation of categorical statements is also discussed.

CHAPTER HIGHLIGHTS

A **mediate inference**, as opposed to an immediate inference, is the drawing of a conclusion from more than one premise. The most basic mediate inference in syllogistic logic was considered to be the syllogism. **Categorical syllogisms** are arguments composed of three categorical statements (one conclusion and two premises). Every categorical syllogism will contain three distinct terms, and each term will occur exactly twice in the syllogism. The subject term of the conclusion is the **minor term** of the syllogism, and the predicate term of the conclusion is the **major term** of the syllogism. The term that appears once in each premise is the **middle term** of the syllogism.

A categorical syllogism is **in standard form** when each of its component categorical statements is in standard form and its major premise occurs first and its minor premise occurs second, followed by its conclusion. The **minor premise** is that premise that contains the minor term, and the **major premise** is that premise that contains the major term. Syllogisms differ in terms of their mood and figure. The **mood** of a syllogism is a designation consisting of a series of three letters: The first letter indicates the form of statement of the major premise; the second letter, the form of statement of the minor premise; and the third letter, the form of statement of the conclusion. (The series of letters will always be made up of the letters "A," "E," "I," and "O".) There are four **figures** of the syllogism. In a syllogism of the **first figure**, the middle term appears in the subject position of the major premise and in the predicate position in the minor premise. A syllogism is in the **second figure** when the middle term appears in the predicate position of both the major and minor premises. In a syllogism of the **third figure**, the middle term appears in the subject position of both the major and minor premises. A syllogism is in the **fourth figure** when the middle term appears in the predicate position of the major premise and in the subject position of the minor premise.

By specifying a syllogism's mood and figure, one completely specifies the form of the syllogism. In writing out just the form of a syllogism, we use the letter "M" to stand for the middle term, the letter "S" to stand for the minor term, and the letter "P" to stand for the major term. Of the 256 possible syllogistic argument forms, only fifteen forms are recognized as valid by both Aristotelian and modern logicians. These are the moods **AAA**, **EAE**, **AII**, and **EIO** in the first figure; the moods **EAE**,

AEE, EIO, and **AOO** in the second figure; the moods **IAI, AII, OAO,** and **EIO** in the third figure; and the moods **AEE, IAI,** and **EIO** in the fourth figure. In addition to these, the Aristotelian logician also recognizes as valid nine more forms. These are the moods **AAI** and **EAO** in the first figure, the moods **AEO** and **EAO** in the second figure, the moods **AAI** and **EAO** in the third figure, and the moods **AEO, EAO,** and **AAI** in the fourth figure. The modern logician does not accept these additional nine forms as valid.

Venn diagrams can be constructed for each of the four kinds of standard-form categorical statements, together with all their stylistic variants. Each such diagram will look like one of the following two-circle diagrams:

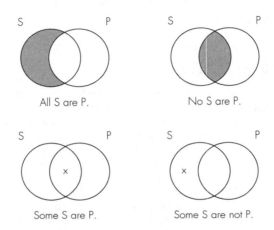

Venn diagrams can be used to show the validity or invalidity of both immediate and mediate (syllogistic) inferences.

To construct a Venn diagram for a categorical syllogism, first draw a three-circle diagram like this one:

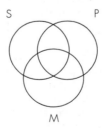

Then diagram each of the premises on this three-circle diagram. Always diagram a universal premise before diagramming a particular premise. (If the syllogism contains two universal or two particular statements, the order in which the premises are diagrammed does not matter.) To diagram a premise, look at only the circle representing the class designated by the middle term and either the circle representing the class designated by the minor term or the circle representing the class designated by the major term, depending on whether you are dealing with, respectively, a minor or a major premise. Shade in a region or place an "×" in a region according to the corresponding two-circle diagram for a statement of the form you are diagramming. Follow the same procedure with the other premise. Once you have diagrammed both premises on the same three-circle diagram, look at the diagram to see whether you have made the conclusion of the syllogism true. If you have made the conclusion true, then the syllogism is valid. If the conclusion is not necessarily true or cannot be true according to the diagram, then the syllogism is invalid.

On the Aristotelian view, an A statement implies its subaltern (its corresponding I statement), but both I and O categorical statements have **existential import** (that is, such statements imply that their subject terms are nonempty). According to Aristotelian logic, an A statement must therefore have existential import, and, since an E statement implies its corresponding O statement, an E statement must also have existential import on the Aristotelian interpretation. Modern logicians reject the existential import of A and E categorical statements because they consider such statements not to imply that there are things in the categories designated by their subject terms. Modern logicians thus reject the idea that corresponding A and I categorical statements and corresponding E and O categorical statements are related by subalternation. By rejecting the existential import of A and E categorical statements, modern logicians also reject the contrary status of corresponding A and E categorical statements and the subcontrary status of corresponding I and O categorical statements. Nevertheless, modern logicians still regard corresponding A and O categorical statements and corresponding E and I categorical statements as contradictory. The **modern square of opposition** thus retains only the contradictory relations depicted in the traditional square of opposition.

Because modern logicians deny the existential import of universal statements, modern logicians also reject the validity of conversion by limitation and contraposition by limitation. In addition, some forms of syllogisms traditionally recognized as valid in Aristotelian logic are no longer recognized as valid in modern logic.

Many actual cases where a person argues from a universal generalization or asserts the truth of a universal generalization involve the presupposition that a subject term is not empty. With regard to such cases, the Aristotelian view of universal statements can be legitimately accepted. Furthermore, by adding these underlying presuppositions as explicit premises to an immediate or mediate inference, it may be possible to show the validity of the inference.

Arguers sometimes omit a premise or even the conclusion in stating an argument. Such an argument is an **enthymeme**, and the missing or implicit step or steps (a step being a premise or a conclusion) must be supplied in restating the argument. In order to interpret an arguer fairly and charitably, you should add as an implicit premise only those premises that are reasonable and are necessary to make the argument an instance of a valid syllogistic form. A missing premise will be either a major or a minor premise and will contain the two terms that appear only once in the argument as originally stated. The unstated premise that is presumably being taken for granted may be false or doubtful, and in this way the implausibility of the argument may be revealed. If what is being assumed is unclear, and you are faced with adding as a premise either a reasonable statement that will make the argument invalid or an improbable statement that will make the argument valid, you should choose the latter as a general rule. When the conclusion of the original argument is left unstated, add as a conclusion the statement that will make the argument a valid syllogism when restated.

A **sorites** is a more complex categorical argument that can be resolved as a series of simpler syllogistic arguments in which the subconclusion of one syllogism enters as a premise in the subsequent syllogism. A sorites is in standard form when (a) its premises and conclusion are all standard-form categorical statements containing two distinct terms, (b) the major term of the conclusion appears in the first premise and the minor term of the conclusion appears in the final premise, and (c) successive premises have a term in common. To analyze a sorites for its potential validity, first put the sorites into standard form, add to the side all subconclusions needed to resolve the sorites as a chain of syllogisms, and then determine the validity or invalidity of all the syllogisms that make up the chain. A sorites is valid if and only if it is resolvable as a series of valid syllogisms.

Some categorical arguments that fail to be syllogisms or standard-form sorites because they contain too many terms for the number of premises may nevertheless contain one or more term-complements of other terms in the argument. Such arguments can often be reconstructed as standard-form syllogisms or sorites by eliminating the unnecessary term-complements. The term-complements in a categorical statement can often be eliminated by using the inferences of conversion, obversion, and/or contraposition to reach an equivalent statement that does not contain the unwanted term-complements.

In lieu of memorizing the valid forms, one can recognize that a categorical syllogism is valid if it conforms to a set of rules. Many of these rules rely on the notion of distribution. A term is **distributed** in a categorical statement if that statement says something about everything that falls under the term. **A** statements distribute only their subject terms; **E** statements distribute both their subject and predicate terms; **I** statements distribute neither their subject nor their predicate terms; and **O** statements distribute only their predicate terms. In the Aristotelian system, these rules and some of their associated fallacies are as follows:

> **Rule 1**: The syllogism must contain exactly three terms, and each occurrence of the same term must designate the same class. The fallacy of equivocation is associated with a violation of this rule.

> **Rule 2**: The middle term must be distributed in at least one of the premises. The fallacy of the undistributed middle is associated with a violation of this rule.

> **Rule 3**: Whatever term (major or minor) is distributed in the conclusion must also be distributed in the premise in which the term occurs. The fallacy of the illicit major and the fallacy of the illicit minor are associated with violations of this rule.

> **Rule 4**: The number of negative premises must be equal to the number of negative conclusions.

The rules for the modern system consist of the preceding four rules together with the following additional rule:

> **Rule 5**: Both premises cannot be universal in quantity if the conclusion is particular in quantity.

DISCUSSION OF KEY CONCEPTS

I. Standard Form, Mood, and Figure

A. *Helpful Reminders*

1. Note the difference between a syllogistic argument form (containing the letters "S," "P," and "M") and a syllogism in standard form. Writing a syllogism in standard form (or putting a syllogism into standard form) does *not* mean writing out the syllogistic argument form of which the syllogism is an instance. Remember that a categorical syllogism is in standard form if its conclusion and premises are all categorical statements in standard form and the major premise occurs first, followed by the minor premise and then the conclusion. The major premise is that premise that contains the major and middle terms. The minor premise is that premise that contains the minor and middle terms. Before attempting to analyze a syllogism, always make sure the syllogism is in standard form.

2. If a syllogism contains a premise or a conclusion that is not in standard form, then you will need to put that categorical statement into standard form in order to put the syllogism into standard form. It may help to review the techniques (discussed in the previous chapter) for putting a non-standard-form categorical statement into standard form. Remember to secure a uniform translation when writing a syllogism in standard form. The major, minor, or middle term of a standard-form categorical syllogism will look the same everywhere it occurs in the syllogism.

3. You can uniquely specify the form of a syllogism by specifying both its mood and its figure. (You do not uniquely specify the form of a syllogism by just specifying its mood.) The mood of a categorical syllogism indicates the type of statement of the major premise, the type of statement of the minor premise, and the type of statement of the conclusion. The figure of a standard-form syllogism depends on the positions of the middle term. There are four possible arrangements of the two occurrences of the middle term, and so there are four figures of the syllogism. As a way of indicating the mood and figure of a categorical syllogism, the letters designating the mood of the syllogism can be written together with a dash followed by the numeral that designates the figure of the syllogism. Thus, an **AAA**-1 syllogism is an **AAA** syllogism in the first figure, and an **OEI**-3 syllogism is an **OEI** syllogism in the third figure. If you know both the mood and the figure of a syllogism and its major, minor, and middle terms, you can write out the syllogism in standard form.

B. *Commonly Asked Questions*

1. How do you know in what order to put the premises when putting a syllogism into standard form?

The order of the premises and the conclusion is always the same in any standard-form categorical syllogism: major premise first, minor premise second, and conclusion last. The major premise is by definition the premise that contains the major term (the predicate term of the conclusion), and the minor premise is by definition the premise that contains the minor term (the subject term of the conclusion). The position of the middle terms in a syllogism (which determines the mood of a syllogism) does not determine the correct order of the premises. The correct order of the premises is thus determined exclusively by the subject and predicate terms of the conclusion.

2. Why is it important to put a syllogism into standard form? (After all, the validity of a syllogism certainly does not depend on its being in standard form.)

Even though the validity or invalidity of a syllogism is not determined by the order of the premises or the standard form of all the categorical statements in the syllogism, a correct analysis of a syllogism requires that it be in standard form. If you attempt to analyze a syllogism that is not in standard form, you may incorrectly identify the mood and figure of the syllogism, and you may incorrectly apply the techniques used to determine a syllogism's validity or invalidity.

C. Exercises

Rewrite each of the following syllogisms in standard form and identify the major, minor, and middle terms as well as the mood and figure of the resulting syllogism.

1. Some Malaysians are Chinese, but no Japanese are Chinese. Hence, no Malaysians are Japanese.
2. All automobiles designed for family use are vehicles that can only be driven at moderate speeds. No automobiles designed for family use are therefore racing cars, since no racing cars are vehicles that can only be driven at moderate speeds.
3. No flightless creatures are mammals, because some birds are flightless creatures but no birds are mammals.
4. Some crocuses bloom in the spring. Some crocuses bloom in the fall. Thus, some fall-blooming flowers bloom in the spring.
5. Not all reptiles lay eggs. Only egg-laying animals have many offspring. It follows that some reptiles do not have many offspring.
6. Everyone who was at the party attended the dance. No one who attended the dance went to the movies. Hence, no one who attended the party went to the movies.
7. Only continuous functions can be integrated, and any function that is continuous is a function that can be differentiated. Therefore, all functions that can be integrated can be differentiated.
8. Students who get up and leave in the middle of class are rude. There are students who almost never come to class who get up and leave in the middle of class. So, some rude students almost never come to class.
9. Anytime customers are dissatisfied, they complain. Every time customers complain, sales are lost. Consequently, when customers are dissatisfied, sales are sometimes lost.
10. Some people who attended the party became drunk and disorderly. Only those who became drunk and disorderly were later arrested for lewd and lascivious behavior. Thus, some partygoers were later arrested for lewd and lascivious behavior.

II. Venn Diagrams and Categorical Statements

A. Helpful Reminders

1. The two circles in the Venn diagram used to depict the logical content of a categorical statement represent the categories or classes designated by the two terms in the categorical statement. It is standard practice to label the left circle with an abbre-

viation of the subject term or the letter "S" and the right circle with an abbreviation of the predicate term or the letter "P." The categorical statement in effect says something about one or more of the regions marked off by the two overlapping circles. It is thus important to recognize what each region of the diagram represents. When you are diagramming a categorical statement, ask yourself what the categorical statement is saying in effect about whatever is within or outside a particular region.

2. In using a Venn diagram to evaluate an immediate inference, draw the standard two overlapping circles and then shade in a region or put an "×" in a region so as to make the premise true. If by making the premise true you have at the same time made the conclusion true, then the inference is valid. If, according to your diagram, you have made the premise true but the conclusion may be, or is, false, then the diagram indicates that the inference is invalid.

B. Commonly Asked Questions

1. What does each of the regions on a two-circle Venn diagram represent?

At the beginning of section 6.2 of *The Power of Logic*, there is a two-circle Venn diagram with the regions of the diagram numbered from 1 to 4. Generalizing from the example discussed there and calling the left circle the "S-circle" and the right circle the "P-circle," we can characterize the various regions as follows: Region 1 represents everything that is in the S-circle and outside the P-circle. Region 2 represents everything that is in both the S-circle and the P-circle. Region 3 represents everything that is outside the S-circle and in the P-circle. Region 4 represents everything that is outside both the S-circle and the P-circle.

2. Since we do not draw a Venn diagram with a circle labeled with a term-complement, how do we construct a diagram for a categorical statement that contains a term-complement?

Even though there is normally no circle labeled with a term-complement in a Venn diagram, there is nevertheless a region of the diagram that represents the category designated by the term-complement. The area outside a circle represents everything not falling in the category designated by the circle and thus represents everything falling within the category designated by the term-complement. To diagram a categorical statement containing a term-complement, treat the region outside a circle as a distinctly separate region (just as you treat the region inside a circle), and shade in or "×" in according to the pattern established for diagramming simpler **A**, **E**, **I**, and **O** categorical statements.

The only significant complication occasionally arises when you need to shade in the region outside a circle. If the categorical statement you are diagramming requires you to shade in region 4 (see comment 1 above), put the two-circle diagram within a rectangle so that you have a bounded region to shade. For example, consider how you would draw a Venn diagram for the statement form "All non-S are P." To say that all non-S are P is to say, in terms of the regions of a Venn diagram, that everything outside the S-circle is within the P-circle. We would need to shade in a region according to how we shade in for an **A** statement, which means that we would need to shade in the region of everything outside the S-circle that is outside the P-circle. To get a bounded region to shade in, we enclose the two-circle diagram in a rectangle. We thus get the following as the Venn diagram for the statement form in question:

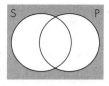

All non-S are P.

C. Exercises

Draw a Venn diagram for each of the following categorical statements. Use appropriate capital letters to abbreviate the subject and predicate terms.

1. All frogs are anurans.
2. All non-anurans are nonfrogs.
3. No whales are fishes.
4. Some nonmammals are birds.
5. All nonmetals are halogens.

III. Venn Diagrams and Categorical Syllogisms

A. Helpful Reminders

1. A Venn diagram for a categorical syllogism will always be a three-circle diagram. Each circle in the diagram represents one of the categories designated by the major, minor, and middle terms of the syllogism. The Venn diagram for a categorical syllogism pictorially represents the relationships between the categories that are indicated by the syllogism's premises. It is thus important to understand what each of the eight regions of a three-circle Venn diagram represents.

2. Here are some pointers and things to bear in mind as you learn how to construct Venn diagrams as a means of determining the validity or invalidity of syllogisms:

a. In a three-circle Venn diagram, always label the circle in the lower middle with a letter standing for the syllogism's middle term, the circle to the upper left with a letter standing for the syllogism's minor term, and the circle to the upper right with a letter standing for the syllogism's major term. This will facilitate communication with your classmates as well as with your instructor.

b. Diagram only the premises of the syllogism. Do not diagram the conclusion. The strategy is to diagram both premises on the same three-circle diagram and then inspect the resulting diagram to see if you have forced the conclusion to be true. If the conclusion is definitely made true by making the premises both true, then the syllogism is valid. If it is still possible for the conclusion to be false in spite of the fact that you have made both premises true according to the diagram, then the syllogism is invalid.

c. When you diagram a universal statement, you will always shade in a region. When you diagram a particular statement, you will always put an "×" in a region. Look at the two circles representing the classes designated by the two terms in the categorical statement, and shade or put an "×" in a region according to how you would produce a two-circle diagram (with a slight modification in the case of particular statements).

d. Never put an "×" in a region that has been shaded. The shading associated with a universal premise may force you to place the "×" associated with a particular premise in a very definite region in order to make both the universal premise and the particular premise true.

e. When the placement of an "×" in any one of two adjoining regions will make a statement true, put the "×" on the line separating the two regions. Note that you will never place an "×" on a line where the region on one side of the line has been shaded.

f. Never shade or put an "×" in a region in such a way as to provide more information in the diagram than there is in the premises. There are eight undivided regions within the Venn diagram; by doing something to only one of these particular regions without any regard to what you have done to other regions, you are in effect making something true that cannot be expressed by any one categorical statement in the syllogism. You are sometimes forced to do something to only one undivided region, but you are not doing so in isolation from what you have done to other regions.

g. If you are faced with the choice of diagramming a universal or a particular premise first, always diagram the universal premise first. By diagramming the universal premise first, you may shade a region in such a way that you will then be forced to put an "×" squarely in a region rather than on a line separating two regions. So, if you diagram the particular premise first, you may be forced later, in diagramming the universal premise, to move the "×" in your diagram.

h. If you have not done anything to a particular region (i.e., you have not shaded it or put an "×" in it), then that particular region either is empty or has something in it, but you don't know which. When an "×" is on a line separating two regions, either both regions have something in them or exactly one of the regions is empty, but, again, you don't know which. Never think that, because you have not shaded a region or have put an "×" on a line separating that region from another, the region must contain something.

i. When diagramming two universal premises, you sometimes have to shade in a region twice. Do not attach any special significance to twice-shaded regions; a twice-shaded region isn't any less empty than a once-shaded region.

B. Commonly Asked Questions

1. By diagramming the premises of a syllogism on a three-circle Venn diagram, we typically do not produce a diagram of the conclusion that looks exactly like a two-circle diagram of that statement. So how do we know if the syllogism we are diagramming is valid?

Do not expect to produce a two-circle representation of the conclusion on a three-circle Venn diagram. The feature of the Venn diagram that determines the validity or invalidity of the syllogism you are diagramming is the pictorial representation of a relationship between the syllogism's minor and major terms. If in diagramming the relationships indicated by the premises you create a pictorial representation of a relationship between the minor and major terms that indicates that the conclusion is true, then the diagram shows the syllogism to be valid. If the pictorial depiction of a relationship does not indicate that the conclusion is true, then the diagram shows the syllogism to be invalid.

2. Why is a Venn diagram, which is, after all, just a drawing, able to tell us that a categorical syllogism is valid?

The validity of a syllogism is determined by the class inclusion and exclusion relationships asserted by the syllogism's premises and conclusion. The physical inclusion and exclusion relations present in a Venn diagram correspond closely to the class inclusion and exclusion relations among the categories designated by the terms of a syllogism. If such a physical relation holds between the left and right circles in virtue of similar relations holding between the left and middle circles and the right and middle circles, then an analogous class relation will hold between the categories designated by the minor and major terms. Hence, if the physical relations that make the premises true result in a physical relation that makes the conclusion true, then the class relations that make the premises true result in a class relation that makes the conclusion true.

C. Exercises

Determine whether the following syllogistic argument forms are valid or invalid by constructing a Venn diagram.

1.
   1. All M are P.
   2. Some S are not M.
   So, 3. Some S are not P.

2.
   1. No P are M.
   2. Some S are M.
   So, 3. Some S are not P.

3.
   1. All M are P.
   2. Some M are S.
   So, 3. Some S are P.

4.
   1. All P are M.
   2. Some S are M.
   So, 3. Some S are P.

5.
   1. All P are M.
   2. No M are S.
   So, 3. No S are P.

6.
   1. All M are P.
   2. All S are M.
   So, 3. All S are P.

7.
   1. Some M are P.
   2. All S are M.
   So, 3. Some S are P.

8.
   1. Some P are M.
   2. Some M are S.
   So, 3. Some S are P.

9.
   1. No M are P.
   2. All S are M.
   So, 3. No S are P.

10.
   1. Some M are not P.
   2. All M are S.
   So, 3. Some S are not P.

IV. The Modern Square of Opposition

A. Helpful Reminders

1. Note the differences between the Aristotelian and modern interpretations of categorical logic. The Aristotelian logician accepts the contrary relation between corresponding **A** and **E** categorical statements, the subcontrary relation between corresponding **I** and **O** categorical statements, the subalternation relation between corresponding **A** and **I** categorical statements and between corresponding **E** and **O** categorical statements, and the contradictory relation between corresponding **A** and **O** categorical statements and between corresponding **E** and **I** categorical statements.

The Aristotelian accepts the validity of conversion by limitation, contraposition by limitation, conversion for **I** and **E** categorical statements, obversion for all four kinds of categorical statements, and contraposition for **A** and **E** categorical statements. In contrast, the modern logician accepts only the contradictory relation between corresponding **A** and **O** categorical statements and between corresponding **E** and **I** categorical statements and recognizes the validity of only conversion for **I** and **E** categorical statements, obversion for all four kinds of categorical statements, and contraposition for **A** and **E** categorical statements. In addition, the Aristotelian logician accepts as valid some syllogistic argument forms that the modern logician does not. However, every syllogistic argument form the modern logician recognizes as valid is a form the Aristotelian logician also recognizes as valid.

2. Venn diagrams constructed according to the techniques developed in sections 6.2 and 6.3 of *The Power of Logic* can show the validity and invalidity of immediate and mediate inference as understood by the modern logician. However, Venn diagramming techniques do not inherently accord with just the methodology of modern logic. By adding to a Venn diagram of an argument what must be the case if all universal premises have existential import, you can construct a diagram that comports with the Aristotelian interpretation of the argument. Thus, Venn diagrams can be modified to show the validity or the invalidity of an inference as interpreted by the Aristotelian logician.

It should be noted that two complications arise due to the fact that universal categorical statements in Aristotelian logic have existential import (that is, such statements imply that their subject terms are not empty). First of all, the existential import of universal categorical statements entails that the predicate terms of universal categorical statements will also be nonempty. Since, for example, the subject term of any **E** statement must not be empty, and "No S are P" implies the **E** statement "No P are S" (the converse), the term "P" must also not be empty. Secondly, what is implied about the nonempty nature of the subject and predicate terms is also implied about their term-complements. For example, because the subject term of any **A** statement must not be empty, and "All S are P" implies the **A** statement "All non-P are non-S" (the contrapositive), the term "non-P" must also not be empty. These complications are significant because they may need to be taken into account when drawing a Venn diagram for an inference interpreted in the Aristotelian fashion. For instance, "No S are P" implies "Some P are not S" (the subaltern of the converse) in Aristotelian logic, and the validity of the inference will be revealed by diagramming the argument "No S are P. There is a P. So, some P are not S." Similarly, in order to show by a Venn diagram the validity of an **AEO**-4 syllogism in the Aristotelian system, you will need to add to the premises a statement to the effect that the minor term is not empty. The minor term in such a syllogism is in the predicate position (not the subject position) of the minor premise.

B. *Commonly Asked Questions*

1. In calling into question the logical relationships in the traditional square of opposition and the validity of certain immediate and mediate inferences, has the modern logician shown that Aristotelian logic is mistaken?

Rather than saying that the modern logician has shown Aristotelian logic to be mistaken, it is more accurate to say that the modern logician has challenged the applicability of the traditional account to the analysis of all categorical arguments. The modern logician sees the Aristotelian account to have its limitations. As long as we are dealing with categorical statements the terms of which we know to be nonempty or can reasonably assume to be nonempty, Aristotelian logic is perfectly applicable to the analysis of inferences made in that context. However, if we are dealing with categorical statements some of the terms of which we know to be empty or cannot just assume are not empty, then we must abandon the Aristotelian account in that context and embrace the modern interpretation of categorical arguments.

2. What motivates the modern logician to change traditional Aristotelian logic?

The Aristotelian logician assumes that all categorical statements have existential import, which implies that, according to Aristotelian logic, every term and term-complement designates a class that is not empty. The modern logician does not make that assumption, for the modern logician, unlike the Aristotelian, accepts the intelligibility of categorical sentences that contain empty terms. This forces the modern logician to reconsider and ultimately to reject portions of the traditional Aristotelian account.

C. Exercises

Draw a Venn diagram to show the validity or the invalidity of the following arguments:

1.
    1. All lizards are reptiles.
    2. There are lizards.
  So, 3. Some reptiles are lizards.

2.
    1. No bats are birds.
    2. There are birds.
  So, 3. Some birds are not bats.

3.
    1. No chairs are tables.
    2. There are chairs.
  So, 3. Some nontables are not nonchairs.

4.
    1. All spiders are arachnids.
    2. No arachnids are vertebrates.
    3. There are spiders.
  So, 4. Some vertebrates are not spiders.

5.
    1. All squares are rectangles.
    2. No rectangles are triangles.
    3. There are triangles.
  So, 4. Some triangles are not squares.

V. Enthymemes

A. Helpful Reminders

1. An enthymeme is an incompletely stated argument. Such an argument is missing a premise or the conclusion. Any such implied or suggested but not explicit statement needs to be added to a categorical syllogism when the syllogism is restated in standard form and analyzed.

2. The rule of thumb when adding a missing premise or conclusion (i.e., a missing step) to a categorical syllogism is to add as a premise only a reasonable statement that makes the syllogism valid, and add as a conclusion only what validly follows from the premises. If you cannot add any plausible statement to make an enthymeme valid, then you will be compelled to add an unreasonable step. (However, try to find a missing premise or conclusion that is not wildly implausible.)

B. Commonly Asked Questions

1. Why would a premise or a conclusion be left out of an argument?

Speakers and writers often want to state their arguments succinctly or to avoid insulting their audience by stating the obvious. As a result, premises that provide information with which the arguer assumes the audience is already familiar and conclusions that are highly suggested by the stated premises are frequently omitted from an argument as presented to an audience.

2. Why always try to add a missing step to an enthymeme in such a fashion as to abide by both the principle of fairness and the principle of charity?

In general, you try to put a speaker or writer's argument in the best possible light in order to avoid misunderstanding and mischaracterizing what he or she is saying. It is a waste of time and effort to analyze an argument that is not actually being offered. Furthermore, the criticism of an argument will be generally more trenchant if it reveals the faults of the strongest possible rendition of the argument presented.

C. Exercises

For each of the following enthymemes, supply the missing step and rewrite the argument as a categorical syllogism in standard form:

1. Spiders are invertebrates because they are arachnids.
2. The prime numbers are all integers, and the integers are all real numbers.
3. Whoever cheats on the test will fail the test, and someone has cheated on the test.
4. Every dog Tony owns is mean since he owns only pit bulls.
5. Some athletes are losers since some beach bums are athletes.

VI. Sorites and Removing Term-Complements

A. Helpful Reminders

1. To analyze a sorites correctly, always begin by putting the sorites into standard form and then proceed to add all the subconclusions necessary to render the sorites as a chain of categorical syllogisms. Make sure the first syllogism in the chain contains the predicate term of the argument's conclusion and the final syllogism in the chain contains the subject term of the argument's conclusion.

2. Putting an invalid sorites into standard form poses no special problems, but adding the subconclusions to an invalid sorites may give you some trouble. The series of syllogisms into which an invalid sorites is resolved will contain at least one invalid syllogism. This means that in resolving an invalid sorites you will need to add at least one subconclusion that does not follow from previous steps. As a result, exactly what subconclusion to add in such circumstances may not be clear. The general rule to follow is: If you cannot add a conclusion that follows from previous steps, then add to the sorites that subconclusion that is either suggested (but not actually implied) by previous steps or needed in a subsequent inference leading to the final conclusion.

3. The strategies to follow to eliminate unwanted term-complements are as follows. If the term-complement appears only in the subject position, use conversion to put the term-complement in the predicate position, followed by obversion to eliminate the term-complement. If the term-complement appears only in the predicate

position, use obversion to eliminate the term-complement. If term-complements appear in both the subject and the predicate positions, use contraposition to eliminate the term-complement. However, always make sure that the inferences you make are valid.

B. Commonly Asked Questions

1. Exactly how does one go about putting a sorites into standard form and resolving it as a series of syllogisms?

After putting all the premises and the conclusion of the sorites into standard categorical form and eliminating all extra term-complements that can be eliminated, you can follow mechanically the procedure outlined below to arrange the steps of the sorites in the proper order:

1. Enter on the first and second lines, respectively, a major premise and a minor premise of a (if possible, valid) syllogism. One of these premises should contain the predicate term of the conclusion of the sorites. Go to 2.
2. Enter on the third line the premise that contains a term in common with one of the premises on the first two lines. Go to 3.
3. Enter on the next line a premise that contains a term in common with the premise immediately preceding it. Go to 4.
4. Determine the number of remaining premises, and then do exactly one of the following:
   a. If no premises remain, enter the conclusion on the last line. Go to 5.
   b. If one or more premises remain, go back to 3.
5. Stop. The sorites is now in standard form.

After writing the sorites in standard form, you will need to add all the appropriate subconclusions to the side of each minor premise (except the last) if you intend to evaluate the sorites for validity. Evaluate the sorites by evaluating each of the resulting syllogisms in the series.

2. Why bother with eliminating unwanted term-complements?

Categorical arguments sometimes contain too many terms and for this reason are not syllogisms, properly speaking. (A syllogism must have only three terms in it, and each term must occur exactly twice.) However, one or more terms in such an argument may be the term-complement of another term or terms. Since the term-complement of a term is the term itself, you may be able to eliminate extra term-complements through conversion, obversion, and/or contraposition. With the reduction of the number of terms, a categorical argument may be written as a categorical syllogism. Hence, the elimination of term-complements may be necessary in order to put a categorical argument into proper syllogistic form.

3. What do you do if you cannot eliminate all the unwanted term-complements from an argument?

Some categorical arguments contain extra terms that are unwanted term-complements that cannot be eliminated in a way that preserves the exact content of the argument. When such an argument cannot be legitimately treated as a sorites with an unstated premise, a syllogistic analysis of the argument typically is not possible. However, in some cases it may be possible to replace the premises of the argument with other categorical statements that are implied by the premises and that imply the conclusion, thereby showing the argument to be valid. For example, consider any argument having the following form.

1. No non-P are non-M.
2. All M are S.
So, 3. Some S are not P.

It is not possible to remove by a valid inference both term-complements in the first premise in such a way as to obtain an equivalent categorical statement. Nevertheless, if we are attempting an Aristotelian analysis of the argument, we can eliminate both term-complements from the first premise by using contraposition by limitation. Even though the resulting categorical statement is not equivalent to the first premise, replacing that premise with its contrapositive by limitation gives us a valid **OAO**-3 syllogism. Since the premises of the former argument imply the premises of the latter argument, which in turn imply the conclusion, the original argument must be valid (given the Aristotelian interpretation anyway).

C. Exercises

Rewrite each of the following arguments as either a categorical syllogism or a sorites in standard form. Add any unstated premises and subconclusions.

1. No reputable scientists are nonmathematicians, and no psychologists are mathematicians. Hence, no psychologists are reputable scientists.
2. Some birds are flightless creatures, and all birds are nonmammals. It follows that no flightless creatures are mammals.
3. All nonvoters are people who don't pay taxes. All voters are citizens. Thus, all citizens are taxpayers.
4. All books healthy in tone are books I recommend reading. All books I recommend reading are bound books, and all bound books are well written. Since all the romances are books healthy in tone, it follows that all the romances are well written.
5. All scholars are great lovers of music, and all editors are scholars. Since people with insensitive souls are neither great lovers of music nor artists, all editors must be artists.

VII. Rules for Evaluating Syllogisms

A. Helpful Reminders

1. Within each of the systems (Aristotelian and modern) containing the rules, any syllogism that conforms to all the rules is valid, while any syllogism that violates at least one rule is invalid. To apply the rules correctly, you need to be able to tell when a term is distributed and when it is not. The most important thing to remember about distribution is the pattern of the distribution of terms among **A**, **E**, **I**, and **O** categorical statements. Only the subject position is distributed in an **A** statement. Both the subject and predicate positions are distributed in an **E** statement. Neither the subject nor the predicate position is distributed in an **I** statement. Only the predicate position is distributed in an **O** statement.

2. Take note of the following remarks about the rules so as not to misapply them.

a. Rules 1–4 are the Aristotelian rules, and rules 1–5 are the modern rules. Appeal to the former set of rules when determining whether a syllogism is valid in the Aristotelian system. Appeal to the latter set of rules when determining whether a syllogism is valid in the modern system.

b. If a syllogism violates any of the rules 1–4, it is invalid from both the Aristotelian and the modern perspectives. If a syllogism satisfies rules 1–4, it is valid from the Aristotelian perspective. If a syllogism satisfies rules 1–4 but violates rule 5, it is valid from the Aristotelian perspective but invalid from the modern perspective. Any syllogism that satisfies all five rules is valid from both the Aristotelian and the modern perspectives. The Aristotelian logician does not, however, accept rule 5.

c. Rule 2 does not say that the middle term must be distributed in both premises. The rule only requires that the middle term be distributed in at least one of the premises.

d. Rule 3 does *not* say that, if the major or minor term is distributed in a premise, then it must be distributed in the conclusion. What the rule says is the other way around: A term that is distributed in the conclusion must be distributed in its associated premise. So, always remember to check the terms from the conclusion to the premises and not the other way around.

e. Rule 4 amounts to two rules: Both premises must not be negative, and the conclusion is negative when and only when a premise is negative. You must check for both of these conditions when applying rule 4.

f. A syllogism that violates rule 5 is sometimes said to be a syllogism that commits the existential fallacy, a formal fallacy recognized only by the modern logician.

B. Commonly Asked Questions

1. Why use the rules to determine the validity or invalidity of a categorical syllogism?

The rules method is a very efficient way to determine whether a categorical syllogism is valid. It is usually quicker and easier to check a syllogism against the rules than it is to construct a Venn diagram. The efficiency of the rules method may not seem obvious at first, but, with some practice applying the rules, the immense practical usefulness of the rules should become apparent.

2. Why is rule 5 accepted by the modern logician but rejected by the Aristotelian logician?

Rule 5 concerns the inferential move from universal premises to a particular conclusion, and no such inference is valid according to the modern account. Modern logic regards any such inference as an invalid move from premises that lack existential import to a conclusion that has existential import. However, since both universal and particular categorical statements have existential import given the Aristotelian interpretation, Aristotelian logic does not regard an inference from universal premises to a particular conclusion to involve the invalid inferential move. Hence, only the modern logician accepts rule 5.

C. Exercises

Determine whether the syllogistic argument forms with the following moods and figures are valid or invalid in the Aristotelian and modern systems. In the case of the invalid forms, identify each rule violated and the reason why the rule is violated. (You will first need to write out the syllogistic argument form with the particular mode and figure and then apply the rules.)

1. **AAA**-3	2. **AAA**-4	3. **AII**-3	4. **AII**-4	5. **AII**-2
6. **AOO**-2	7. **AOO**-1	8. **AOO**-3	9. **EIO**-1	10. **EIO**-2
11. **EOO**-2	12. **EOO**-1	13. **EOO**-4	14. **EEE**-1	15. **EAE**-4
16. **EAE**-2	17. **AEE**-2	18. **AEE**-1	19. **IOO**-3	20. **IOI**-2
21. **AEO**-3	22. **EAO**-3	23. **EAO**-1	24. **EEO**-3	25. **OAI**-4

ANSWERS TO EXERCISES

Answers to Selected Exercises in the Text

Exercise 6.1
Part D

1.   1. No Catholic priests are women.
       2. Some unmarried people are Catholic priests.
      So, 3. Some unmarried people are not women.
      EIO-1 valid syllogism

2.   1. All functions that can be integrated are functions that can be differentiated.
       2. No discontinuous functions are functions that can be differentiated.
      So, 3. No discontinuous functions are functions that can be integrated.
      AEE-2 valid syllogism

3.   1. Some stars are centers of planetary systems.
       2. All stars are nuclear furnaces.
      So, 3. Some nuclear furnaces are centers of planetary systems.
      IAI-3 valid syllogism

4.   1. No alcoholic beverages are beverages suitable for children.
       2. All beverages suitable for children are wholesome drinks.
      So, 3. No wholesome drinks are alcoholic beverages.
      EAE-4 invalid syllogism

5.   1. All arachnids are invertebrates.
       2. All spiders are arachnids.
      So, 3. No spiders are invertebrates.
      AAE-1 invalid syllogism

6.   1. No celestial objects that twinkle are planets.
       2. Some celestial objects are planets.
      So, 3. Some celestial objects are not celestial objects that twinkle.
      EIO-2 valid syllogism

7. 1. Some aquatic animals are not fish.
    2. All aquatic animals are freshwater animals.
    So, 3. Some freshwater animals are not fish.
    OAO-3 valid syllogism

8. 1. Some conifers are deciduous trees.
    2. All deciduous trees are broadleaf trees.
    So, 3. Some broadleaf trees are conifers.
    IAI-4 valid syllogism

9. 1. No sedimentary rocks are igneous rocks.
    2. No volcanic rocks are sedimentary rocks.
    So, 3. All volcanic rocks are igneous rocks.
    EEA-1 invalid syllogism

10. 1. All snakes are squamates.
    2. Some reptiles are not squamates.
    So, 3. Some reptiles are not snakes.
    AOO-2 valid syllogism

Exercise 6.7
Part A

1. This form violates rule 4 by having a negative conclusion but two negative premises. It is an invalid form in both the Aristotelian and modern systems.
4. This form violates rule 2 by having an undistributed middle. It is an invalid form in both the Aristotelian and modern systems.
7. This form violates none of the rules. It is a valid form in both the Aristotelian and modern systems.
10. This form violates rule 3 by having an illicit major and violates rule 4 by having two negative premises. It is an invalid form in both the Aristotelian and modern systems.
13. This form violates rule 2 by having an undistributed middle. It is an invalid form in both the Aristotelian and modern systems.
16. This form violates only rule 5 by having two universal premises and a particular conclusion. It is an invalid form in the modern system and a valid form in the Aristotelian system.
19. This form violates rule 2 by having an undistributed middle. It is an invalid form in both the Aristotelian and modern systems.

Part B

7. 1. All M are P.
    2. All S are M.
    So, 3. Some S are P.

This syllogism violates only rule 5 by having two universal premises and a particular conclusion. It is an invalid syllogism according to the modern interpretation and a valid syllogism according to the Aristotelian interpretation.

Answers to Supplemental Exercises

I

1. 1. No Japanese are Chinese.
    2. Some Malaysians are Chinese.
    So, 3. No Malaysians are Japanese.

    (major term—Japanese; minor term—Malaysians; middle term—Chinese; **EIE**-2 syllogism)

2. 1. No racing cars are vehicles that can only be driven at moderate speeds.
    2. All automobiles designed for family use are vehicles that can only be driven at moderate speeds.
    So, 3. No automobiles designed for family use are racing cars.

    (major term—racing cars; minor term—automobiles designed for family use; middle term—vehicles that can only be driven at moderate speeds; **EAE**-2 syllogism)

3. 1. No birds are mammals.
    2. Some birds are flightless creatures.
    So, 3. No flightless creatures are mammals.

    (major term—mammals; minor term—flightless creatures; middle term—birds; **EIE**-3 syllogism)

4. 1. Some crocuses are flowers that bloom in the spring.
    2. Some crocuses are flowers that bloom in the fall.
    So, 3. Some flowers that bloom in the fall are flowers that bloom in the spring.

    (major term—flowers that bloom in the spring; minor term—flowers that bloom in the fall; middle term—crocuses; **III**-3 syllogism)

5. 1. All animals that have many offspring are egg-laying animals.
    2. Some reptiles are not egg-laying animals.
    So, 3. Some reptiles are not animals that have many offspring.

    (major term—animals that have many offspring; minor term—reptiles; middle term—egg-laying animals; **AOO**-2 syllogism)

6. 1. No people who attended the dance are people who went to the movies.
    2. All people who were at the party are people who attended the dance.
    So, 3. No people who were at the party are people who went to the movies.

    (major term—people who went to the movies; minor term—people who were at the party; middle term—people who attended the dance; **EAE**-1)

7. 1. All continuous functions are functions that can be differentiated.
    2. All functions that can be integrated are continuous functions.
    So, 3. All functions that can be integrated are functions that can be differentiated.

    (major term—functions that can be differentiated; minor term—functions that can be integrated; middle term—continuous functions; **AAA**-1)

8.   1. Some students who almost never come to class are students who get up and leave in the middle of class.
      2. All students who get up and leave in the middle of class are rude students.
  So, 3. Some rude students are students who almost never come to class.

  (major term—students who almost never come to class; minor term—rude students; middle term—students who get up and leave in the middle of class; **IAI**-4)

9.   1. All times customers complain are times sales are lost.
      2. All times customers are dissatisfied are times customers complain.
  So, 3. Some times customers are dissatisfied are times sales are lost.

  (major term—times sales are lost; minor term—times customers are dissatisfied; middle term—times customers complain; **AAI**-1)

10.   1. All people who were later arrested for lewd and lascivious behavior are people who became drunk and disorderly.
       2. Some partygoers are people who became drunk and disorderly.
  So, 3. Some partygoers are people who were later arrested for lewd and lascivious behavior.

  (major term—people who were later arrested for lewd and lascivious behavior; minor term—partygoers; middle term—people who became drunk and disorderly; **AII**-2)

II

1.

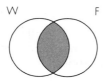

All frogs are anurans.

2.

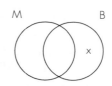

All non-anurans are nonfrogs.

3.

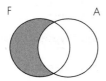

No whales are fishes.

4.

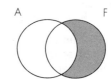

Some nonmammals are birds.

5.

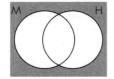

All nonmetals are halogens.

III

1.

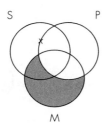

The syllogistic argument form is invalid.

2.

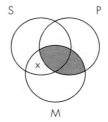

The syllogistic argument form is valid.

3.

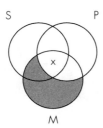

The syllogistic argument form is valid.

4.

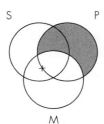

The syllogistic argument form is invalid.

5.

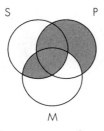

The syllogistic argument form is valid.

6.

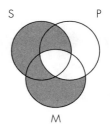

The syllogistic argument form is valid.

7.

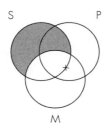

The syllogistic argument form is invalid.

8.

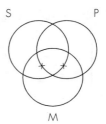

The syllogistic argument form is invalid.

9.

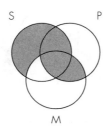

The syllogistic argument form is valid.

10.

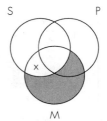

The syllogistic argument form is valid.

IV

1.

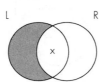

The argument is valid.

2.

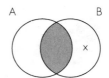

The argument is valid.

3.

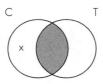

The argument is valid.

4.

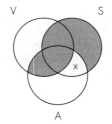

The argument is invalid.

5.

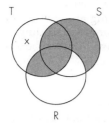

The argument is valid.

V

1.   1. All arachnids are invertebrates.
        2. All spiders are arachnids.
   So, 3. All spiders are invertebrates.

2.   1. All integers are real numbers.
        2. All prime numbers are integers.
   So, 3. All prime numbers are real numbers.

3.   1. All persons who have cheated on the test are persons who will fail the test.
        2. Some persons are persons who have cheated on the test.
   So, 3. Some persons are persons who will fail the test.

4.   1. All pit bulls are mean dogs.
        2. All dogs Tony owns are pit bulls.
   So, 3. All dogs Tony owns are mean dogs.

5.   1. All beach bums are losers.
        2. Some beach bums are athletes.
   So, 3. Some athletes are losers.

VI

1.   1. All reputable scientists are mathematicians.
        2. No psychologists are mathematicians.
   So, 3. No psychologists are reputable scientists.

2.   1. No birds are mammals.
        2. Some birds are flightless creatures.
   So, 3. No flightless creatures are mammals.

3.   1. All residents are taxpayers.
        2. All non-aliens are residents.   Sub. 1: All non-aliens are taxpayers.
        3. All citizens are non-aliens. (unstated premise)
   So, 4. All citizens are taxpayers.

4. 1. All bound books are well-written books.
    2. All books I recommend reading are bound books.
        Sub. 1: All books I recommend reading are well-written books.
    3. All books healthy in tone are books I recommend reading.
        Sub. 2: All books healthy in tone are well-written books.
    4. All the romances are books healthy in tone.
    So, 5. All the romances are well-written books.

5. 1. No people with insensitive souls are artists.
    2. No people with insensitive souls are great lovers of music.
        Sub. 1: All great lovers of music are artists.
    3. All scholars are great lovers of music.
        Sub. 2: All scholars are artists.
    4. All editors are scholars.
    5. All editors are artists.

VII

1. This form is invalid in both the Aristotelian and modern systems. It violates rule 3 by having an illicit minor.
2. This form is invalid in both the Aristotelian and modern systems. It violates rule 3 by having an illicit minor.
3. This form is valid in both the Aristotelian and modern systems.
4. This form is invalid in both the Aristotelian and modern systems. It violates rule 2 by having an undistributed middle.
5. This form is invalid in both the Aristotelian and modern systems. It violates rule 2 by having an undistributed middle.
6. This form is valid in both the Aristotelian and modern systems.
7. This form is invalid in both the Aristotelian and modern systems. It violates rule 3 by having an illicit major.
8. This form is invalid in both the Aristotelian and modern systems. It violates rule 3 by having an illicit major.
9. This form is valid in both the Aristotelian and modern systems.
10. This form is valid in both the Aristotelian and modern systems.
11. This form is invalid in both the Aristotelian and modern systems. It violates rule 4 by having two negative premises.
12. This form is invalid in both the Aristotelian and modern systems. It violates rule 4 by having two negative premises.
13. This form is invalid in both the Aristotelian and modern systems. It violates rule 4 by having two negative premises.
14. This form is invalid in both the Aristotelian and modern systems. It violates rule 4 by having two negative premises.
15. This form is invalid in both the Aristotelian and modern systems. It violates rule 3 by having an illicit minor.
16. This form is valid in both the Aristotelian and modern systems.
17. This form is valid in both the Aristotelian and modern systems.
18. This form is invalid in both the Aristotelian and modern systems. It violates rule 3 by having an illicit major.

19. This form is invalid in both the Aristotelian and modern systems. It violates rule 2 by having an undistributed middle and violates rule 3 by having an illicit major.
20. This form is invalid in both the Aristotelian and modern systems. It violates rule 4 by having a negative premise with an affirmative conclusion.
21. This form is invalid in both the Aristotelian and modern systems. It violates rule 3 by having an illicit major and violates the modern system's rule 5 by having two universal premises with a particular conclusion.
22. This form is valid in the Aristotelian system and invalid in the modern system. In the modern system, it violates rule 5 by having two universal premises with a particular conclusion.
23. This form is valid in the Aristotelian system and invalid in the modern system. In the modern system, it violates rule 5 by having two universal premises with a particular conclusion.
24. This form is invalid in both the Aristotelian and modern systems. It violates rule 4 by having two negative premises. In the modern system, it also violates rule 5 by having two universal premises with a particular conclusion.
25. This form is invalid in both the Aristotelian and modern systems. It violates rule 4 by having a negative premise with an affirmative conclusion.

FOR FURTHER CONSIDERATION

How do you analyze a categorical argument that contains singular statements as premises or a conclusion? (Singular statements were discussed in the study guide at the very end of the previous chapter.) For instance, consider the following famous argument, which is not really a categorical syllogism but a kind of categorical argument that has been called a "quasi-syllogism."

All men are mortal. Socrates is a man. Therefore, Socrates is mortal.

A quasi-syllogism like the above will contain one categorical statement and one or more singular statements. Rewriting the above argument as a well-crafted quasi-syllogism in standard form, we obtain the following.

    1. All human beings are mortal beings.
    2. Socrates is a human being.
So, 3. Socrates is a mortal being.

The middle term is "human beings." The minor term is "Socrates." The major term is "mortal beings." Notice that we disregard the difference between the plural "human beings" and "mortal beings" and the singular "a human being" and "a mortal being." The time-honored method of dealing with such quasi-syllogisms is this: Determine the mood and figure of the syllogism as if affirmative singular statements were **A** statements and negative singular statements were **E** statements, and then determine whether that mood and figure is valid in the Aristotelian system. You must check for validity in the Aristotelian system since singular statements always have existential import. Both the modern and Aristotelian logician recognize this feature of singular statements, but only the Aristotelian logician treats **A** and **E** categorical statements as having existential import. Any such quasi-syllogism that is valid in the Aristotelian system is also valid in the modern system. Thus, the above quasi-syllogism is valid in both the Aristotelian and modern systems since an **AAA**-1 syllogism is valid in the Aristotelian system.

CHAPTER 7

Statement Logic: Truth Tables

The primary aim of chapter 7 of The Power of Logic *is to enable you to translate English-language arguments into the notation of state-ment logic and then to construct truth tables for the purpose of deter-mining the validity or invalidity of those arguments. In chapter 7, you are also shown how to use truth tables to sort statements into the three logically significant categories of contingencies, contradictions, and tautologies.*

CHAPTER HIGHLIGHTS

In statement logic, the most fundamental elements out of which arguments are built are atomic statements. An **atomic statement** is one that contains no other statement as a part. For instance, the statement "Snow is white" contains no other statement as a part. The subject "Snow" is a noun, not a complete sentence, and the predicate "is white" contains a linking verb and an adjective and is not a complete sentence. Statements such as this are atomic because they cannot be decomposed into other statements as parts. In contrast, the statement "Snow is not white" does contain a statement as a part, namely, "Snow is white." The English word "not" functions as a negation particle and is symbolized in the language of statement logic by the **tilde** (~). Thus, "Snow is not white" is a logically compound statement even though it is a grammatically simple sentence.

We may understand a **compound statement**, then, to be any statement in which there occurs at least one logical operator. The tilde, used to translate "not" and its stylistic variants, is known as a **singulary operator** because it combines with single statements, whether atomic or compound, to form new statements. For example, "Snow is white and grass is green" is a compound statement because it contains two (atomic) statements as parts. Similarly, "It is not the case that snow is white and grass is green" is simply the negation of that compound statement. Logical opera-tors that connect two statements, i.e., the **dot** (•), the **vee** (∨), the **arrow** (→), and the **double-arrow** (↔), are known as **binary operators**.

The point of translating an argument from natural language into logical notation is to lay bare the logical form of the argument. In terms of logical form, there are five types of compound statements: negations, conjunctions, disjunctions, conditionals, and biconditionals. Atomic statements are abbreviated by capital letters (statement letters) known as "constants" because they stand for specific statements. Each of the five types of connectives used to form compound statements is represented by a spe-cial symbol or operator. Whereas constants represent the specific content of state-ments, the logical operators are used to indicate the logical form of compound statements. The word "therefore" and its cognates, which signal conclusions, are all represented by the triple-dot (∴).

The six rules that specify what a WFF is in statement logic determine which sequences of symbols count as grammatical or **well formed**. Note that in stating these rules we are not using the symbols and sequences of symbols of statement logic themselves, since we are talking about them. To do this clearly, we use statement variables instead of statement constants. These variables are the letters "p" and "q," and they represent stand-ins for any of a potentially infinite number of symbolic statements.

Truth tables can be constructed to determine the validity or invalidity of arguments. The truth value of a compound statement is a function of the truth values of its component statements, and this is what it means to say that a compound statement is **truth-functional**. A truth table for a statement gives us the truth conditions of that statement (i.e., its truth value under every combination of truth values that is possible for its parts). For example, the truth table for a negation tells us the conditions under which the negation is true. We know that a **negation** is true if and only if the statement it negates is false, and we know that a negation is false if and only if the statement it negates is true. For example, since "$3 + 6 = 10$" is false, its negation, "It is not the case that $3 + 6 = 10$," is true. Similarly, since "$3 + 6 = 9$" is true, its negation, "It is not the case that $3 + 6 = 9$," is false. So we can see that the truth value of a negation is a function of the truth value of the statement being negated. Negation, then, is said to be truth functional.

Any statement that is a **conjunction** is true if and only if all of its conjuncts are true (and is false otherwise). A **disjunction** is true if and only if at least one of its disjuncts is true (and is false only when all of its disjuncts are false). A **conditional** is true if and only if either its antecedent is false or its consequent is true (and is false only when its antecedent is true and its consequent is false). Finally, a **biconditional** is true if and only if both its right- and left-hand sides have the same truth value (and is false otherwise).

In setting up a **truth table** for a compound statement, one must first determine all the possible ways the two truth values, true (T) and false (F), can be assigned to all of the atomic statements in the compound. All the possible combinations of truth values are given in the rows of the columns on the far left side of the table. In a truth table for an argument, the premises and the conclusion occur at the top of the table to the right of the series of statement letters. Each row in such a truth table gives the truth value of each premise and the conclusion as they are determined by the assignment of truth values to the statement letters contained in the argument. If a truth table for an argument has no row on which all the premises are true and the conclusion is false, then the combination of all true premises and false conclusion is not possible, since each row gives all the ways the premises and conclusion can come out true or false. The truth table in such a case would show that the argument is valid. Furthermore, the truth table would actually show more than the mere fact that the particular argument evaluated is valid, for any argument with the same form as this argument will also be a valid argument. It does not matter what the content (subject matter) of an argument is as long as the argument has a valid form. (Logic, then, is not discipline specific.) If, however, an argument is invalid, then there will be at least one row in its truth table on which all the premises are true and the conclusion is false.

Truth tables are a definitive way to test for validity or invalidity, but they can be impractical to use when the number of letters becomes very large. An argument containing just four statement letters will require a truth table with 16 rows; one with five letters, 32 rows; and so on. Fortunately, the abbreviated truth table method alleviates this difficulty. The central idea in using the **abbreviated truth table method** is to attempt to "make" a given argument invalid by first translating it into logical notation and then assigning truth values to its component statement letters in such a way that the conclusion comes out false and all the premises come out true. If this attempt is successful, then it is clearly possible for all the premises to be true and the conclusion to be false, in which case the argument is, by definition, invalid. However, if every truth value assignment that makes the conclusion false also makes at least one premise false, then the combination of all true premises and a false conclusion is not possible. In such a case, the abbreviated truth table method can be used to show that the argument is valid.

Three important kinds of statements are tautologies, contradictions, and contingencies. A **tautology** is a compound statement that is true and remains true under every possible assignment of truth values to its component statement letters. In other words, a tautology is a compound statement that has a "T" on every row of its truth table in the column of truth values under the main operator. For example, "A ∨ ~A" is a tautology because, whether "A" is true or false, there will always be one true disjunct, and thus the disjunction will always evaluate as true. An interesting property of tautologies is that any argument whose conclusion is a tautology is a valid argument. A **contradiction** is a compound statement that is false and remains false under every assignment of truth values to its component statement letters. In other words, a contradiction is a compound statement that has an "F" on every row of its truth table in the column of truth values under the main operator. For example, "A • ~A" is a contradiction because, whether "A" is true or false, there will always be one false conjunct, and thus the conjunction will always evaluate as false. If the conjunction of an argument's premises is a contradiction, then the argument has premises that are **inconsistent**. Interestingly enough, any argument having a contradiction as a premise or having inconsistent premises is a valid argument. A **contingency** is a statement that has a truth table that contains at least one "T" and at least one "F" in the column of truth values under the main operator. For example, "A ∨ B" is contingent because it comes out true when either "A" or "B" is true and comes out false when both "A" and "B" are false.

Two statements are **logically equivalent** if and only if they each validly imply the other. Statements that are truth-functionally equivalent will have truth tables that have the same column of truth values under the main operator. This means that, within statement logic, two statements are logically equivalent if and only if the biconditional with the statements as its left- and right-hand sides is a tautology.

DISCUSSION OF KEY CONCEPTS

I. Symbolizing English Arguments

A. Helpful Reminders

1. Note that statement letters are normally used to translate only atomic (logically simple) English statements, which have no translatable logical structure within statement logic. Furthermore, when translating from English into statement logic, be

sure to assign the same statement letter to the same simple English statement for every occurrence of that statement in a compound statement. Never assign the same letter to different atomic statements or assign different letters to the same atomic statement. Be consistent and uniform in your assignments, and remember to provide a scheme of translation, since any translation is relative to the scheme of translation used to generate it.

2. Parentheses and brackets function as punctuation devices and need to be present in a symbolic statement whenever there would be ambiguity in their absence. For instance, the parentheses are needed in the statement "(A • B) → C" since the statement "A • B → C" is ambiguous. The latter statement could be read either as a conjunction whose left conjunct is "A" and whose right conjunct is "B → C" or as a conditional whose antecedent is "A → B" and whose consequent is "C." Note, however, that, according to the rules for the formation of WFFs, parentheses are not added to a statement when forming a negation. Thus, such expressions as "(~A)" and "~(A)" are not well formed. If, though, we want to form the negation of a symbolic statement that has been abbreviated, we may need to add parentheses. Thus, the negation of the disjunction "A ∨ B" should be written as "~(A ∨ B)" and not as "~A ∨ B."

3. English statements may be grammatically simple but have a compound subject or predicate containing the word "and" or the word "or" (or a stylistic variant of one of these). Many, but not all, of these statements can be restated as equivalent statements that are grammatically compound and contain "and" or "or" as the coordinating conjunction. For instance, the statement "Tom and Sally both drive new cars" can be legitimately restated as "Tom drives a new car, and Sally drives a new car." Similarly, the statement "The officer either pulled out his gun or displayed his badge" can be reasonably rephrased as "The officer pulled out his gun, or the officer displayed his badge." Such a restatement of an English statement with a compound subject or predicate may help when translating the statement into the symbolic notation of statement logic.

4. Do not confuse the notion of a "consequent" with the notion of a "consequence." A consequent is a statement occurring in the right-hand side of a material conditional. A consequence is the conclusion of an argument (or is the result or effect of something).

5. In addition to the stylistic variants of the five kinds of compound statements, there are a few other kinds of English constructions that may give you some trouble when translating them into symbolic notation. If we let the upper case letters "*P*" and "*Q*" be stand-ins for English statements and the lower case letters "*p*" and "*q*" be stand-ins for the symbolic statements used to translate *P* and *Q*, respectively, we can represent these special kinds of English statements and their translations as follows:

1. Not both *P* and *Q*. This statement is a denial of the conjunction of *P* and *Q* and should thus be translated as "~(*p* • *q*)."
2. Both not *P* and *Q*. This statement is a conjunction whose left conjunct is a denial of *P* and whose right conjunct is *Q*. This statement should thus be translated as "~*p* • *q*."
3. Neither *P* nor *Q*. This statement is both a denial of *P* and a denial of *Q* or, what amounts to the same thing, a denial of the disjunction of *P* and *Q*. So, this statement should be translated either as "~*p* • ~*q*" or as "~(*p* ∨ *q*)."

4. Not either P or Q. This statement is equivalent to "Neither P nor Q" and should be translated accordingly.
5. Either not P or Q. This statement is a disjunction whose left disjunct is a denial of P and whose right disjunct is Q. This statement should therefore be translated as "$\sim p \vee q$."

B. Commonly Asked Questions

1. Since such words as "although," "but," "however," "while," and "yet" do not mean the same as "and," why do we use the dot in translating statements containing these words?

The word "and" as well as these other words all normally have conjunctive force in an English statement, and that fact justifies translating these words with the dot. Granted, many of these conjunctive words other than "and" are often used to introduce a discount into an argument (see Chapter 2) and thus have an additional component meaning, but this surplus meaning does not affect their truth-functional meaning, which is just the meaning of the dot (see section 7.2 of *The Power of Logic*).

2. Why do we use the vee to translate statements containing the word "unless"?

When a speaker asserts "P unless Q," what he or she is saying is that P is the case as long as Q is not the case. (Note that such a speaker is not making a commitment about the truth or falsity of P if Q happens to be the case.) As a result, the statement "P unless Q" means the same as the statement "If not Q, then P." This latter statement can be shown to be equivalent to "P or Q." Thus, we can use the vee to translate the word "unless."

3. Why is the statement "P only if Q" translated as "$p \rightarrow q$" instead of "$q \rightarrow p$"?

In asserting that P only if Q, one is claiming that Q is a necessary condition for P (in other words, P cannot be the case without Q being the case). Thus, if it is true that P only if Q, then the truth of P ensures the truth of Q (not the other way around). Hence, we translate the statement "P only if Q" as "$p \rightarrow q$." That this makes sense is apparent if we consider an example. It may well be true to say that Mary will attend class only if she is enrolled in the course (since enrollment in a course is typically necessary in order to be permitted to attend the class). The statement "If Mary will attend class, then she is enrolled in the course" is true, but the statement "If Mary is enrolled in the course, then she will attend class" may be false (since some students who are enrolled do not always attend class). Therefore, the former statement and not the latter must be the correct translation of "Mary will attend class only if she is enrolled in the course."

C. Exercises

Translate the following statements into the language of statement logic. You are provided with a scheme of translation below.

A: Albert goes to the party.   B: Bart goes to the party.
C: Albert drinks too much.   D: Bart drinks too much.
E: Bart gets sick.   F: Albert gets rowdy.
G: Bart gets rowdy.

1. If Albert goes to the party, he will drink too much.
2. Albert goes to the party only if he drinks too much.

3. Albert drinks too much on the condition that he goes to the party.
4. Bart gets sick unless he does not drink too much.
5. Neither Albert nor Bart goes to the party.
6. Either Bart does not drink too much, or both he and Albert get rowdy.
7. Albert gets rowdy if and only if he goes to the party.
8. It is not true that, if Bart goes to the party, he gets sick.
9. Either Albert or Bart get rowdy, but not both of them.
10. If either Albert or Bart goes to the party, then Bart gets sick unless he does not drink too much.
11. Bart fails to go to the party provided that Albert gets rowdy.
12. Neither Albert nor Bart drinks too much only if both of them fail to go to the party.

II. Truth Tables

A. Helpful Reminders

1. The vertical columns of "T"s and "F"s under the statement letters on the far left side of a truth table are sometimes called "guide columns." You should standardize the way you fill in the guide columns, for doing so, among other things, will ensure that you enter into your table every possible combination of truth values for the number of statement letters you have. For example, suppose we are constructing a truth table for the statement "(A ∨ ~K) ↔ (A → L)." We begin by listing the statement letters on a truth table in the order in which they appear in the statement. Since we have a total of three letters ("A," "K," and "L") occurring in the statement, this will require a truth table with eight (2^3) horizontal rows. In the right most guide column (under "L"), we fill in these rows by alternating "T"s and "F"s down the column. In the next guide column to the left (under "K"), we fill in the rows by alternating two "T"s followed by two "F"s down the column. Finally, in the left most guide column (under "A"), we fill in the rows by alternating four "T"s followed by four "F"s down the column. The completed guide columns of the table should look like this:

A	K	C	$(A \lor \sim K) \leftrightarrow (A \to L)$
T	T	T	
T	T	F	
T	F	T	
T	F	F	
F	T	T	
F	T	F	
F	F	T	
F	F	F	

A statement containing four statements letters would require a sixteen-row truth table, but the procedure just outlined should be followed so that the guide columns are filled in correctly.

2. The truth tables for the statement forms "~p," "p ∨ q," "p • q," "p → q," and "p ↔ q" give the truth conditions (the conditions under which a statement of the form is true or false) of, respectively, negations, conjunctions, disjunctions, conditionals, and biconditionals. These tables in effect define the meaning of the five logi-

cal operators. When constructing a truth table for a particular statement, you use the information contained on the rows of these tables to fill in the columns of "T"s and "F"s under the operators (what are sometimes referred to as "evaluation columns"). It is important to memorize the information these tables provide in order to determine the truth or falsity of a statement, just as it is important to memorize the multiplication tables in order to determine the product of two numbers. (It will be easier to commit these tables to memory if you think of the logical operators in terms of their English-language analogues.) When determining the truth value of a compound statement, be sure to determine the truth values of the smallest component statements first and then work outward. For example, if you have a conjunction whose conjuncts are both compounds, evaluate the conjuncts first and then the conjunction itself.

3. Of the five logical operators, the sign for the material conditional, the arrow, seems to be the most difficult to understand. The arrow departs more radically from its English-language counterpart than any of the other logical operators. There are several distinct kinds of conditionals expressible in the English language, and most of these conditionals are meaningful or true only if there is either a conceptual or a causal connection between what is mentioned in the antecedent and what is mentioned in the consequent. In section 7.2 of *The Power of Logic*, three examples are offered of English if-then statements that are true when interpreted strictly as material conditionals but appear to be false as ordinarily understood. It is true that each of these compound statements has what you might call a "surplus meaning" in addition to its truth-functional meaning. If you found yourself wondering what relevance the claim "1 + 1 = 2" has to the claim "The Eiffel Tower is in France," then you were being influenced by this surplus meaning. From the standpoint of truth-functional meaning alone—that is, disregarding any surplus meaning—we know that the conditional "If the Eiffel Tower is in Germany, then it is in the U.S.A." is false when and only when its antecedent is true and its consequent false. This conditional is therefore true. This may seem odd, but logically speaking, it is correct. A material conditional is used to assert just a relationship between the *truth value* of its antecedent and the *truth value* of its consequent and nothing more. If you know that a material conditional is true, then you know only that its antecedent is false and/or its consequent is true. In asserting a material conditional, one asserts no other kind of connection between antecedent and consequent.

It may help to think of the material conditional in the following way. Suppose someone made a promise to a friend by saying to her, "If it rains, I'll come pick you up." Under what conditions would the person have broken the promise? If it did rain, and the person did pick up his friend, then clearly the promise was kept. If it did not rain, and the person did not pick up his friend, then clearly the promise was not broken. If it did not rain, but the person picked up his friend anyway, then the promise was not actually broken or compromised, since the person never said what he would do if it did not rain. Only if it did rain and the person did not pick up his friend would the promise be broken. Thus, only when the antecedent is true and the consequent is false is this "promissorial conditional" false. The material conditional behaves in the same fashion.

B. *Commonly Asked Questions*

1. Why construct truth tables for symbolic statements?

As will be discussed in the next section, the techniques involved in the construction of a truth table for an argument are just an extension of the techniques involved in the construction of a truth table for a statement. A mastery of the latter is consequently needed for a mastery of the former. In addition, symbolic statements can be categorized according to how they come out true and false on a truth table, a topic that is discussed in the last section of the present chapter.

2. Why is the particular truth table given for the material conditional the one used to specify the truth-functional meaning of the arrow?

Within statement logic, the validity of arguments is analyzed as it turns on just the truth-functional meaning of the various kinds of compound statements. Thus, the only component meaning of conditionals that matters in statement logic is their truth-functional meaning. Given the way conditional statements are used in common kinds of valid and invalid arguments, the truth-functional aspect of the conditional defines the material conditional and is fully captured by the definition of the arrow as provided by its truth table.

C. *Exercises*

Given that A, B, and C are true statements and X, Y, and Z are false statements, find the truth value of each of the following compound statements:

1. ~(Y ∨ Y)	2. ~~(A ∨ B)
3. ~[A ∨ (Z ∨ X)]	4. (A ∨ Z) • B
5. (A ∨ X) • (B ∨ Z)	6. (A • Z) ∨ (B • Z)
7. ~Z ∨ (Z • A)	8. ~[A ∨ ~(X ∨ Z)]
9. A ∨ [(~B • C) ∨ ~[~B ∨ ~(B ∨ Y)]]	10. A • [(~B • C) ∨ ~[~B ∨ ~(Y ∨ B)]]

III. Using Truth Tables to Evaluate Arguments

A. *Helpful Reminders*

1. What amounts to the same English statement may occur more than once in an argument but may not always occur in exactly the same words. Don't be confused by this situation. When translating an argument from English into the language of statement logic, you should translate the atomic statements in a way that secures the same kind of uniform translation that you were asked to provide in Chapter 2 when constructing a well-crafted version of an argument. In fact, it may help to rewrite an argument as a well-crafted one before producing a scheme of translation and translating the argument.

2. To construct a truth table for an argument, you do what you normally do to construct a truth table for a statement except that you add as a heading an entire argument instead of a single statement. The series of statement letters entered as a heading to the left of the argument should consist of all the statement letters occurring in the argument in the alphabetical order in which they occur. After filling in the guide columns, you evaluate each of the premises and the conclusion so that you end up with a column of truth values under the main operator of each compound statement.

3. Students are often confused about the difference between truth and validity. The two are related but are certainly not identical. Truth is a property of statements, while validity is a property of arguments. It makes no sense, at least in the present context, to speak of an argument being true or of a statement being valid. (See Chapter 1.) In a certain sense, truth is easy to understand. If you have ever caught anyone in a lie, you know what truth is: It is what that individual should have told you but did not. Since a valid argument can have all false premises and a false conclusion, validity obviously does not require of an argument that it have true premises and a true conclusion. Nevertheless, with respect to arguments, there is a combination of truth values that validity rules out as impossible, and that is the combination in which all of the premises are true and the conclusion is false. So validity is concerned with truth, but only at one remove: If we know that an argument is valid, then we know which combinations of truth values are possible and which are not. The truth table for an argument presents all the possible ways the premises and the conclusion can be true or false, and thus we use a truth table to determine whether an argument is valid.

B. *Commonly Asked Questions*

1. When constructing a truth table for an argument that contains a single-statement letter as a premise or a conclusion, do we repeat the column of truth values under the letter that appears in the guide columns to the left?

In order to avoid overlooking the truth value of a premise or the conclusion when determining whether an argument is valid from its truth table, you should evaluate every premise and the conclusion. Thus, you should evaluate a single-statement letter when it is a premise or a conclusion even though that means constructing an evaluation column that is just a repetition of one of the guide columns.

2. On a truth table for an argument, what do we look for to determine whether the argument is valid?

If, when evaluating an argument for validity, you discover a row in which all of the premises are true and the conclusion is false, then the argument is *invalid*. The argument is not merely invalid "in that row." If the evaluation yields no row in which all of the premises are true and the conclusion is false, then the argument is *valid*. So the only row that will tell you anything about the validity or invalidity of an argument is a row in which all the premises are true and the conclusion is false. Note that any other kind of row, and in particular a row in which the premises are all false and the conclusion is true, does not tell you anything about an argument's validity or invalidity.

C. *Exercises*

Determine whether the following arguments are valid or invalid. Justify your answer with a truth table evaluation.

1. $A \cdot B$, $\sim A \vee \sim B$ $\therefore B$
2. $(A \vee B) \rightarrow (A \cdot B)$, $A \cdot B$ $\therefore A \vee B$
3. $A \rightarrow B$, $A \rightarrow \sim B$ $\therefore \sim A$
4. $\sim(A \cdot B)$, $\sim B$ $\therefore A$
5. $(A \vee B) \cdot \sim(A \cdot B)$ $\therefore A \vee B$

6. $A \to B, \sim(B \lor C)$ $\therefore \sim A$
7. $A \to B, B \to \sim C$ $\therefore A \to \sim C$
8. $A \lor B, (A \to \sim C) \bullet (B \to \sim C)$ $\therefore \sim C$
9. $(A \lor B) \bullet (A \lor C)$ $\therefore A \bullet (B \lor C)$
10. $A \to (B \to C), B \to (C \to D)$ $\therefore A \to D$

IV. Abbreviated Truth Tables

A. Helpful Reminders

1. To show that an argument is valid, we need to show that the combination of its premises all being true and its conclusion being false is not possible. We can show that such a combination is not possible if we can show that, in every case in which the conclusion is false, at least one premise is false as well. We accomplish the latter by demonstrating that the assumption of the falsehood of the conclusion leads inevitably to the falsehood of at least one premise. In demonstrating this, we in effect show that, in the truth table for the argument, for any row in which the conclusion comes out false, at least one of the premises also comes out false in that row. It is in just such a fashion that the abbreviated truth table method can be used to determine the validity of an argument.

2. To show that an argument is invalid, we need to show that the combination of its premises all being true and its conclusion being false is indeed possible. We can show that such a combination is possible if we can show that a truth table for the argument will contain a row in which every premise is true and the conclusion is false. We accomplish the latter by finding such a row, and we find such a row by assigning truth values to the statement letters occurring in the argument in such a way that all the premises evaluate as true and the conclusion evaluates as false. It is in this fashion that the abbreviated truth table method can be used to demonstrate the invalidity of an argument.

B. Commonly Asked Questions

1. What is the basic strategy of the abbreviated truth table method?

The basic strategy is to begin with the supposition that the conclusion is false and all the premises are true, and then try to assign to the statement letters truth values that are consistent with that supposition. (Thus, regardless of whether or not you know the argument to be invalid, you begin with the hypothesis that the argument is invalid.) If you are able to assign truth values to each statement letter consistently based on that supposition, then you have confirmed your hypothesis that the argument is invalid. You have in effect produced a row in the argument's truth table that shows the argument to be invalid. However, if, for each truth value assignment that makes the conclusion false, you are forced to make at least one premise false, then you have refuted the hypothesis. That is, you have shown that it is not possible, on pain of inconsistency, for all the premises to be true and the conclusion false, which means that the argument is valid. Note that, in the case of demonstrating validity, you may need to produce what amounts to more than one row of the argument's truth table to ensure that you have examined all the relevant cases.

2. Why construct an abbreviated truth table when a standard truth table works to determine the validity or invalidity of an argument?

The abbreviated truth table method helps circumvent the impracticalities of the full-blown truth table method. As the number of statement letters in an argument increases, the size of its truth table increases dramatically. An argument containing just six statement letters, for example, will require a truth table with sixty-four (2^6) rows. We can alleviate most of the work involved in constructing a complete truth table for an argument if we can either find a row in such a table in which all the premises are true and the conclusion is false or convince ourselves that there can be no such row. The abbreviated truth table method in effect enables us to do just that.

C. Exercises

(a) Show that the following arguments are valid by using the abbreviated truth table method.

1. A ∨ B, A → ~C, B → ~C ∴ ~C
2. M → N, O • M ∴ N ∨ P
3. C • D, ~D ∨ F ∴ ~(~F • ~G)
4. A → (B ∨ C), ~B, ~C ∴ ~A
5. A ∨ B, C → ~A, C → ~B ∴ ~C

(b) Show that the following arguments are invalid by using the abbreviated truth table method.

1. A → B, ~A ∴ ~B
2. A → B, B ∴ A
3. A ∨ R, R ∨ E ∴ A ∨ E
4. P ↔ Q ∴ P • Q
5. A → B, A → C ∴ C → B

V. Tautology, Contradiction, Contingency, and Logical Equivalence

A. Helpful Reminders

1. Remember that a tautology is a compound statement that must be true; a contradiction is a compound statement that must be false; and a contingency is a statement that can be either true or false. In a truth table for a statement, the evaluation column under the main operator is sometimes called the "main column." Thus, the truth table for a tautology will have a main column that has only "T"s in it; the truth table for a contradiction will have a main column that has only "F"s in it; and the truth table for a contingency will have a main column that has at least one "T" and at least one "F" in it.

2. Remember that two statements are logically equivalent if and only if each one of them validly implies the other. This mutual implication ensures that equivalent statements must always agree in truth value. As a result, in statement logic anyway, two equivalent statements will have truth tables with the same main column, which in turn means that a biconditional with equivalent statements as its left- and right-hand sides is a tautology.

3. The premises of an argument are consistent if it is possible that they are all true, while an argument's premises are inconsistent if it is not possible for them all to be true. If the truth table for an argument has a row in which all of the premises are

true, then the argument has consistent premises. If the truth table for an argument does not have such a row, then the argument has inconsistent premises.

B. Commonly Asked Questions

1. Aren't there other kinds of statements that are always true besides the tautologies of statement logic (or their English counterparts)?

There are indeed other kinds of statements that will always be true due to the nature of their logical form, regardless of the way the world is. You will encounter statements in predicate logic (the topic of Chapter 9), for instance, that are always true for the same reason but are not recognized as tautologies in statement logic.

2. Why is an argument having a tautology as a conclusion always a valid argument?

An argument having a tautology as a conclusion is an argument the conclusion of which cannot be false. Any argument having a conclusion that cannot be false is an argument that cannot have all true premises and a false conclusion and is therefore by definition a valid argument.

3. Why is an argument having a contradiction as a premise or having inconsistent premises always a valid argument?

Any argument having a contradiction as a premise or having inconsistent premises is an argument the premises of which cannot all be true. Any argument the premises of which cannot all be true is an argument that cannot have all true premises and a false conclusion and is therefore by definition a valid argument. By the way, note that any argument having a contradiction among its other premises will have inconsistent premises, but an argument having inconsistent premises may not have a contradiction as a premise.

C. Exercises

(a) Determine whether each of the following statements is a tautology, a contradiction, or a contingency by constructing a truth table.

1. $[(A \lor B) \bullet {\sim}A] \to B$
2. $[{\sim}(A \lor B) \bullet A] \to B$
3. $[({\sim}A \lor B) \bullet A] \to {\sim}B$
4. $[{\sim}(A \bullet B) \bullet B] \to {\sim}A$
5. $[(A \bullet B) \lor (A \bullet C)] \to [A \bullet (B \lor C)]$

(b) Use truth tables to determine whether the following biconditionals are tautologies:

1. $(A \lor {\sim}A) \leftrightarrow {\sim}(A \bullet {\sim}A)$
2. $A \leftrightarrow [A \bullet (B \lor {\sim}B)]$
3. $A \leftrightarrow [A \lor (B \bullet {\sim}B)]$
4. $[A \bullet (B \lor C)] \leftrightarrow [A \lor (B \bullet C)]$
5. $[A \bullet (B \bullet C)] \leftrightarrow [(A \bullet B) \bullet C]$

ANSWERS TO EXERCISES

Answers to Selected Exercises in the Text

Exercise 7.1
Part C

10. This can also be translated as "~B • ~S", which literally reads "Birds are not animals, and snakes are not animals."
19. Translate the subordinating conjunction "while" as the dot, which will be the main operator.

Part D

10. The words "given that" and the comma at the end of the subordinate clause indicate that the arrow is the main operator. The "only if" indicates that the antecedent is itself a conditional.

Exercise 7.2 Part A

4. Remember that the material conditional comes out false only in the case where its antecedent is true and its consequent false.
10. Here the main operator is the negation sign, so be sure to evaluate it last. The only condition under which a disjunction comes out false is when both disjuncts are false. Therefore, "C ∨ D" is false, which makes "~(C ∨ D)" come out true.
22. Notice that this statement is a disjunction whose left disjunct is a biconditional and whose right disjunct is a conditional. So be sure to evaluate both disjuncts before you evaluate the entire disjunction.

Part B

7. This statement is true because it is the negation of a false conjunction.

Exercise 7.3 Part A

1. You should immediately recognize this argument as an instance of disjunctive syllogism, a valid argument form.
4. In both the first and fourth rows, all the premises are true and the conclusion is false. However, don't forget that only one such row is required to show invalidity. An argument does not become "more invalid" just because there is more than one row having all true premises and a false conclusion.
10. The only row that is relevant here is the last row, where the premise is true. Since the conclusion is not false, and since in no other row is the premise true, it follows that the argument is valid.
19. If you recall the definition of validity, you can see that only rows 1, 3, and 5 are relevant, because only in these rows are all the premises true. In none of these rows is the conclusion false, and therefore the argument is valid.

Part B

10. Since there is at least one row where all the premises are true and the conclusion is false, the argument is invalid.

Part C

4. Notice how in the first premise the word "unless" is translated as a disjunction. The third row of the truth table shows the argument to be invalid.
7. Whenever one thing is claimed to be both a necessary and a sufficient condition for another thing, as occurs in the first premise, the statement should always be translated as a biconditional. The only relevant rows of the truth table are the last two, and in neither case are all the premises true and the conclusion false. The argument is therefore valid.

Exercise 7.4
Part A

19. This is a complicated argument. Notice that the first premise is a negation of a disjunction, the second premise is a disjunction, and the third premise is a conditional whose antecedent is a conjunction. The conclusion is a conjunction whose left conjunct is itself a conjunction. Assign "F" to the conclusion, then "T" to each of the three premises. All the rest is detail. Just make sure you do not assign different truth values to different occurrences of the same statement letter! No statement can be both true and false.

Part B

10. The conclusion is a biconditional, so to make it false, be sure that "P" and "Z" disagree in truth value. Whatever values you assign to them, be sure to assign those same truth values to each occurrence of these statement letters throughout the argument.

Part C

1. Even though you are proving an argument valid here, your strategy is the same: Hypothesize that the conclusion is false and the premise is true. What happens in this case is that you are forced to assign inconsistent truth values to the premise. You have refuted your hypothesis. The premise can't be true when the conclusion is false. The argument is thus valid.

Part D

7. In translating the first premise, translate the first occurrence of "if" as a left-hand bracket, and the comma immediately preceding the word "then" as the arrow, in this case the main operator. Translate the second "if" as a left-hand parenthesis indicating another arrow. The final result is a conditional whose consequent is itself a conditional. In the second premise, translate "But it is not true" as "~" and then "either" as a left-hand parenthesis. The rest is easy.

Exercise 7.5
Part A

1. Let's reason through this one to see why it is a tautology. If the antecedent "~A" is true, then the consequent "(A → B)" must be true since "A" is false. Since all conditionals with true consequents are true, it follows that, when "~A" is true, the entire conditional is true. On the other hand, if "~A" is false, then, again, the entire conditional is true because all conditionals with false antecedents are true. Thus, since "~A" must be either true or false but not both, it follows that the conditional as a whole must always be true and is therefore by definition a tautology.

7. Since there occurs at least one "T" and one "F" in the main column of the truth table for this statement, it follows that the statement is contingent. It will be either true or false, depending on the specific assignments of truth values to its statement letters.

Part B

1. Notice that, since the biconditional has a "T" in every row of its truth table, it is a tautology. The two statements comprising the two sides of the biconditional are thus logically equivalent.

Part C

1. This argument has a conclusion that is a tautology. Any argument with a tautology as a conclusion is a valid argument. Since the conclusion cannot be false, it cannot be false when the premises are all true.

4. The premise of this argument is a contradiction. Any argument whose premise is a contradiction is a valid argument. Since it is impossible for such a premise to be true, it is thus impossible for it to be true when the conclusion is false.

Answers to Supplemental Exercises

I

1. $A \rightarrow C$
2. $A \rightarrow C$
3. $A \rightarrow C$
4. $E \vee \sim D$
5. $\sim A \cdot \sim B$ or $\sim(A \vee B)$
6. $\sim D \vee (G \cdot F)$
7. $F \leftrightarrow A$
8. $\sim(B \rightarrow E)$
9. $(F \vee G) \cdot \sim(F \cdot G)$
10. $(A \vee B) \rightarrow (E \vee \sim D)$
11. $F \rightarrow \sim B$
12. $(\sim C \cdot \sim D) \rightarrow (\sim A \cdot \sim B)$ or $\sim(C \vee D) \rightarrow \sim(A \vee B)$

II

1. True   ~(Y ∨ Y)
           T F F F

2. True   ~~(A ∨ B)
           TF T T T

3. False   ~[A ∨ (Z ∨ X)]
           F T T F F F

4. True   (A ∨ Z) • B
           T T F T T

5. True   (A ∨ X) • (B ∨ Z)
           T T F T T T F

6. False   (A • Z) ∨ (B • Z)
           T F F F T F F

7. True   ~Z ∨ (Z • A)
           TF T F F T

8. False   ~[A ∨ ~(X ∨ Z)]
           F T T T F F F

9. True   A ∨ [(~B • C) ∨ ~[~B ∨ ~(B ∨ Y)]]
           T T FT FT T T FT FF T T F

10. True   A • [(~B • C) ∨ ~[~B ∨ ~(Y ∨ B)]]
           T T FT FT T T FT FF FT T

III

1.

A	B	A • B.	~A ∨ ~B	∴ B
T	T	T	F FF	T
T	F	F	F TT	F
F	T	F	T TF	T
F	F	F	T TT	F

The argument is valid.

2.

A	B	(A ∨ B) → (A • B).	A • B	∴ A ∨ B
T	T	T T T	T	T
T	F	T F F	F	T
F	T	T F F	F	T
F	F	F T F	F	F

The argument is valid.

3.

A	B	A → B.	A → ~B	∴ ~A
T	T	T	F F	F
T	F	F	T T	F
F	T	T	T F	T
F	F	T	T T	T

The argument is valid.

4.

A	B	~(A•B).	~B	∴ A
T	T	F T	F	T
T	F	T F	T	T
F	T	T F	F	F
F	F	T F	T	F

The argument is invalid.

5.

A	B	(A ∨ B) • ~(A • B)	∴ A ∨ B
T	T	T FF T	T
T	F	T TT F	T
F	T	T TT F	T
F	F	F FT F	F

The argument is valid.

6.

A	B	C	A → B.	~(B ∨ C)	∴ ~A
T	T	T	T	F T	F
T	T	F	T	F T	F
T	F	T	F	F T	F
T	F	F	F	T F	F
F	T	T	T	F T	T
F	T	F	T	F T	T
F	F	T	T	F T	T
F	F	F	T	T F	T

The argument is valid.

7.

A	B	C	A → B.	B → ~C	∴ A → ~C
T	T	T	T	F F	F F
T	T	F	T	T T	T T
T	F	T	F	T F	F F
T	F	F	F	T T	T T
F	T	T	T	F F	T F
F	T	F	T	T T	T T
F	F	T	T	T F	T F
F	F	F	T	T T	T T

The argument is valid.

8.

A	B	C	A∨B.	(A→~C)•(B→~C)	∴ ~C
T	T	T	T	F F F F F	F
T	T	F	T	T T T T T	T
T	F	T	T	F F F T F	F
T	F	F	T	T T T T T	T
F	T	T	T	T F F F F	F
F	T	F	T	T T T T T	T
F	F	T	F	T F T T F	F
F	F	F	F	T T T T T	T

The argument is valid.

9.

A	B	C	(A∨B)•(A∨C)	∴ A•(B∨C)
T	T	T	T T T	T T
T	T	F	T T T	T T
T	F	T	T T T	T T
T	F	F	T T T	F F
F	T	T	T T T	F T
F	T	F	T F F	F T
F	F	T	F F T	F T
F	F	F	F F F	F F

The argument is invalid.

10.

A	B	C	D	A→(B→C).	B→(C→D)	∴ A→D
T	T	T	T	T T	T T	T
T	T	T	F	T T	F F	F
T	T	F	T	F F	T T	T
T	T	F	F	F F	T T	F
T	F	T	T	T T	T T	T
T	F	T	F	T T	T F	F
T	F	F	T	T T	T T	T
T	F	F	F	T T	T T	F
F	T	T	T	T T	T T	T
F	T	T	F	T T	F F	T
F	T	F	T	T F	T T	T
F	T	F	F	T F	T T	T
F	F	T	T	T T	T T	T
F	F	T	F	T T	T F	T
F	F	F	T	T T	T T	T
F	F	F	F	T T	T T	T

The argument is invalid.

IV(a)

1. A ∨ B.   A → ~C.   B → ~C   ∴ ~C   valid
   T T F   T(T/F)FT F T FT   FT   ↑
   (line connecting)

The argument is valid. The second premise is both T and F.

2. M → N.   O • M   ∴ N ∨ P   valid
   F T F   T(T/F)F   F F F   ↑

The argument is valid. The second premise is both T and F.

3. C • D.   ~D ∨ F   ∴ ~(~F • ~G)   valid
   T(T/F)F TF T F   F TFT TF   ↑

The argument is valid. The first premise is both T and F.

4. A → (B ∨ C).   ~B.   ~C   ∴ ~A   valid
   T(T/F)F F F   TF   TF   FT   ↑

The argument is valid. The first premise is both T and F.

5. A ∨ B.   C → ~A.   C → ~B   ∴ ~C   valid
   F T T   T T TF   T(T/F)FT   F T   ↑

The argument is valid. The third premise is both T and F.

IV(b)

1.
A	B	A → B.	~A	∴ ~B
F	T	F T T	TF	FT

The argument is invalid. The assignment of "F" to A and "T" to B makes the premises true and the conclusion false.

2.
A	B	A → B.	B	∴ A
F	T	F T T	T	F

The argument is invalid. The assignment of "F" to A and "T" to B makes the premises true and the conclusion false.

3.
A	R	E	A ∨ R.	R ∨ E	∴ A ∨ E
F	T	F	F T T	T T F	F F F

The argument is invalid. The assignment of "F" to A and E and "T" to R makes the premises true and the conclusion false.

4.

P	Q	$P \leftrightarrow Q$	$\therefore P \cdot Q$
F	F	F T F	F F F

The argument is invalid. The assignment of "F" to both P and Q makes the premises true and the conclusion false.

5.

A	B	C	$A \rightarrow B$.	$A \rightarrow C$	$\therefore C \rightarrow B$
F	F	T	F T F	F T T	T F F

The argument is invalid. The assignment of "F" to A and B and "T" to C makes the premises true and the conclusion false.

V(a)

1.

A	B	$[(A \vee B) \cdot \sim A] \rightarrow B$
T	T	T F F T
T	F	T F F T
F	T	T T T T
F	F	F F T T

The statement is a tautology.

2.

A	B	$[\sim(A \vee B) \cdot A] \rightarrow B$
T	T	F T F T
T	F	F T F T
F	T	F T F T
F	F	T F F T

The statement is a tautology.

3.

A	B	$[(\sim A \vee B) \cdot A] \rightarrow \sim B$
T	T	F T T F F
T	F	F F F T T
F	T	T T F T F
F	F	T T F T T

The statement is a contingency.

4.

A	B	$[\sim(A \cdot B) \cdot B] \rightarrow \sim A$
T	T	F T F T F
T	F	T F F T F
F	T	T F T T T
F	F	T F F T T

The statement is a tautology.

5.

A	B	C	[(A • B) ∨ (A • C)] → [A • (B ∨ C)]					
T	T	T	T	T	T	T	T	T
T	T	F	T	T	F	T	T	T
T	F	T	F	T	T	T	T	T
T	F	F	F	F	F	T	F	F
F	T	T	F	F	F	T	F	T
F	T	F	F	F	F	T	F	T
F	F	T	F	F	F	T	F	T
F	F	F	F	F	F	T	F	F

The statement is a tautology.

V(b)

1.

A	(A ∨ ~A) ↔ ~(A • ~A)					
T	T F	T T	F F
F	T T	T T	F T

The biconditional is a tautology, so "A ∨ ~A" is equivalent to "~(A • ~A)."

2.

A	B	A ↔ [A • (B ∨ ~B)]		
T	T	T	T	T F
T	F	T	T	T T
F	T	T	F	T F
F	F	T	F	T T

The biconditional is a tautology, so "A" is equivalent to "A • (B ∨ ~B)."

3.

A	B	A ↔ [A ∨ (B • ~B)]		
T	T	T	T	F F
T	F	T	T	F T
F	T	T	F	F F
F	F	T	F	F T

The biconditional is a tautology, so "A" is equivalent to "A ∨ (B • ~B)."

4.

A	B	C	[A • (B ∨ C)] ↔ [A ∨ (B • C)]				
T	T	T	T	T	T	T	T
T	T	F	T	T	T	T	F
T	F	T	T	T	T	T	F
T	F	F	F	F	F	T	F
F	T	T	F	T	F	T	T
F	T	F	F	T	T	F	F
F	F	T	F	T	T	F	F
F	F	F	F	F	T	F	F

The biconditional is not a tautology, so "A • (B ∨ C)" is not equivalent to "A ∨ (B • C)."

5.

A	B	C	[A • (B • C)]	↔	[(A • B) • C]

A	B	C	[A	•	(B	•	C)]	↔	[(A	•	B)	•	C]
T	T	T		T		T	T	T		T		T	T
T	T	F		F		F	T	T		T		T	F
T	F	T		F		F	T	T		F		F	F
T	F	F		F		F	T	T		F		F	F
F	T	T		F		T	T	T		F		F	F
F	T	F		F		F	T	T		F		F	F
F	F	T		F		F	T	T		F		F	F
F	F	F		F		F	T	T		F		F	F

The biconditional is a tautology, so "A • (B • C)" is equivalent to "(A • B) • C."

FOR FURTHER CONSIDERATION

You learned in this chapter that when two statements are logically equivalent their truth tables will contain exactly the same sequence of "T"s and "F"s under the main operator. Thus, from a truth-functional point of view, "P ↔ Q" says the same thing as "(P → Q) • (Q → P)" because they always have the same truth value under the same assignment of truth values to their component statement letters. Since a truth table gives you the truth conditions of a compound statement and the logical meaning of an operator amounts to the truth conditions of a compound statement formed from the operator, the double-arrow is said to be definable in terms of the arrow and the dot. Theoretically, the double-arrow can thus be eliminated from our collection of operators, but we keep it because it provides us a briefer way to express what we would otherwise have to express by a logically equivalent conjunction both conjuncts of which are conditionals. Likewise, the arrow can be eliminated in favor of the vee and the negation sign. To demonstrate this, simply show that the truth tables for "P → Q" and "~P ∨ Q" have the same column of truth values under the main operator or that the biconditional formed from them is a tautology. Furthermore, the vee can be eliminated in favor of the dot and the negation sign, as you can see if you construct truth tables for the two statements "P ∨ Q" and "~(~P • ~Q)." From a theoretical standpoint, a mere two operators are sufficient to express anything we can express using all five operators. Because of this, we say that the set of operators containing the negation sign and the dot is functionally or expressively complete. You may find it interesting to know that we can take this a step further and eliminate this set of operators in favor of a set containing just one operator. Two operators are actually expressively complete by themselves: the dagger (↓), which is a sign for nondisjunction, and the Sheffer's stroke (|), which is a sign for nonconjunction. For further discussion of these matters, see pages 49–51 of Gerald J. Massey's *Understanding Symbolic Logic* (1970, Harper and Row) and page 74 of E. J. Lemmon's *Beginning Logic* (1978, Hackett).

Certain English conditionals present problems when we attempt to translate arguments containing them into the notation of statement logic. The material conditional expresses only the truth-functional meaning of the English conditional, that meaning which is essential for the validity of the basic argument forms of statement logic involving conditionals. However, as alluded to earlier, there are certain other conditionals whose truth conditions are much more difficult to determine, and these apparently cannot be translated as material conditionals. There are, for instance, what philosophers and grammarians call subjunctive or counterfactual conditionals because their antecedents mention what is contrary to fact. Typically, these sentences have the form "If A were (or had been) the case, then B would be (or not be) the case." To assess the truth value of such conditionals, we must imagine a situation, or "possible world," as philosophers would say, which is just like our actual world except that, in this possible world, the antecedent is true. We then try to determine whether the consequent is also true in this possible world. For example, one might argue that the counterfactual "If Hitler had been French, then he would not have been a Nazi" is true. We know that if Hitler was French but also a Nazi, then the counterfactual is false, which corroborates the fact that all conditionals with true antecedents and false consequents are false. However, one cannot translate this counterfactual conditional into a material conditional without ignoring its counter-factuality. After all, one cannot let the antecedent "Hitler had been French" be abbreviated by a statement letter, because such letters must stand for complete English sentences, and neither the antecedent nor the consequent of this conditional is a complete sentence.

Unlike material conditionals, counterfactual conditionals are not logically well behaved. Consider the following example inspired by one provided by R. M. Martin in his entertaining book *There Are Two Errors in the the Title of This Book* (1992, Broadview Press) (Yes, the title is correct!) Everyone knows that George Bush and Al Gore do not belong to the same political party. Bush is a Republican, and Gore is a Democrat. However, supposing that they had been members of the same political party, which of the following two sentences would be true?

1. If Bush and Gore had been members of the same political party, then Bush would have been a Democrat.
2. If Bush and Gore had been members of the same political party, then Gore would have been a Republican.

They cannot both be true, for if they were, then in a world in which Bush and Gore belong to the same political party, Bush the Democrat and Gore the Republican would be members of the same political party, which is absurd. So, are they both false? If not, which one is true, and how should it be decided?

Statement Logic: Proofs

*Although you can always use truth tables to determine the validity
or invalidity of an argument in statement logic, the truth table
method is not very efficient, particularly for arguments that contain many different atomic statements. Chapter 8 discusses another
method of demonstrating validity, the method of proof, and presents
the various inference rules that can be used to construct proofs. The
chapter also discusses theorems and their relation to tautologies and
valid arguments.*

CHAPTER HIGHLIGHTS

The system of natural deduction for proving arguments valid has several advan-
tages over the truth table method. In a **natural deduction system**, we can prove that
a conclusion follows from a given set of premises by way of certain **inference rules**.
The inference rules are themselves valid, which means that any argument whose
conclusion can be proved by using the inference rules will certainly be valid.

A proof within the context of a natural deduction system is always a proof of a
symbolic argument—that is, an argument the premises and conclusion of which are
sentences in the language of statement logic (SL for short). In this technical sense, a
proof is a series of steps, each one of which is either a premise of the argument (or a
temporarily assumed premise) or validly deduced from one or more previous steps
by the application of an inference rule. The last line of a completed proof is the argument's conclusion, which follows validly from the premises. Since the inference
rules are valid, they are truth preserving—that is, they cannot ever lead from truths to
falsehoods. By showing that a conclusion can be derived from an argument's premises by virtue of the inference rules, we have thus shown that, if all the premises
should be true, the conclusion would have to be true, and the argument is valid.

The eight **implicational inference rules** are *modus ponens* (MP), *modus tollens*
(MT), hypothetical syllogism (HS), disjunctive syllogism (DS), constructive dilemma
(CD), simplification (Simp), conjunction (Conj), and addition (Add). The ten **equivalence rules** are double-negation (DN), commutation (Com), association (As), De
Morgan's laws (DeM), contraposition (Cont), distribution (Dist), exportation (Ex),
redundancy (Re), material equivalence (ME), and material implication (MI). To this
set of rules are also added two additional rules: conditional proof (CP) and *reductio
ad absurdum* (RAA).

The distinction between implicational and equivalence rules is fairly simple to
grasp, yet it is crucial for applying the rules correctly. First, an implicational rule
must be applied to an entire line or lines of a proof. Second, implicational rules are
one-directional, which means that, although a statement *p* may validly follow from

another statement *q* according to an implicational inference rule, *q* may not validly follow from *p*. So, the inference may well be valid in only one direction. In contrast, equivalence rules are two-directional, and they can be applied to parts of lines.

In a natural deduction system with just the eighteen implicational and equivalence inference rules, some arguments that are valid in SL cannot be proved valid. However, with the addition of the rule of **conditional proof**, every argument within SL that is valid can be proved valid. Hence, the inclusion of CP makes our system complete. Specifically, CP is required for many arguments whose conclusions are conditional statements. In a proof in which you use CP, first assume the antecedent of the conditional you wish to prove as an extra but temporary premise. Next, prove the consequent of the conditional you wish to prove from that assumption together with any other previous steps that may be required. Last, infer the conditional you wish to prove by applying the rule CP and entering that conditional on the next line of the proof. Upon inferring the conditional, you discharge the temporarily assumed premise and box off the line where the assumption was made, along with each subsequent line that followed from that assumption. These boxed-off lines cannot be used again in the proof.

The rule of *reductio ad absurdum* does not enable you to prove any arguments valid that cannot already be proved valid with CP and the other eighteen rules already at hand, but it can significantly shorten otherwise lengthy proofs. It is a fairly simple rule. If you are to prove a certain conclusion C from certain premises, and you intend to use RAA, first assume the "opposite" of C, and then derive a contradiction (any statement of the form "p • ~p") from that assumption together with any previous lines that may be required. The opposite of C cannot then be true since it entails a contradiction, and RAA allows us to infer that C is true on the next line of the proof. As is also the case with CP, the temporarily assumed premise is discharged, and the line where that assumption is made, together with every line following from that assumption, is boxed off. If the conclusion you are after is not a negation, then assume its negation, and derive a contradiction. If your desired conclusion is a negation, assume the statement that results from dropping the negation sign, and derive a contradiction. So, the "opposite" of a conclusion C will be its negation, "~C," and the opposite of "~C" will be C.

A **theorem** is a statement that can be proved independently of any premises. As it turns out, to every theorem there corresponds a tautology. In fact, the set of theorems and the set of tautologies are exactly the same set. The notion of a corresponding conditional can be introduced in order to explicate an important connection between valid arguments and theorems. An argument's corresponding conditional is the conditional whose antecedent is the premise (or a conjunction of all the premises) of the argument and whose consequent is the conclusion of the argument. If an argument is valid in SL, then its corresponding conditional can be proven as a theorem. Furthermore, if an argument's corresponding conditional can be proved as a theorem in SL, then the argument is valid. Since all valid SL arguments correspond to theorems in SL and all theorems in SL correspond to valid SL arguments, it follows that an argument is valid in SL if and only if its corresponding conditional is a theorem in SL.

DISCUSSION OF KEY CONCEPTS

I. Implicational Rules of Inference

A. Helpful Reminders

1. The eight implicational inference rules are the rules of *modus ponens* (MP), *modus tollens* (MT), hypothetical syllogism (HS), disjunctive syllogism (DS), constructive dilemma (CD), simplification (Simp), conjunction (Conj), and addition (Add). Be sure to learn these rules and the abbreviations of the names of these rules. You should also keep in mind that these eight rules are one-directional and cannot be applied to just part of a line.

2. We write the triple-dot symbol (∴) and the conclusion of the argument we wish to prove to the side of the line where we enter the final premise of the argument. This symbolic statement to the side is not a part of the proof and is there only to remind us what we must prove as the final conclusion of the proof.

3. Notice that all the inference rules are completely general in that they are potentially applicable to any step of any argument in SL. Because of this, statement variables instead of statement letters are used to characterize the inference rules. Notice also that a line of a proof has been correctly justified by an application of an inference rule if and only if the statement on that line, together with the statement(s) on the line(s) mentioned in the justification, constitute an instance of the argument form corresponding to the rule.

B. Commonly Asked Questions

1. How do you get started with a proof?

Of course, the very first thing you should do is enter the premises of the argument on the initial lines of the proof and write your conclusion to the side of the last line that contains a premise. If, upon inspecting the premises and conclusion, you do not automatically see the inferential path to follow to get to the conclusion, then follow Rule of Thumb 2, and break down the premises. Make as many inferences as you can to obtain smaller statements as conclusions. Since a single statement letter or its negation can typically be used in a variety of possible inferences, try to derive individual statement letters and/or their negations from the premises. By having more lines to work with, you can do more, and thus you may be able to see your way to the conclusion. If you still do not see how to get the conclusion, then follow Rule of Thumb 1 and work backward from the conclusion to the premises until an appropriate proof strategy to follow emerges.

2. Is it always best to attempt a proof of an argument by routinely working backward from the conclusion?

Although working backward from the conclusion may well help, this technique of proof construction does have its limitations. By starting with the conclusion and figuring out first what lines would be needed to derive the conclusion, then what other lines would be needed to derive the former lines, and so on, you may not always be able to get back to the premises. When you reach a line that may be derived from more than one possible combination of prior lines, given the premises, you are at an impasse, and the technique of working backward from the conclusion has broken down. When this happens, you need to start working the proof from the beginning until it becomes clear how the first parts of the proof connect with the last parts of the proof. So, although you should definitely look at the conclusion and the premises and consider how to derive the former from the latter, you should not expect in every case to be able to construct a complete proof from the conclusion to the premises.

C. Exercises

(a) Indicate which implicational rule of inference was used to derive the last line of each of the following proofs.

1. 1. $A \rightarrow B$
   2. A $\therefore B$
   3. B

2. 1. $C \vee D$
   2. $\sim D$ $\therefore C$
   3. C

3. 1. $A \vee B$
   2. $A \rightarrow C$
   3. $B \rightarrow D$ $\therefore C \vee D$
   4. $C \vee D$

4. 1. $C \rightarrow D$
   2. $D \rightarrow E$ $\therefore C \rightarrow E$
   3. $C \rightarrow E$

5. 1. $(B \cdot A) \rightarrow C$
   2. $\sim C$ $\therefore \sim(B \cdot A)$
   3. $\sim(B \cdot A)$

6. 1. A
   2. B $\therefore A \cdot B$
   3. $A \cdot B$

7. 1. $(C \leftrightarrow D) \vee \sim(A \rightarrow B)$
   2. $\sim(C \leftrightarrow D)$ $\therefore \sim(A \rightarrow B)$
   3. $\sim(A \rightarrow B)$

8. 1. $D \cdot C$ $\therefore (D \cdot C) \vee \sim(E \leftrightarrow F)$
   2. $(D \cdot C) \vee \sim(E \leftrightarrow F)$

9. 1. $\sim(D \rightarrow E) \rightarrow \sim(C \vee F)$
   2. $\sim\sim(C \vee F)$ $\therefore \sim\sim(D \rightarrow E)$
   3. $\sim\sim(D \rightarrow E)$

10. 1. $\sim(A \rightarrow C) \cdot (D \vee \sim F)$ $\therefore D \vee \sim F$
    2. $D \vee \sim F$

(b) Indicate whether the following statements are true or false.

1. The inference rule DS can be used only when a disjunction occurs on one line and the negation of one of the disjuncts occurs on another.
2. The rule ADD tells you to take a statement occurring on one line and another statement occurring on another line and form a disjunction of the two statements on another line.
3. MT can be used only when a conditional occurs on one line and the negation of its antecedent on another line.
4. MP can be used only when a conditional occurs on a line and the antecedent of that conditional occurs on another line.
5. CD can be used only when you have a disjunction on one line and two conditionals occur on separate lines, the antecedent of one conditional being the left disjunct and the antecedent of the other conditional being the right disjunct.

(c) Annotate each of the following proofs by indicating from which line(s) each inference is drawn and by which implicational inference rule.

1. 1. A → B
   2. A ∨ C
   3. ~B   ∴ C
   4. ~A
   5. C

2. 1. B → C
   2. ~A ∨ B
   3. C → D
   4. ~A → M   ∴ [(M ∨ D) • (B → C)] ∨ E
   5. B → D
   6. M ∨ D
   7. (M ∨ D) • (B → C)
   8. [(M ∨ D) • (B → C)] ∨ E

3. 1. E
   2. F
   3. (E • F) → G
   4. G → M   ∴ M ∨ N
   5. E • F
   6. G
   7. M
   8. M ∨ N

4. 1. $(D \lor E) \rightarrow \sim A$
    2. $A \lor \sim B$
    3. $C \rightarrow B$
    4. D $\therefore \sim C \lor E$
    5. $D \lor E$
    6. $\sim A$
    7. $\sim B$
    8. $\sim C$
    9. $\sim C \lor E$

5. 1. $\sim(A \leftrightarrow B)$
    2. $\sim(C \rightarrow D)$
    3. $\sim(A \leftrightarrow B) \rightarrow (C \rightarrow D)$ $\therefore N \bullet \sim\sim(A \leftrightarrow B)$
    4. $\sim(A \leftrightarrow B) \lor N$
    5. $\sim\sim(A \leftrightarrow B)$
    6. N
    7. $N \bullet \sim\sim(A \leftrightarrow B)$

(d) Some of the following proofs contain lines on which there are errors. Find and identify these errors. The proofs employ only the eight implicational inference rules.

1. 1. $(A \bullet B) \rightarrow C$
    2. $C \rightarrow D$
    3. D
    4. $B \lor D$ $\therefore B$
    5. C 2, 3, MP
    6. $\sim D$ 2, 5, MP
    7. C 2, 6, MP
    8. B 1, Simp

2. 1. $(A \lor D) \lor C$
    2. $C \rightarrow E$
    3. $\sim E$ $\therefore A \lor D$
    4. $\sim C$ 2, 3, MT
    5. E 2, 4, MP
    6. C 1, Simp
    7. $A \lor D$ 1, 4, DS

3. 1. $M \lor N$
    2. $M \rightarrow O$
    3. $N \rightarrow P$
    4. $\sim P$ $\therefore O$
    5. $O \lor P$ 1, 2, 3, CD
    6. $\sim N$ 3, 4, MT
    7. M 2, Simp
    8. $\sim P \bullet \sim N$ 4, 6, Add
    9. M 1, 6, DS
    10. O 2, 9, MP

4. 1. $(A \lor B)$ $\therefore (A \lor B) \lor (C \bullet D)$
    2. $(A \lor B) \lor (C \bullet D)$ 1, Add

5. 1. $(A \bullet B) \bullet (C \bullet D)$ $\therefore C$
    2. C 1, Simp

(e) Prove each of the following using only the eight implicational inference rules.

1. 1. $A \to B$
    2. $A \bullet D$ $\therefore B \lor (P \bullet Q)$

2. 1. $B \to C$
    2. $\sim C \bullet M$
    3. $\sim B \to N$
    4. $(N \bullet M) \to L$ $\therefore L$

3. 1. $\sim(H \to \sim J)$
    2. $\sim G \lor K$
    3. $\sim G \to (H \to \sim J)$ $\therefore K \bullet \sim\sim G$

4. 1. $\sim C \bullet \sim F$
    2. $(\sim C \lor D) \to (\sim E \to F)$ $\therefore \sim\sim E$

5. 1. $(P \bullet N) \lor O$
    2. $\sim O$
    3. $P \to M$ $\therefore M \lor A$

(f) By using the suggested letters, symbolize the following arguments, and then construct proofs to show that they are valid. You need use only the eight implicational inference rules.

1. Liberal Democrats love to spend money on big government programs (L) only if the money spent for such programs is someone else's money (M). If the money spent on big government programs is someone else's money, those government programs are free (F). However, no big government program is free. Hence, liberal Democrats do not love to spend money on big government programs.

2. Atheism will come to an end (A) only if conservative Republicans have the power (P). Conservative Republicans have the power only if conservative Republicans help out the tobacco industry (T). Thus, if atheism comes to an end, conservative Republicans help out the tobacco industry.

3. Delbert went to the bank today (D). Delbert is broke today (B). If Delbert went to the bank today and is broke today, then he is a spendthrift (S). Therefore, either Delbert is a spendthrift or he should stay away from the mall (M).

4. Bevis takes an IQ test either on Monday (M) or on Tuesday (T), but not on both days. Bevis does not take the test on Tuesday. So, Bevis takes the test on Monday.

5. God sees to it that the ambient temperature of hell is 2000 degrees Kelvin (K). If God sees to it that the ambient temperature of hell is 2000 degrees Kelvin, then God allows millions of people to suffer eternal torment (T). If God allows millions of people to suffer eternal torment, then God does not love his creatures (N). If God does not love his creatures, then the Bible is mistaken (B). Therefore, the Bible is mistaken.

II. Five Equivalence Rules

A. *Helpful Reminders*

1. A new symbol—the four-dot symbol (::)—is introduced in stating the equivalence rules. Do not confuse this symbol with the triple-dot symbol (∴). The four-dot symbol is used to indicate that equivalence rules work both ways. For instance, we can replace a statement *p* on any line of a proof with its double-negation, "~~*p*," and vice versa, for these expressions are mutually implicative or logically equivalent. The rule that allows us to do this is, of course, the rule of double-negation (DN).

2. The five equivalence rules that are first introduced are the rules of double-negation (DN), commutation (Com), association (As), De Morgan's laws (DeM), and contraposition (Cont). Be sure to learn these rules and the abbreviations of the names of these rules.

3. Remember to apply one equivalence rule to one line or part of a line at a time. If two or more parts of a line need to be transformed, be sure to apply the equivalence rule or rules in a series of separate steps, for only one transformation at a time is permitted.

B. *Commonly Asked Questions*

1. What exactly is "part of a line"?

A statement of SL is "part of a line" if and only if it is negated or is a conjunct in a conjunction, a disjunct in a disjunction, an antecedent of a conditional, or one of the sides of a biconditional.

2. Why can you use an equivalence rule to replace part of a line with another statement?

Equivalent statements will always have the same truth value (since such statements imply each other), and the truth value of any compound statement is determined only by the truth values of its component statements (since the logical operators are truth-functional). Hence, the replacement of a component statement with an equivalent statement will result in a compound statement that must have the same truth value as the original. The original and the resulting compound statements will thus imply one another.

C. *Exercises*

(a) Indicate which of the five equivalence rules was used to derive the last line of each of the following proofs.

1. 1. $(A \leftrightarrow B) \rightarrow \sim(M \vee N)$ ∴ $\sim\sim(M \vee N) \rightarrow \sim(A \leftrightarrow B)$
   2. $\sim\sim(M \vee N) \rightarrow \sim(A \leftrightarrow B)$

2. 1. $\sim\sim\sim(\sim C \leftrightarrow \sim E)$ $\therefore \sim(\sim C \leftrightarrow \sim E)$
  2. $\sim(\sim C \leftrightarrow \sim E)$

3. 1. $(B \bullet A) \vee (C \bullet \sim D)$ $\therefore (C \bullet \sim D) \vee (B \bullet A)$
  2. $(C \bullet \sim D) \vee (B \bullet A)$

4. 1. $\sim[P \bullet (Q \vee R)]$ $\therefore \sim P \vee \sim(Q \vee R)$
  2. $\sim P \vee \sim(Q \vee R)$

5. 1. $G \vee (H \vee J)$ $\therefore (G \vee H) \vee J$
  2. $(G \vee H) \vee J$

(b) Annotate the following proofs. Remember that the last premise is to the left of the conclusion indicator, the triple-dot.

1.   1. $\sim A \bullet \sim B$
    2. $P \rightarrow (A \vee B)$ $\therefore \sim(Q \bullet P)$
    3. $\sim(A \vee B)$
    4. $\sim(A \vee B) \rightarrow \sim P$
    5. $\sim P$
    6. $\sim P \vee \sim Q$
    7. $\sim Q \vee \sim P$
    8. $\sim(Q \bullet P)$

2.   1. $R \bullet (Q \bullet P)$
    2. $(N \bullet M) \rightarrow O$
    3. $(P \vee R) \rightarrow \sim(\sim M \vee \sim N)$ $\therefore O$
    4. $(R \bullet Q) \bullet P$
    5. P
    6. $P \vee R$
    7. $\sim(\sim M \vee \sim N)$
    8. $\sim\sim M \bullet \sim\sim N$
    9. $M \bullet \sim\sim N$
    10. $M \bullet N$
    11. $N \bullet M$
    12. O

3.   1. $\sim R \rightarrow \sim Q$
    2. $R \rightarrow P$
    3. $(\sim P \rightarrow \sim Q) \rightarrow (S \vee M)$ $\therefore M \vee S$
    4. $Q \rightarrow R$
    5. $Q \rightarrow P$
    6. $\sim P \rightarrow \sim Q$
    7. $S \vee M$
    8. $M \vee S$

(c) Some of the following inferences are in error and some are not. If the inference is not correct, explain why.

1. 1. ~(P • R)   ∴ ~(~P • ~R)
   2. ~(~P • ~R)   1, DeM

2. 1. (A ∨ B) ∨ C   ∴ A ∨ (B ∨ C)
   2. A ∨ (B ∨ C)   1, As

3. 1. ~(F • D) → ~T   ∴ T → (F • D)
   2. T → (F • D)   1, Cont

4. 1. ~~~~~(P ↔ Q)   ∴ ~~~(P ↔ Q)
   2. ~~~(P ↔ Q)   1, DN

5. 1. A → B   ∴ B → A
   2. B → A   1, Com

(d) Construct proofs to show that the following arguments are valid.

1. 1. A → ~(~P • ~Q)
   2. ~(P ∨ Q)
   3. D → A   ∴ ~(C • D)

2. 1. (P ∨ Q) ∨ ~R
   2. ~P
   3. ~(R • ~Q) → S   ∴ ~~S

3. 1. ~~(M • N) → ~O
   2. O
   3. M   ∴ ~N

III. Five More Equivalence Rules

A. Helpful Reminders

1. The remaining five equivalence rules are the rules of distribution (Dist), exportation (Ex), redundancy (Re), material equivalence (ME), and material implication (MI). Be sure to learn these rules and the abbreviations of the names of these rules.

2. If you are having trouble with a rather complex proof, distribution may help, as Rule of Thumb 7 suggests. Also, material equivalence allows you to replace a biconditional with either a disjunction whose disjuncts are conjunctions or a conjunction whose conjuncts are conditionals. You may find it easier to work with the equivalent conjunction than the biconditional or the equivalent disjunction.

B. Commonly Asked Questions

1. Why use equivalence rules in a proof?

Equivalence rules may allow you to transform lines of a proof into other lines that you can deal with more easily. These rules may enable you to put a statement into the form needed in order to apply a particular inference rule. You may also be able to use an equivalence rule in a proof to transform a line into the conclusion you are after, hence the usefulness of Rule of Thumb 4.

2. How do you know what equivalence rule to use and what statement to use as a replacement for a line or part of a line?

What equivalence rule you use and how you apply it will depend on the nature of the line of proof and the proof strategy you are pursuing. Do not misapply a rule, and always keep in mind what you hope to accomplish by applying a rule. The long-range goals involved in constructing a proof often determine most of the particular steps of a proof.

C. Exercises

(a) Annotate each of the following short proofs.

1. 1. $P \vee (Q \bullet R)$ $\therefore (P \vee Q) \bullet (P \vee R)$
   2. $(P \vee Q) \bullet (P \vee R)$

2. 1. $(P \bullet Q) \vee (\sim P \bullet \sim Q)$ $\therefore P \leftrightarrow Q$
   2. $P \leftrightarrow Q$

3. 1. $P \rightarrow (Q \rightarrow R)$ $\therefore (P \bullet Q) \rightarrow R$
   2. $(P \bullet Q) \rightarrow R$

4. 1. $(A \bullet B) \vee (A \bullet C)$ $\therefore A \bullet (B \vee C)$
   2. $A \bullet (B \vee C)$

5. 1. $\sim(A \rightarrow B) \rightarrow C$ $\therefore \sim\sim(A \rightarrow B) \vee C$
   2. $\sim\sim(A \rightarrow B) \vee C$

(b) Some of the following proofs contain lines on which there are errors. Identify the errors.

1. 1. $P \leftrightarrow Q$ $\therefore \sim\sim(P\leftrightarrow\leftrightarrow Q) \bullet \sim\sim(P \leftrightarrow Q)$
   2. $(P \rightarrow Q) \vee (Q \rightarrow P)$ 1, ME
   3. $P \rightarrow Q$ 2, Simp
   4. $\sim\sim(P \leftrightarrow Q)$ 1, DN
   5. $\sim\sim(P \leftrightarrow Q) \bullet \sim\sim(P \leftrightarrow Q)$ 4, Re

2. 1. P $\therefore \sim(\sim P \bullet P)$
   2. $P \bullet P$ 1, Re
   3. $\sim\sim(P \bullet P)$ 2, DN
   4. $\sim(\sim P \bullet P)$ 3, As

3. 1. P → Q
    2. (P ∨ Q) • (P ∨ R)
    3. ~Q   ∴ Q → (R → ~P)
    4. ~Q → P   1, Cont
    5. P   3, 4, MP
    6. P ∨ (Q • R)   2, As
    7. ~P → (Q • R)   6, MI
    8. (Q • R) → ~P   7, Com
    9. Q → (R → ~P)   8, Ex

4. 1. A ↔ B   ∴ ~A → B
    2. (A ∨ B) • (~A ∨ ~B)   1, ME
    3. A ∨ B   2, Simp
    4. ~~A ∨ B   3, DN
    5. ~A → B   4, MI

5. 1. (M • N) ∨ ~(P ↔ Q)
    2. ~N
    3. P   ∴ ~Q
    4. (M • N) ∨ ~[(P • Q) ∨ (~P • ~Q)]   1, ME
    5. ~N ∨ ~M   2, Add
    6. ~(N • M)   5, DeM
    7. ~(M • N)   6, Com
    8. ~[(P • Q) ∨ (~P • ~Q)]   4, 7 DS
    9. ~(P • Q) • ~(~P • ~Q)   8, DeM
    10. ~(P • Q)   9, Simp
    11. ~P ∨ ~Q   10, DeM
    12. ~~P   3, DN
    13. ~Q   11, 12, DS

(c) Construct proofs for each of the following valid arguments.

1. 1. A ∨ (B • C)
    2. (A ∨ B) → (~D ∨ E)   ∴ D → E

2. 1. P ↔ Q
    2. P
    3. (P • Q) → R   ∴ Q → R

3. 1. (A • B) ∨ (A • C)
    2. (B ∨ C) → D   ∴ E → D

4. 1. P
    2. Q
    3. (P • Q) → (R ↔ ~S)
    4. S   ∴ ~R

5.　1.　$M \bullet (N \vee O)$
　　2.　$\sim(M \bullet O)$
　　3.　$N \rightarrow P$　　　　　　　　$\therefore P \vee P$

IV. Conditional Proof

A. Helpful Reminders

1. Rule of Thumb 9 tells us that, whenever we have an argument whose conclusion is a conditional, we should use the rule of conditional proof (CP) to prove the conditional. Thus, to prove "$p \rightarrow q$" from a set of premises, assume p as a temporary premise, deduce q, then discharge the assumption by inferring "$p \rightarrow q$" on the next line and boxing off every previous line that either involved or was derived from the assumption. You should cite the line numbers where you assumed p and subsequently deduced q and the rule CP to justify the line on which "$p \rightarrow q$" is inferred. What you have shown is that the conditional conclusion follows from the original set of premises.

2. Remember that any assumption made on a line of proof must be discharged somewhere in the proof, and remember not to use lines that are boxed off in subsequent derivations in a proof.

3. A conditional proof strategy is often pursued in order to prove a conclusion that is a biconditional. The standard strategy is to assume the left side of the biconditional, prove the right side, and use CP to infer the conditional, and then assume the right side of the biconditional, prove the left side, and again use CP to infer the conditional. The conjunction of the two conditionals obtained by CP is equivalent to the desired biconditional, and so the rule ME is used to infer the biconditional.

B. Commonly Asked Questions

1. How do you know what to assume to set up a subsequent application of the rule CP?

The rule CP always authorizes an inference to a conditional, so the assumption you make will always become the antecedent of the conditional you later infer by CP. The line you reach from the assumption prior to inferring the conditional will be the consequent of the conditional you infer. You therefore make a particular assumption with a view toward inferring a particular conditional later on in the proof.

2. Will you use the rule CP only when the conclusion of the argument you are trying to prove is a conditional?

You will often but not always use the rule CP to prove an argument that has a conditional as a conclusion. You should thus consider using CP whenever the argument you are attempting to prove has a conditional conclusion, and other strategies of proving a conditional do not seem very promising. Sometimes, though, the conclusion of the argument you wish to prove is not a conditional, but proving a certain conditional will allow you to infer the conclusion on a subsequent line of the proof. For example, proving a conditional may enable you to use the rule MI to prove a disjunction as a conclusion. The rule CP can also be used in such a case to prove the desired conditional. You will thus tend to use CP whenever it will allow you to prove a conditional, regardless of whether or not the conditional is the conclusion of the argument.

C. Exercises

Prove that the following arguments are valid using any of the implicational or equivalence inference rules together with CP.

1. 1. $(G \vee H) \rightarrow I$
   2. $J \rightarrow G$ $\therefore \sim I \rightarrow \sim J$

2. 1. $A \rightarrow B$ $\therefore [A \rightarrow (A \cdot B)] \vee C$

3. 1. $A \rightarrow (B \rightarrow C)$
   2. $A \rightarrow (B \rightarrow D)$
   3. $A \rightarrow B$ $\therefore A \rightarrow (C \cdot D)$

4. 1. $(A \vee B) \rightarrow (C \cdot D)$
   2. $(E \vee F) \rightarrow G$ $\therefore A \rightarrow [F \rightarrow (D \cdot G)]$

5. 1. $N \rightarrow O$
   2. $(O \cdot P) \rightarrow \sim M$ $\therefore M \rightarrow (\sim N \vee \sim P)$

V. *Reductio ad Absurdum*

A. *Helpful Reminders*

1. According to Rule of Thumb 10, if your conclusion is not a conditional, and a direct proof would be too long and difficult, then use an indirect proof or *reductio ad absurdum* (RAA). A corollary to this rule of thumb may also be helpful: If no strategy of direct or conditional proof seems to work or to be fairly easy, then try an indirect proof.

2. Remember, when using RAA, assume the opposite of your conclusion, deduce a contradiction, and then discharge the assumption by inferring your conclusion on the next line and boxing off all previous lines where the assumption was made and conclusions were derived from that assumption. You justify the line on which you infer your conclusion, and discharge the assumption, by citing the line numbers where you made the assumption and subsequently derived the contradiction and the rule RAA.

3. Remember that any assumption entered on a line of proof must later be discharged, and remember to refrain from using boxed-off lines in further deductions in a proof.

4. The rules of thumb, summarized in section 8.5 of *The Power of Logic*, are just that—rules of thumb. They do not allow one to produce a proof of an argument in a purely mechanical fashion. (Techniques of mechanical proof construction can be developed for statement logic, but the proofs constructed by such means are typically very complex and involve more work than truth table evaluations.) The rules of thumb are no substitute for experience with the system of natural deduction developed for statement logic. As you prove more arguments valid and thereby gain more experience with the system, you should find that constructing proofs becomes easier.

B. Commonly Asked Questions

1. What should you assume on a line of a proof in order to apply RAA on a subsequent line of the proof?

To set up a future application of RAA in a proof, you always assume that the statement you are trying to prove is false. Thus, you should always enter as an assumption a statement such that either the statement is the negation of what you are trying to prove or the negation of the statement is what you are trying to prove. Note that a use of RAA can occur somewhere in the middle of a proof, so what you are trying to prove by using RAA may not be the conclusion of the argument.

2. Is a direct proof better than a proof by RAA?

As a demonstration of an argument's validity, any correctly constructed proof is just as good as any other, so a correct proof by RAA is in this respect just as acceptable as a correct direct proof. A direct proof, however, often (although not always) involves fewer steps than a proof using RAA, and thus, generally speaking, an indirect proof should be tried only when it is not apparent how to construct a direct proof.

C. Exercises

Prove that the following arguments are valid by using RAA and any of the implicational or equivalence inference rules.

1. 1. $A \cdot B$ $\therefore \sim(\sim A \vee \sim B)$

2. 1. $M \rightarrow (N \rightarrow O)$
   2. $\sim O \rightarrow (M \rightarrow N)$
   3. $\sim M \rightarrow O$ $\therefore O$

3. 1. $\sim(R \vee S)$
   2. $T \rightarrow (\sim S \rightarrow R)$ $\therefore \sim T$

4. 1. $(A \vee B) \rightarrow C$
   2. $C \rightarrow D$ $\therefore \sim(\sim D \cdot A)$

5. 1. $D \rightarrow (E \vee \sim F)$
   2. $\sim(D \cdot \sim F)$
   3 $\sim E$ $\therefore \sim D$

VI. Proving Theorems

A. Helpful Reminders

1. We prove theorems using only assumptions that, by definition, are temporarily introduced into a proof. This being the case, one must use either CP or RAA when proving theorems. In a completed proof of a theorem, every line is boxed off except the line where the theorem itself occurs, and this in effect shows that a theorem is true independently of the truth value of any other statement. To indicate that a statement is a theorem, we write it to the right of the triple-dot symbol. For example, "$P \vee \sim P$" is a theorem, and we indicate this by writing "$\therefore P \vee \sim P$."

2. Remember that, in a proof of a theorem, the theorem proved will occur on the last line of the proof, and every assumption made will be discharged at or before this last line.

B. Commonly Asked Questions

1. Why do we bother to prove theorems, as opposed to valid arguments?

The nature of the theorems tells us something about our deduction system. It can be shown that the theorems of statement logic are all tautologies. Since the corresponding conditional of any valid argument can be proved as a theorem, the conditional theorems that correspond to valid arguments are all tautologies. This fact indicates that our system of deduction is safe in that the rules of inference will never lead from true premises to a false conclusion.

2. Are all theorems conditional statements?

The theorems that are the corresponding conditionals of valid arguments are obviously conditional theorems, but there are other theorems of statement logic that are not conditional in form. In fact, any tautology of SL, including such a statement as "~(P • ~P)" or " P ↔ P," can be proved as a theorem of SL.

3. What is the difference between the theorems of statement logic and mathematical theorems?

The theorems of a natural deduction system are provable from the rules of inference alone, whereas the derivation of the theorems of mathematics depends fundamentally on the mathematical axioms and definitions.

C. Exercises

Prove that the following statements are theorems.

1. ∴ P → ~~P

2. ∴ (A → B) → (~B → ~A)

3. ∴ (P • ~P) → Q

4. ∴ P ∨ (P → Q)

5. ∴ P → (Q → P)

ANSWERS TO EXERCISES

Answers to Selected Exercises in the Text

Exercise 8.1
Part A

1. The conclusion is "F → H." The antecedent of this conditional occurs in premise 1, and the consequent occurs in premise 2. The only rule that will work with these two premises is HS. Line 3 should thus be justified by citing lines 1 and 2 and the rule HS.

10. Notice that the conclusion contains a statement letter not occurring in any of the premises. Appealing to Rule of Thumb 3, we can surmise that Add was used here. The first inference drawn is at line 3, where "W" occurs. "W" occurs in both premises but cannot be derived from the first premise. Deriving "W" from the second premise allows us to apply MP to lines 1 and 3 to derive "X ∨ ~Y" at line 4. Why do you use Simp on line 2 to get line 5? Line 5 together with line 4 gives us our much needed "X," which then sets us up for one application of Add.

Exercise 8.2
Part C

10. Com must be applied to either the consequent of the first premise or the antecedent of the second premise. It does not matter to which one of these you apply Com, as long as the antecedent and consequent match up exactly prior to applying HS.
19. Com must be applied twice before Cont is applied, but it does not matter in this case which is done first.

Part D

10. The conclusion is a disjunction, so it will probably (but not necessarily) be derived by either Add or CD. Since both disjuncts occur in the premises, Add is not necessary, and so Rule of Thumb 3 is not applicable. Working backward, you can see that "E" is the consequent of line 2, and "F" is the consequent of line 4. The antecedents of these lines both occur at line 6 as the disjuncts of a disjunction; thus, CD justifies line 7, "F ∨ E." The rest is cake.

Exercise 8.3
Part C

13. The desired conclusion is "H," which occurs as a consequent in two conditionals in the premises of this argument. You should suspect a usage of CD here because all you need to apply it are the antecedents of these conditionals occurring as the disjuncts of a disjunction. Looking at premise 2, you can determine that this will give you the desired disjunction provided that you apply the rule of Dist. Applying CD yields line 5, "H ∨ H." Applying Re completes the proof of this argument.

Part D

7. Whenever you see a statement of the same form as the statement on line 1 of this proof, think of Rule of Thumb 7, and transform the statement into a conjunction to set up an application of simplification. The smaller the statements, the easier they are to work with, and conjunctions are typically easier to decompose than disjunctions. This also means that, as a general rule, you should transform biconditionals into their equivalent conjunctions rather than their equivalent disjunctions.

Exercise 8.4
Part A

1. Since your desired conclusion is a conditional, use Rule of Thumb 9: If the conclusion is a conditional, use CP. At line 6, what has been shown is that if "Z" is true—within the context of the proof—then so is "X." This "if . . . then" is then restated at line 7 as a material conditional, and the truth of this material conditional does not depend on the truth of the antecedent "Z" because, even if it is false, the conditional is still true. The truth of the conclusion, then, depends only on the truth of the two premises. Remember also that none of the information contained within lines 3 through 6 can be used again once these lines are boxed off.

16. In this proof, we have nested applications of CP. It is important that you discharge your assumptions in the reverse order in which you assumed them (discharging the most recent assumption first). If you don't do this, you may end up using boxed-off material, and that is a no-no. This is why the assumption at line 4 is discharged first.

Exercise 8.5
Part A

1. The conclusion is a negation, so we assume the statement being negated, "A • ~B." Our assumption is a conjunction and thus will be easy to decompose. At line 6, what has been shown is that if "A • ~B" is true, so is the contradiction, "B • ~B." A contradiction, though, cannot be true and is therefore false. Hence, "A • ~B" is false, which means that its negation is true. Notice the similarity of this reasoning to *modus tollens*.

Part B

1. You should be able to determine that the second argument of the pair (problem 2) is invalid by using the abbreviated truth table method. Merely assign false to "F," to "G," and to "H." Under this assignment, the premise is true and the conclusion false. The first argument of the pair (problem 1) is valid, as the text proves. This proof is a good illustration of the usefulness of Rule of Thumb 10: When the conclusion is not a conditional, and a direct proof would be too difficult, try RAA. After you assume both "F" and "G," there is no apparent way to derive "H." So, we assume its negation at line 4 in order to derive a contradiction at line 9, thus concluding "H" at line 10. The three assumptions are discharged by applications of RAA and CP in the reverse order in which they entered the proof.

Exercise 8.6
Part B

1.   ∴ $(T \rightarrow U) \lor (U \rightarrow T)$

   ┌ 1. T   Assume (CP)
   │ 2. $T \rightarrow T$ 1-1 CP
   │ 3. $\sim T \lor T$ 2, MI
   │ 4. $(\sim T \lor T) \lor U$ 3, Add

5. U ∨ (~T ∨ T)	4, Com
6. (U ∨ ~T) ∨ T	5, As
7. (~T ∨ U) ∨ T	6, Com
8. [(~T ∨ U) ∨ T] ∨ ~U	7, Add
9. [(T → U) ∨ T] ∨ ~U	8, MI
10. (T → U) ∨ (T ∨ ~U)	9, As
11. (T → U) ∨ (~U ∨ T)	10, Com
12. (T → U) ∨ (U → T)	11, MI

4. ∴ [P ∨ (~P • Q)] ↔ (P ∨ Q)

1. P ∨ (~P • Q)	Assume (CP)
2. (P ∨ ~P) • (P ∨ Q)	1, Dist
3. P ∨ Q	2, Simp
4. [P ∨ (~P • Q)] → (P ∨ Q)	1-3 CP
5. P ∨ Q	Assume (CP)
6. P	Assume (CP)
7. P → P	6-6 CP
8. ~P ∨ P	7, MI
9. P ∨ ~P	8, Com
10. (P ∨ ~P) • (P ∨ Q)	5, 9, Conj
11. P ∨ (~P • Q)	10, Dist
12. (P ∨ Q) → [P ∨ (~P • Q)]	5-11 CP
13. [[P ∨ (~P • Q)] → (P ∨ Q)] • [(P ∨ Q) → [P ∨ (~P • Q)]]	4, 12, Conj
14. [P ∨ (~P • Q)] ↔ (P ∨ Q)	13, ME

6. ∴ [(S ∨ T) • (Q ∨ R)] → ([(S • Q) ∨ (S • R)] ∨ [(T • Q) ∨ (T • R)])

1. (S ∨ T) • (Q ∨ R)	Assume (CP)
2. (Q ∨ R) • (S ∨ T)	1, Com
3. [(Q ∨ R) • S] ∨ [(Q ∨ R) • T]	2, Dist
4. [S • (Q ∨ R)] ∨ [(Q ∨ R) • T]	3, Com
5. [S • (Q ∨ R)] ∨ [T • (Q ∨ R)]	4, Com
6. [(S • Q) ∨ (S • R)] ∨ [T • (Q ∨ R)]	5, Dist
7. [(S • Q) ∨ (S • R)] ∨ [(T • Q) ∨ (T • R)]	6, Dist
8. [(S ∨ T) • (Q ∨ R)] → ([(S • Q) ∨ (S • R)] ∨ [(T • Q) ∨ (T • R)])	1-7 CP

7. ∴ ([(L • M) ∨ (L • N)] ∨ [(P • M) ∨ (P • N)]) → [(L ∨ P) • (M ∨ N)]

1. [(L • M) ∨ (L • N)] ∨ [(P • M) ∨ (P • N)]	Assume (CP)
2. [L • (M ∨ N)] ∨ [(P • M) ∨ (P • N)]	1, Dist
3. [L • (M ∨ N)] ∨ [P • (M ∨ N)]	2, Dist
4. [(M ∨ N) • L] ∨ [P • (M ∨ N)]	3, Com
5. [(M ∨ N) • L] ∨ [(M ∨ N) • P]	4, Com
6. (M ∨ N) • (L ∨ P)	5, Dist
7. (L ∨ P) • (M ∨ N)	6, Com
8. ([(L • M) ∨ (L • N)] ∨ [(P • M) ∨ (P • N)]) → [(L ∨ P) • (M ∨ N)]	1-7 CP

8.   ∴ [(K → J) • (Q → R)] → ([(~K • ~Q) ∨ (~K • R)] ∨ [(J • ~Q) ∨ (J • R)])

    1. (K → J) • (Q → R)   Assume (CP)
    2. (~K ∨ J) • (Q → R)   1, MI
    3. (~K ∨ J) • (~Q ∨ R)   2, MI
    4. (~Q ∨ R) • (~K ∨ J)   3, Com
    5. [(~Q ∨ R) • ~K] ∨ [(~Q ∨ R) • J]   4, Dist
    6. [~K • (~Q ∨ R)] ∨ [(~Q ∨ R) • J]   5, Com
    7. [~K • (~Q ∨ R)] ∨ [J • (~Q ∨ R)]   6, Com
    8. [(~K • ~Q) ∨ (~K • R)] ∨ [J • (~Q ∨ R)]   7, Dist
    9. [(~K • ~Q) ∨ (~K • R)] ∨ [(J • ~Q) ∨ (J • R)]   8, Dist
  10. [(K → J) • (Q → R)] → ([(~K • ~Q) ∨ (~K • R)] ∨
     [(J • ~Q) ∨ (J • R)])   1-9 CP

9.   ∴ ([(~E • ~G) ∨ (~E • H)] ∨ [(F • ~G) ∨ (F • H)]) → [(E → F) • (G → H)]

    1. [(~E • ~G) ∨ (~E • H)] ∨ [(F • ~G) ∨ (F • H)]   Assume (CP)
    2. [(~E • ~G) ∨ (~E • H)] ∨ [(F • H) ∨ (F • ~G)]   1, Com
    3. ([(~E • ~G) ∨ (~E • H)] ∨ (F • H)) ∨ (F • ~G)   2, As
    4. (F • ~G) ∨ ([(~E • ~G) ∨ (~E • H)] ∨ (F • H))   3, Com
    5. ((F • ~G) ∨ [(~E • ~G) ∨ (~E • H)]) ∨ (F • H)   4, As
    6. ([(F • ~G) ∨ (~E • ~G)] ∨ (~E • H)) ∨ (F • H))   5, As
    7. [(F • ~G) ∨ (~E • ~G)] ∨ [(~E • H) ∨ (F • H)]   6, As
    8. [(~G • F) ∨ (~E • ~G)] ∨ [(~E • H) ∨ (F • H)]   7, Com
    9. [(~G • F) ∨ (~G • ~E)] ∨ [(~E • H) ∨ (F • H)]   8, Com
  10. [(~G • F) ∨ (~G • ~E)] ∨ [(H • ~E) ∨ (F • H)]   9, Com
  11. [(~G • F) ∨ (~G • ~E)] ∨ [(H • ~E) ∨ (H • F)]   10, Com
  12. [~G • (F ∨ ~E)] ∨ [(H • ~E) ∨ (H • F)]   11, Dist
  13. [~G • (F ∨ ~E)] ∨ [H • (~E ∨ F)]   12, Dist
  14. [~G • (~E ∨ F)] ∨ [H • (~E ∨ F)]   13, Com
  15. [(~E ∨ F) • ~G] ∨ [H • (~E ∨ F)]   14, Com
  16. [(~E ∨ F) • ~G] ∨ [(~E ∨ F) • H]   15, Com
  17. (~E ∨ F) • (~G ∨ H)   16, Dist
  18. (E → F) • (~G ∨ H)   17, MI
  19. (E → F) • (G → H)   18, MI
  20. ([(~E • ~G) ∨ (~E • H)] ∨ [(F • ~G) ∨ (F • H)]) →
     [(E → F) • (G → H)]   1-19 CP

10. ∴ [(A • B) ∨ (C • D)] → ([(A ∨ C) • (A ∨ D)] • [(B ∨ C) • (B ∨ D)])

    1. (A • B) ∨ (C • D)   Assume (CP)
    2. (C • D) ∨ (A • B)   1, Com
    3. [(C • D) ∨ A] • [(C • D) ∨ B]   2, Dist
    4. [A ∨ (C • D)] • [(C • D) ∨ B]   3, Com
    5. [A ∨ (C • D)] • [B ∨ (C • D)]   4, Com
    6. [(A ∨ C) • (A ∨ D)] • [(B ∨ C) • (B ∨ D)]   5, Dist
    7. [(A • B) ∨ (C • D)] → ([(A ∨ C) • (A ∨ D)] •
     [(B ∨ C) • (B ∨ D)])   1-6 CP

Answers to Supplemental Exercises

I(a)

1. 1, 2, MP
2. 1, 2, DS
3. 1, 2, 3, CD
4. 1, 2, HS
5. 1, 2, MT
6. 1, 2, Conj
7. 1, 2, DS
8. 1, Add
9. 1, 2, MT
10. 1, Simp

I(b)

1. True
2. False
3. False
4. True
5. True

I(c)

1.
   1. $A \rightarrow B$
   2. $A \vee C$
   3. $\sim B$ $\therefore C$
   4. $\sim A$ 1, 3, MT
   5. C   2, 4 DS

2.
   1. $B \rightarrow C$
   2. $\sim A \vee B$
   3. $C \rightarrow D$
   4. $\sim A \rightarrow M$ $\therefore [(M \vee D) \bullet (B \rightarrow C)] \vee E$
   5. $B \rightarrow D$ 1, 3, HS
   6. $M \vee D$ 2, 4, 5, CD
   7. $(M \vee D) \bullet (B \rightarrow C)$ 1, 6, Conj
   8. $[(M \vee D) \bullet (B \rightarrow C)] \vee E$ 7, Add

3.
   1. E
   2. F
   3. $(E \bullet F) \rightarrow G$
   4. $G \rightarrow M$ $\therefore M \vee N$
   5. $E \bullet F$ 1, 2, Conj
   6. G   3, 5, MP
   7. M   4, 6, MP
   8. $M \vee N$ 7, Add

4. 1. $(D \lor E) \to \sim A$
    2. $A \lor \sim B$
    3. $C \to B$
    4. D $\therefore \sim C \lor E$
    5. $D \lor E$ 4, Add
    6. $\sim A$ 1, 5, MP
    7. $\sim B$ 2, 6, DS
    8. $\sim C$ 3, 7, MT
    9. $\sim C \lor E$ 8, Add

5. 1. $\sim(A \leftrightarrow B)$
    2. $\sim(C \to D)$
    3. $\sim(A \leftrightarrow B) \to (C \to D)$ $\therefore N \cdot \sim\sim(A \leftrightarrow B)$
    4. $\sim(A \leftrightarrow B) \lor N$ 1, Add
    5. $\sim\sim(A \leftrightarrow B)$ 2, 3, MT
    6. N 4, 5, DS
    7. $N \cdot \sim\sim(A \leftrightarrow B)$ 5, 6, Conj

I(d)

1. 1. $(A \cdot B) \to C$
    2. $C \to D$
    3. D
    4. $B \lor D$ $\therefore B$
    5. C 2, 3, MP   Misapplication of MP.
    6. $\sim D$ 2, 5, MP   Misapplication of MP; it should be "D."
    7. C 2, 6, MP   This should be "$\sim C$" by MT.
    8. B 1, Simp   You cannot do Simp on part of a line.

2. 1. $(A \lor D) \lor C$
    2. $C \to E$
    3. $\sim E$ $\therefore A \lor D$
    4. $\sim C$ 2, 3, MT   Correct.
    5. E 2, 4, MP   Misapplication of MP.
    6. C 1, Simp   Simp cannot be done with a disjunction.
    7. $A \lor D$ 1, 4, DS   Correct.

3. 1. $M \lor N$
    2. $M \to O$
    3. $N \to P$
    4. $\sim P$ $\therefore O$
    5. $O \lor P$ 1, 2, 3, CD   Correct.
    6. $\sim N$ 3, 4, MT   Correct.
    7. M 2, Simp   Simp cannot be done on a conditional.
    8. $\sim P \cdot \sim N$ 4, 6, Add   Add is applied to only one line and
                                           forms a disjunction.
    9. M 1, 6, DS   Correct.
    10. O 2, 9, MP   Correct.

4.　1.　A ∨ B　　　　　　　∴ (A ∨ B) ∨ (C • D)
　　2.　(A ∨ B) ∨ (C • D)　　1, Add　　　　　　　Correct.

5.　1.　(A • B) • (C • D)　　∴ C
　　2.　C　　　　　　　　　　1, Simp　　　　　　　Simp cannot be done
　　　　　　　　　　　　　　　　　　　　　　　　on part of a line.

I(e)

1.　1.　A → B
　　2.　A • D　　　　　　　∴ B ∨ (P • Q)
　　3.　A　　　　　　　　　2, Simp
　　4.　B　　　　　　　　　1, 3, MP
　　5.　B ∨ (P • Q)　　　　4, Add

2.　1.　B → C
　　2.　~C • M
　　3.　~B → N
　　4.　(N • M) → L　　　　∴ L
　　5.　M　　　　　　　　　2, Simp
　　6.　~C　　　　　　　　2, Simp
　　7.　~B　　　　　　　　1, 6, MT
　　8.　N　　　　　　　　　3, 7, MP
　　9.　N • M　　　　　　　5, 8, Conj
　10.　L　　　　　　　　　4, 9, MP

3.　1.　~(H → ~J)
　　2.　~G ∨ K
　　3.　~G → (H → ~J)　　∴ K • ~~G
　　4.　~~G　　　　　　　1, 3, MT
　　5.　K　　　　　　　　2, 4, DS
　　6.　K • ~~G　　　　　4, 5, Conj

4.　1.　~C • ~F
　　2.　(~C ∨ D) → (~E → F)　∴ ~~E
　　3.　~C　　　　　　　　1, Simp
　　4.　~C ∨ D　　　　　　3, Add
　　5.　~E → F　　　　　　2, 4, MP
　　6.　~F　　　　　　　　1, Simp
　　7.　~~E　　　　　　　5, 6, MT

5.　1.　(P • N) ∨ O
　　2.　~O
　　3.　P → M　　　　　　∴ M ∨ A
　　4.　P • N　　　　　　　1, 2, DS
　　5.　P　　　　　　　　　4, Simp
　　6.　M　　　　　　　　　3, 5, MP
　　7.　M ∨ A　　　　　　6, Add

I(f)

1. 1. L → M
   2. M → F
   3. ~F   ∴ ~L
   4. ~M   2, 3, MT
   5. ~L   1, 4, MT

2. 1. A → P
   2. P → T   ∴ A → T
   3. A → T   1, 2, HS

3. 1. D
   2. B
   3. (D • B) → S   ∴ S ∨ M
   4. D • B   1, 2, Conj
   5. S   3, 4, MP
   6. S ∨ M   5, Add

4. 1. (M ∨ T) • ~(M • T)
   2. ~T   ∴ M
   3. M ∨ T   1, Simp
   4. M   2, 3, DS

5. 1. K
   2. K → T
   3. T → N
   4. N → B   ∴ B
   5. T   1, 2, MP
   6. N   3, 5, MP
   7. B   4, 6, MP

II(a)

1. Cont
2. DN
3. Com
4. DeM
5. As

II(b)

1. 1. ~A • ~B
   2. P → (A ∨ B)   ∴ ~(Q • P)
   3. ~(A ∨ B)   1, DeM
   4. ~(A ∨ B) → ~P   2, Cont
   5. ~P   3, 4, MP
   6. ~P ∨ ~Q   5, Add
   7. ~Q ∨ ~P   6, Com
   8. ~(Q • P)   7, DeM

2.　1.　R • (Q • P)
　　2.　(N • M) → O
　　3.　(P ∨ R) → ~(~M ∨ ~N)　　　∴ O
　　4.　(R • Q) • P　　　　　　　　1, As
　　5.　P　　　　　　　　　　　　4, Simp
　　6.　P ∨ R　　　　　　　　　　5, Add
　　7.　~(~M ∨ ~N)　　　　　　　3, 6, MP
　　8.　~~M • ~~N　　　　　　　　7, DeM
　　9.　M • ~~N　　　　　　　　　8, DN
　　10.　M • N　　　　　　　　　　9, DN
　　11.　N • M　　　　　　　　　　10, Com
　　12.　O　　　　　　　　　　　　2, 11, MP

3.　1.　~R → ~Q
　　2.　R → P
　　3.　(~P → ~Q) → (S ∨ M)　　　∴ M ∨ S
　　4.　Q → R　　　　　　　　　　1, Cont
　　5.　Q → P　　　　　　　　　　2, 4, HS
　　6.　~P → ~Q　　　　　　　　　5, Cont
　　7.　S ∨ M　　　　　　　　　　3, 6, MP
　　8.　M ∨ S　　　　　　　　　　7, Com

II(c)

1.　1.　~(P • R)　　　　　　　∴ ~(~P • ~R)
　　2.　~(~P • ~R)　　　　　　1, DeM　　　　The dot should be a vee, and there should be no negation sign on the outside.

2.　1.　(A ∨ B) ∨ C　　　　　∴ A ∨ (B ∨ C)
　　2.　A ∨ (B ∨ C)　　　　　1, As　　　　　Correct.

3.　1.　~(F • D) → ~T　　　　∴ T → (F • D)
　　2.　T → (F • D)　　　　　1, Cont　　　　Correct.

4.　1.　~~~~~(P ↔ Q)　　　　∴ ~~~(P ↔ Q)
　　2.　~~~(P ↔ Q)　　　　　1, DN　　　　　Correct.

5.　1.　A → B　　　　　　　　∴ B → A
　　2.　B → A　　　　　　　　1, Com　　　　Cannot use Com with the arrow.

II(d)

1. 1. A → ~(~P • ~Q)
    2. ~(P ∨ Q)
    3. D → A   ∴ ~(C • D)
    4. ~P • ~Q   2, DeM
    5. ~~(~P • ~Q)   4, DN
    6. ~A   1, 5, MT
    7. ~D   3, 6, MT
    8. ~D ∨ ~C   7, Add
    9. ~C ∨ ~D   8, Com
    10. ~(C • D)   9, DeM

2. 1. (P ∨ Q) ∨ ~R
    2. ~P
    3. ~(R • ~Q) → S   ∴ ~~S
    4. P ∨ (Q ∨ ~R)   1, As
    5. Q ∨ ~R   2, 4, DS
    6. ~R ∨ Q   5, Com
    7. ~R ∨ ~~Q   6, DN
    8. ~(R • ~Q)   7, DeM
    9. S   3, 8, MP
    10. ~~S   9, DN

3. 1. ~~(M • N) → ~O
    2. O
    3. M   ∴ ~N
    4. ~~O   2, DN
    5. ~~~(M • N)   1, 4, MT
    6. ~(M • N)   5, DN
    7. ~M ∨ ~N   6, DeM
    8. ~~M   3, DN
    9. ~N   7, 8, DS

III(a)

1. 1. P ∨ (Q • R)   ∴ (P ∨ Q) • (P ∨ R)
    2. (P ∨ Q) • (P ∨ R)   1, Dist

2. 1. (P • Q) ∨ (~P • ~Q)   ∴ P ↔ Q
    2. P ↔ Q   1, ME

3. 1. P → (Q → R)   ∴ (P • Q) → R
    2. (P • Q) → R   1, Ex

4. 1. $(A \bullet B) \vee (A \bullet C)$ $\therefore A \bullet (B \vee C)$
   2. $A \bullet (B \vee C)$ 1, Dist

5. 1. $\sim(A \rightarrow B) \rightarrow C$ $\therefore \sim\sim(A \rightarrow B) \vee C$
   2. $\sim\sim(A \rightarrow B) \vee C$ 1, MI

III(b)

1. 1. $P \leftrightarrow Q$ $\therefore \sim\sim(P \leftrightarrow Q) \bullet \sim\sim(P \leftrightarrow Q)$
   2. $(P \rightarrow Q) \vee (Q \rightarrow P)$ 1, ME   Should be "[(P → Q) •
                                              (Q → P)]."
   3. $P \rightarrow Q$ 2, Simp   Cannot do Simp with
                                              the vee.
   4 $\sim\sim(P \leftrightarrow Q)$ 1, DN   Correct.
   5. $\sim\sim(P \leftrightarrow Q) \bullet \sim\sim(P \leftrightarrow Q)$ 4, Re   Correct.

2. 1. P $\therefore \sim(\sim P \bullet P)$
   2. $P \bullet P$ 1, Re   Correct.
   3. $\sim\sim(P \bullet P)$ 2, DN   Correct.
   4. $\sim(\sim P \bullet P)$ 3, As   Incorrect.

3. 1. $P \rightarrow Q$
   2. $(P \vee Q) \bullet (P \vee R)$
   3. $\sim Q$ $\therefore Q \rightarrow (R \rightarrow \sim P)$
   4. $\sim Q \rightarrow P$ 1, Cont   Incorrect. "P" should also be
                                            negated.
   5. P 3, 4, MP   Correct.
   6. $P \vee (Q \bullet R)$ 2, As   No, this can be obtained by Dist
                                            from line 2.
   7. $\sim P \rightarrow (Q \bullet R)$ 6, MI   Line 6 needs to be
                                            "$\sim\sim P \vee (Q \bullet R)$."
   8. $(Q \bullet R) \rightarrow \sim P$ 7, Com   Cannot use Com with the
                                            arrow.
   9. $Q \rightarrow (R \rightarrow \sim P)$ 8, Ex   Correct.

4. 1. $A \leftrightarrow B$ $\therefore \sim A \rightarrow B$
   2. $(A \vee B) \bullet (\sim A \vee \sim B)$ 1, ME   Incorrect. Should be "$(A \bullet B) \vee$
                                            $(\sim A \bullet \sim B)$."
   3. $A \vee B$ 2, Simp   Correct.
   4. $\sim\sim A \vee B$ 3, DN   Correct.
   5. $\sim A \rightarrow B$ 4, MI   Correct.

5. 1. $(M \cdot N) \vee \sim(P \leftrightarrow Q)$
    2. $\sim N$
    3. P $\therefore \sim Q$
    4. $(M \cdot N) \vee \sim[(P \cdot Q) \vee (\sim P \cdot \sim Q)]$ 1, ME   Correct.
    5. $\sim N \vee \sim M$ 2, Add   Correct.
    6. $\sim(N \cdot M)$ 5, DeM   Correct.
    7. $\sim(M \cdot N)$ 6, Com   Correct.
    8. $\sim[(P \cdot Q) \vee (\sim P \cdot \sim Q)]$ 4, 7 DS   Correct.
    9. $\sim(P \cdot Q) \cdot \sim(\sim P \cdot \sim Q)$ 8, DeM   Correct.
    10. $\sim(P \cdot Q)$ 9, Simp   Correct.
    11. $\sim P \vee \sim Q$ 10, DeM   Correct.
    12. $\sim\sim P$ 3, DN   Correct.
    13. $\sim Q$ 11, 12, DS   Correct.

III(c)

1. 1. $A \vee (B \cdot C)$
    2. $(A \vee B) \rightarrow (\sim D \vee E)$ $\therefore D \rightarrow E$
    3. $(A \vee B) \cdot (A \vee C)$ 1, Dist
    4. $A \vee B$ 3, Simp
    5. $\sim D \vee E$ 2, 4, MP
    6. $D \rightarrow E$ 5, MI

2. 1. $P \leftrightarrow Q$
    2. P
    3. $(P \cdot Q) \rightarrow R$ $\therefore Q \rightarrow R$
    4. $(P \rightarrow Q) \cdot (Q \rightarrow P)$ 1, ME
    5. $P \rightarrow Q$ 4, Simp
    6. Q 2, 5, MP
    7. $P \cdot Q$ 2, 6, Conj
    8. R 3, 7, MP
    9. $R \vee \sim Q$ 8, Add
    10. $\sim Q \vee R$ 9, Com
    11. $Q \rightarrow R$ 10, MI

3. 1. $(A \cdot B) \vee (A \cdot C)$
    2. $(B \vee C) \rightarrow D$ $\therefore E \rightarrow D$
    3. $A \cdot (B \vee C)$ 1, Dist
    4. $B \vee C$ 3, Simp
    5. D 2, 4, MP
    6. $D \vee \sim E$ 5, Add
    7. $\sim E \vee D$ 6, Com
    8. $E \rightarrow D$ 7, MI

4. 1. P
    2. Q
    3. $(P \cdot Q) \rightarrow (R \leftrightarrow \sim S)$
    4. S $\therefore \sim R$
    5. $P \cdot Q$ 1, 2, Conj

```
        6. R ↔ ~S                    3, 5, MP
        7. (R → ~S) • (~S → R)       6, ME
        8. R → ~S                    7, Simp
        9. ~~S                       4, DN
       10. ~R                        8, 9, MT

  5.   1. M • (N ∨ O)
       2. ~(M • O)
       3. N → P                      ∴ P ∨ P
       4. (M • N) ∨ (M • O)          1, Dist
       5. M • N                      2, 4, DS
       6. N                          5, Simp
       7. P                          3, 6, MP
       8. P ∨ P                      7, Re
```

IV

```
  1.   1. (G ∨ H) → I
       2. J → G                      ∴ ~I → ~J
       3. J                          Assume
       4. G                          2, 3, MP
       5. G ∨ H                      4, Add
       6. I                          1, 5 MP
       7. J → I                      3-6, CP
       8. ~I → ~J                    7, Cont

  2.   1. A → B                      ∴ [A → (A • B)] ∨ C
       2. A                          Assume
       3. B                          1, 2, MP
       4. A • B                      2, 3, Conj
       5. A → (A • B)                2-4, CP
       6. [A → (A • B)] ∨ C          5, Add

  3.   1. A → (B → C)
       2. A → (B → D)
       3. A → B                      ∴ A → (C • D)
       4. A                          Assume
       5. B                          3, 4, MP
       6. (A • B) → C                1, Ex
       7. (A • B) → D                2, Ex
       8. A • B                      4, 5, Conj
       9. C                          6, 8, MP
      10. D                          7, 8, MP
      11. C • D                      9, 10, Conj
      12. A → (C • D)                4-11, CP
```

4. 1. $(A \lor B) \to (C \bullet D)$
    2. $(E \lor F) \to G$ $\therefore A \to [F \to (D \bullet G)]$
    3. A   Assume
    4. F   Assume
    5. $A \lor B$ 3, Add
    6. $C \bullet D$ 1, 5, MP
    7. $F \lor E$ 4, Add
    8. $E \lor F$ 7, Com
    9. G   2, 8, MP
    10. D   6, Simp
    11. $D \bullet G$ 9, 10, Conj
    12. $F \to (D \bullet G)$ 4-11, CP
    13. $A \to [F \to (D \bullet G)]$ 3-12, CP

5. 1. $N \to O$
    2. $(O \bullet P) \to \sim M$ $\therefore M \to (\sim N \lor \sim P)$
    3. M   Assume
    4. $\sim\sim M$ 3, DN
    5. $\sim(O \bullet P)$ 2, 4, MT
    6. $\sim O \lor \sim P$ 5, DeM
    7. $O \to \sim P$ 6, MI
    8. $N \to \sim P$ 1, 7, HS
    9. $\sim N \lor \sim P$ 8, MI
    10. $M \to (\sim N \lor \sim P)$ 3-9, CP

V

1. 1. $A \bullet B$ $\therefore \sim(\sim A \lor \sim B)$
    2. $\sim A \lor \sim B$ Assume
    3. A   1, Simp
    4. $\sim\sim A$ 3, DN
    5. $\sim B$ 2, 4, DS
    6. B   1, Simp
    7. $B \bullet \sim B$ 5, 6, Conj
    8. $\sim(\sim A \lor \sim B)$ 2-7, RAA

2. 1. $M \to (N \to O)$
    2. $\sim O \to (M \to N)$
    3. $\sim M \to O$ $\therefore O$
    4. $\sim O$ Assume
    5. $M \to N$ 2, 4, MP
    6. $\sim\sim M$ 3, 4, MT
    7. M   6, DN
    8. N   5, 7, MP
    9. $N \to O$ 1, 7, MP
    10. O   8, 9, MP
    11. $O \bullet \sim O$ 4, 10, Conj
    12. O   4-11, RAA

3. 1. ~(R ∨ S)
    2. T → (~S → R)   ∴ ~T
    3. T   Assume
    4. ~S → R   2, 3, MP
    5. ~R • ~S   1, DeM
    6. ~R   5, Simp
    7. ~S   5, Simp
    8. R   4, 7, MP
    9. R • ~R   6, 8, Conj
    10. ~T   3-9, RAA

4. 1. (A ∨ B) → C
    2. C → D   ∴ ~(~D • A)
    3. ~D • A   Assume
    4. ~D   3, Simp
    5. A   3, Simp
    6. ~C   2, 4, MT
    7. A ∨ B   5, Add
    8. C   1, 7, MP
    9. C • ~C   6, 8, Conj
    10. ~(~D • A)   3-9, RAA

5. 1. D → (E ∨ ~F)
    2. ~(D • ~F)
    3. ~E   ∴ ~D
    4. D   Assume
    5. E ∨ ~F   1, 4, MP
    6. ~F   3, 5, DS
    7. ~D ∨ ~~F   2, DeM
    8. ~~D   4, DN
    9. ~~F   7, 8, DS
    10. F   9, DN
    11. F • ~F   6, 10, Conj
    12. ~D   4-11, RAA

VI

1. ∴ P → ~~P
    1. P   Assume
    2. ~~P   1, DN
    3. P → ~~P   1-2, CP

2. ∴ (A → B) → (~B → ~A)
    1. A → B   Assume
    2. ~B → ~A   1, Cont
    5. (A → B) → (~B → ~A)   1-2, CP

3. $\therefore (P \cdot \sim P) \to Q$

1.	$P \cdot \sim P$	Assume
2.	P	1, Simp
3.	$\sim P$	1, Simp
4.	$P \vee Q$	2, Add
5.	Q	3, 4, DS
6.	$(P \cdot \sim P) \to Q$	1-5, CP

4. $\therefore P \vee (P \to Q)$

1.	$\sim P$	Assume
2.	$\sim P \vee Q$	1, Add
3.	$P \to Q$	2, MI
4.	$\sim P \to (P \to Q)$	1-3, CP
5.	$\sim\sim P \vee (P \to Q)$	4, MI
6.	$P \vee (P \to Q)$	5, DN

5. $\therefore P \to (Q \to P)$

1.	P	Assume
2.	$P \vee \sim Q$	1, Add
3.	$\sim Q \vee P$	2, Com
4.	$Q \to P$	3, MI
5.	$P \to (Q \to P)$	1-4, CP

FOR FURTHER CONSIDERATION

An appeal to our valid inference rules provides an objective criterion for deciding whether or not an argument is valid. Therefore, if a skeptic questions an inference of yours, and you can show it to be an instance of one of our valid inference rules, then this should quell the skeptic's doubts. Now suppose the skeptic questions the validity of one of the inference rules themselves, say, *modus tollens*. Suppose also that he or she wishes to convince you beyond a shadow of a doubt that MT is not a valid inference rule. This being the case, the skeptic has to justify his or her doubt with the most powerful kind of argument, and that is one such that, if its premises should be true, its conclusion would have to be true. So, the skeptic can't be questioning validity in general, at least not if the skeptic intends to convince you once and for all with a valid argument.

Still, the skeptic might try to make his or her point by showing that MT has a counterexample. After all, only one counterexample is needed to refute a generalization. The easiest way for the skeptic to do this would be to demonstrate that an argument whose form is *modus tollens* can have all true premises and a false conclusion, and this is best done with the truth table method. However, we have already shown that MT is a valid argument form (or a valid inference rule) with this method; it cannot have all true premises and a false conclusion. Is the skeptic defeated?

Being a contentious sort, the skeptic presses on. The skeptic thinks that the truth table method is just an abstract manipulation of symbols that is too far removed from everyday arguments to be a convincing method. You, having had some logic, should not be impressed with this response, but the skeptic has more up his or her sleeve. The skeptic proceeds to give the following counterexample to MT:

1. If Bevis studies, then Bevis does not study hard.
2. It is not true that Bevis does not study hard (i.e., Bevis studies hard).
3. So, Bevis does not study.

The skeptic seems to be on a roll. He or she has apparently offered a counterexample to MT. What has happened here? There appears to be nothing wrong with the premises. The conclusion just doesn't seem to follow from them, yet it must follow from them if the argument is an instance of MT. Is the conditional expressed in the first premise not a material conditional? Does the problem lie in the meaning of the nonlogical words "study" or "hard"? Is the argument not really of the form MT? Is there something wrong with the inference from "Bevis studies hard" to "Bevis studies"? Certainly that inference is valid, but is there any way to capture its validity within statement logic?

One possible response to the skeptic would be to point out that the statement "Bevis does not study hard" is ambiguous and that, when the statement is interpreted properly, the argument is not really an instance of *modus tollens*. The statement "Bevis does not study hard" is ambiguous because the scope of the negation particle "not" is unclear. The statement could be a denial that Bevis both studies and does it diligently, or, alternatively, the statement could be only a denial that Bevis's studying is diligent. Thus, "Bevis does not study hard" could mean (a) "Either Bevis does not study or his studying is not diligent" or (b) "Bevis studies, but his studying is not diligent." Given the nature of the antecedent in the first premise, the most likely interpretation of "Bevis does not study hard" as it occurs in the consequent is (b). However, if the second premise is to mean "Bevis studies hard," then the second premise must be interpreted as the negation of (a). Thus, the argument is not really an instance of *modus tollens*. To see this, symbolize the argument using the following scheme of abbreviation. S: Bevis studies; D: Bevis's studying is diligent.*

*For further examples of this sort of alleged counterexample and additional references, see page 154 in the fifth edition of *Understanding Arguments: An Introduction to Informal Logic* (Harcourt Brace, 1997) by Robert J. Fogelin and Walter Sinnott-Armstrong.

CHAPTER 9

Predicate Logic

*Statement logic is the study of how validity and other related notions
are determined by the logical properties of the five truth-functional
operators. Predicate logic, or "quantification logic," as it is sometimes called, is a categorical logic that is, oddly enough, an extension
of statement logic. Predicate logic, though, goes well beyond both
syllogistic and statement logic in that predicate logic provides us
with the tools to represent the inner structure of atomic statements
and to render the logical form of categorical statements in a more
elaborate fashion. Predicate logic also allows us to prove the validity
of categorical arguments that are not provable within statement
logic and are difficult or impossible to prove using the techniques
of syllogistic logic.*

CHAPTER HIGHLIGHTS

The language of predicate logic (PL) is a symbolic language and contains as logical
symbols the five truth-functional operators of SL, **individual variables** (lowercase
letters "v" through "z"), **universal quantifiers** such as "(x)" and "(y)," **existential
quantifiers** such as "(∃x)" and "(∃y)," and the grouping indicators (the parentheses
and brackets). The non-logical symbols of the language are the **predicate letters**
(capital letters "A" through "Z") and the **individual constants** (lowercase letters "a"
through "u"). A well-formed formula (WFF) of PL is any formula that is constructed
in conformity with the relevant conditions. A statement that has a universal quantifier as its main logical symbol is a **universal statement**, and a statement that has an
existential quantifier as its main logical symbol is a **particular statement**. The non-
statement that results from removing a quantifier from a universal or particular
statement is a **statement function**. Statement functions contain a **free** variable, while
the variables in universal and particular statements are **bound**.

Two steps are involved in translating English-language statements into the symbolic notation of predicate logic (PL):

1. Translate the English statements into logicese.
2. Translate the statements of logicese into the language of PL.

Logicese is logical language that is a sort of hybrid of English and the purely symbolic language of PL. Although awkward sounding, logicese is easier than English
to render into the notation of PL. Four important points must be kept in mind as you
attempt to translate from English into logicese and then into the language of PL:

1. Universal statements usually translate with the arrow as their main truth-functional operator.
2. Particular statements almost always translate with the dot as their main truth-functional operator.
3. Parentheses must be used with care to indicate the proper **scope** of a quantifier. The scope of a quantifier is the statement function that contains the occurrences of the variable bound by the quantifier.
4. The grammatical and logical subjects of English-language statements are not always the same. The logical subject of English-language statements in which there occur quantifiers like "all" and "some" is the first item of which "all" or "some" is said. This means that, in PL-language statements, the logical subject is the first statement function that occurs within the scope of the main quantifier.

Let us examine these points with the help of a few examples. The following argument is intuitively valid:

1. All mammals are warm blooded.
2. Some aquatic animals are mammals.
So, 3. Some aquatic animals are warm blooded.

Following our two-step process, we first translate the statements of this argument into statements of logicese:

1. For all x, if x is a mammal, then x is warm blooded.
2. For some x, x is both an aquatic animal and a mammal.
So, 3. For some x, x is both an aquatic animal and warm- blooded.

Next, we translate these statements (using obvious abbreviations) into the language of PL as follows:

1. $(x)(Mx \rightarrow Wx)$
2. $(\exists x)(Ax \bullet Mx)$
∴ 3. $(\exists x)(Ax \bullet Wx)$

The translation of the previous argument into the language of PL illustrates the four points concerning translation. The first premise, a universal statement, requires the arrow as its main truth-functional operator and is thus a universally quantified conditional statement. The second premise and the conclusion, both particular statements, require the dot as their main truth-functional operator and are thus existentially quantified conjunctions. The parentheses are required around the conditional "$(Px \rightarrow Ux)$" to indicate that both occurrences of "x" are bound by the quantifier and are thus within its scope. Parentheses are required for similar reasons in the second premise and in the conclusion. Note, though, that parentheses never go around a statement formed by adding a quantifier to an atomic statement. The grammatical and logical subjects of the first premise are the same. The first premise is about mammals, so according to point 4, "Mx" is the first statement function that occurs within the scope of the quantifier. Furthermore, what is said of mammals is that they are warm-blooded, so "Wx," the logical predicate, occurs as the consequent of the universally quantified conditional. Similar remarks may be made in regard to the second premise and the conclusion.

The four traditionally recognized types of categorical statements (discussed in Chapter 5) and their translations into the language of PL can be summarized in the following manner:

1. Universal Affirmative   PL Translation
   All S are P. $(x)(Sx \rightarrow Px)$
2. Universal Negative   PL Translation
   No S are P. $(x)(Sx \rightarrow \sim Px)$
3. Particular Affirmative   PL Translation
   Some S are P. $(\exists x)(Sx \bullet Px)$
4. Particular Negative   PL Translation
   Some S are not P. $(\exists x)(Sx \bullet \sim Px)$

An argument is invalid if and only if it is possible for all its premises to be true and its conclusion false. An argument containing universal and particular generalizations will thus be invalid if the argument can be interpreted to be about a possible universe in which the premises are all true and the conclusion is false. The main idea, then, behind the **finite universe method** is to show the invalidity of an argument containing generalizations by finding a possible situation (or universe) involving a finite number of individuals in which all the premises are true and the conclusion is false. The following argument is clearly invalid:

Something is square. Hence, everything is square.

Let U be a universe with only two objects, a square and a triangle, and assume the generalizations in our argument are about the things in U. The universe U represents a specific, albeit an imaginary, situation in which the premise is true and the conclusion is false. This shows that it is *possible* for the premise to be true and the conclusion false, and the mere possibility of this, you will recall, is all we need concern ourselves with when demonstrating invalidity. The argument is therefore invalid.

To use the finite universe method in a completely symbolic fashion, you must begin with an argument the premises and conclusion of which are in the language of PL and first interpret the argument's generalizations as conjunctions or disjunctions before subsequently applying the abbreviated truth table method for demonstrating invalidity. Using obvious abbreviations, we can translate our argument as follows:

    1. $(\exists x)Sx$
∴ 2. $(x)Sx$

Next, we interpret our symbolic PL argument in U. Universal statements, when interpreted to be about things in a universe of two or more objects, are equivalent to conjunctions, and particular statements (existentially quantified statements), when interpreted to be about things in such a universe, are equivalent to disjunctions.

Letting "a" name the square and "b" name the triangle present in U, we thus interpret the premise and conclusion, respectively, as follows.

1. Sa ∨ Sb
∴ 2. Sa • Sb

Given that "Sa" is true and "Sb" is false, which is the case in the situation imagined, the resulting premise is true (since the left disjunct is true), but the conclusion is false (since its right conjunct is false). We thus construct the following abbreviated truth table for this argument as interpreted to be about the universe imagined:

Sa	Sb	Sa ∨ Sb	∴ Sa • Sb
T	F	T T F	T F F

Since the premise is true and the conclusion is false in this universe, the argument is invalid.

The finite universe method has its limitations. There are arguments that are invalid that cannot be proved invalid using this method. In addition, the demonstration of invalidity for some arguments would require a universe with so large a number of members that this method would be impractical without the assistance of a computer. In spite of its limitations, the finite universe method can be used to help us understand the logical relations that hold, or do not hold, among categorical statements on the modern interpretation (specifically, those relations depicted in the traditional and modern squares of opposition discussed in Chapters 5 and 6).

In order to construct proofs of validity in PL, four new implicational inference rules are introduced. The first two rules, **universal instantiation** (UI) and **existential instantiation** (EI), allow us in effect to remove outermost quantifiers from generalizations so that we end up with atomic statements or statements that have a truth-functional operator as the main logical symbol. The other two rules, **universal generalization** (UG) and **existential generalization** (EG), allow us in effect to add quantifiers so as to reach a generalization as a conclusion.

The rule UI allows us to infer any instance of a universally quantified statement. For example, from "(x)[(Hx • Gx) → Fx]," we may validly infer by UI a statement such as "(Hx • Gx) → Fx," "(Hy • Gy) → Fy," or "(Hb • Gb) → Fb." The idea behind UI is that whatever is true of all the individuals in a domain is true of any specific or unknown individual in the domain. It is very important to keep in mind the following two restrictions when using UI:

1. Replace all and only free occurrences of the relevant variable with either the same variable, other variables of a uniform type, or constants of a uniform type.
2. Never use UI on part of a line.

The rule EI allows us to infer any arbitrary instance from an existentially quantified statement. For example, from "(∃x)(Hx • Gx)," we may validly use EI to infer a statement such as "Hx • Gx," "Hy • Gy," or "Hz • Gz." The idea behind EI is that if something is true of some individuals in a domain, then we can use an indefinite (arbitrary) name, such as "x," to designate any one of these unknown individuals. When using EI, keep in mind the following restrictions.

1. Replace all and only free occurrences of the relevant variable with either the same variable or other variables of a uniform type.
2. Never instantiate with a variable that occurs free previously in the proof.
3. Never instantiate with an individual constant.
4. Be sure that, when you instantiate with a variable, the variable does not accidentally become bound by another quantifier. For example, it would be incorrect to infer "(y)Fyy" from "(∃x)(y)Fxy" because the variable used to replace "x" is now bound by the universal quantifier "(y)."
5. Never use EI on part of a line.

The rule UG allows us to infer a universally quantified statement from an instance of the generalization. For example, a valid use of UG may enable us to infer "(x)Fx" from "Fx." The idea behind UG is that whatever is true of any randomly chosen individual in a domain is true of all individuals in the domain. Some restrictions should be kept in mind when using UG to infer a universal statement:

1. Never use UG to generalize universally over a position occupied by an individual constant (e.g., do not infer "(x)Bx" from "Ba").
2. Never use UG to generalize universally over a position occupied by a variable that is free in a line obtained by EI.
3. Never use UG on part of a line.
4. Never use UG to generalize universally over a position occupied by a variable that occurs free within the scope of an assumption for RAA or CP.

The rule EG allows us to infer an existentially quantified statement from an instance of the generalization. For example, from "Ba" or "By" we can validly infer "(∃x)Bx" by EG. The idea behind EG is that whatever is true of a specific or an unknown individual is true of some individual. (This makes sense, for, surely, given that Albert is bald, someone is bald.) The only restriction on the use of EG is that it must never be used on part of a line.

Two equivalence rules can be especially useful when constructing a proof by either CP or RAA. Clearly, to say that no thing is purple is to say that everything is not purple. Thus, the rule of **quantifier negation** (QN) allows us to infer "(x)~Px" from "~(∃x)Px," and vice versa. Similarly, to say that not everything is purple is to say that something is not purple. Thus, the rule QN also allows us to infer "(∃x)~Px" from "~(x)Px," and vice versa.

A formal account of the logic of relations requires the introduction of **polyadic predicates**, i.e., predicates with two or more places. Letting "Lxy" be the two-place predicate "x loves y," we can symbolize the statement "Bevis loves Daria" as "Lbd," where "b" is "Bevis" and "d" is"Daria." However, there are cases in which the grammatical and logical subjects are not the same. Consider, for instance, the statement "Bevis loves all women." This statement can be translated into logicese as "For all x, if x is a woman, then Bevis loves x." Letting "Lxy" be the predicate "x loves y," "Wx" be the predicate "x is a woman," and "b" be "Bevis," we can translate this statement into the language of PL as "(x)(Wx → Lbx)." Notice that the grammatical subject of the English statement is "Bevis," but the logical subject is "women," since "Wx" is the first statement function over which we quantify in the PL-language statement.

A relation **R** is **symmetrical** if and only if, for any x and y, "Ryx" is true if "Rxy" is true. A relation **R** is **asymmetrical** if and only if, for any x and y, "Ryx" is not true if "Rxy" is true. A relation is **nonsymmetrical** if and only if it is neither symmetrical nor asymmetrical. A relation **R** is **reflexive** if and only if, for all x, "Rxx" is true, and is **irreflexive** if and only if, for all x, "Rxx" is not true. A relation is **nonreflexive** if and only if it is neither reflexive nor irreflexive. A relation **R** is **transitive** if and only if, for any x, y, and z, it is the case that, if "Rxy" and "Ryz" are both true, "Rxz" is also true. A relation **R** is **intransitive** if and only if, for any x, y, and z, it is the case that, if "Rxy" and "Ryz" are both true, "Rxz" is not true. A relation is **nontransitive** if and only if it is neither transitive nor intransitive.

The **identity relation** is very important in logic, and we use a special symbol, the **identity sign** (=) to designate that relation. There are some common kinds of English-language constructions that cannot be translated into the language of PL without the use of the identity sign. The following list presents examples of some of these constructions and provides their translations first into logicese and then into the language of PL:

Only

English: Only Bevis failed the exam. (b: Bevis; Fx: x failed the exam)
Logicese: Bevis failed the exam, and for all x, if x failed the exam, x is Bevis.
Symbols: $Fb \bullet (x)(Fx \rightarrow x = b)$

The only

English: The only beer that is drinkable is Meister Brau. (m: Meister Brau; Bx: x is a beer; Dx: x is drinkable)
Logicese: Meister Brau is a beer, and Meister Brau is drinkable, and for all x, if x is a beer and x is drinkable, then x is identical to Meister Brau.
Symbols: $(Bm \bullet Dm) \bullet (x)[(Bx \bullet Dx) \rightarrow x = m]$

No . . . except

English: No person except Bill feels your pain. (Px: x is a person; Fx: x feels your pain; b: Bill)
Logicese: Bill is a person and Bill feels your pain, and for all x, if x is a person and x feels your pain, then x is identical to Bill.
Symbols: $(Pb \bullet Fb) \bullet (x)[(Px \bullet Fx) \rightarrow x = b]$

All . . . except

English: All people except Jessie Helms are funny. (Px: x is a person; Fx: x is funny; j: Jessie Helms)
Logicese: Jesse Helms is a person, and Jesse Helms is not funny, and for all x, if x is a person, and x is not identical to Jesse Helms, then x is funny.
Symbols: $(Pj \bullet \sim Fj) \bullet (x)[(Px \bullet \sim x = j) \rightarrow Fx]$

Superlatives

English:	The smartest man is Albert Einstein. (Sxy: x is smarter than y; Mx: x is a man; a: Albert Einstein)
Logicese:	Albert Einstein is a man, and for all x, if x is a man, and x is not identical to Albert Einstein, then Albert Einstein is smarter than x.
Symbols:	Ma • (x)[(Mx • ~x = a) → Sax]

At most

English:	There is at most one Devil. (Dx: x is a Devil)
Logicese:	For all x and for all y, if x is a Devil and y is a Devil, then x is identical to y.
Symbols:	(x)(y)[(Dx • Dy) → x = y]

Exactly one

English:	There is exactly one Devil. (Dx: x is a Devil)
Logicese:	There is an x such that x is a Devil, and for all y, if y is a Devil, then x is identical to y.
Symbols:	(∃x)[Dx • (y)(Dy → x = y)]

Definite Descriptions

English:	The discoverer of Kansas was a communist. (Dxy: x discovered y; Cx: x is a communist; k: Kansas)
Logicese:	There is an x such that x discovered Kansas, and for all y, if y discovered Kansas, then x is identical to y, and x is a communist.
Symbols:	(∃x)([Dxk • (y)(Dyk → x = y)] • Cx)

The use of statements of identity in proofs is governed by three new inference rules. The first new rule is **Leibniz' law** (LL), which states that, if x and y are one and the same or identical, then whatever is true of the one is also true of the other. Hence, we can, for example, infer "Fb" from the statements "Fa" and "a = b" by applying LL. The reasoning behind Leibniz' law should be fairly clear. If, for instance, Ben Franklin was the inventor of bifocals, and Ben Franklin was intelligent, then it seems reasonable to infer that the inventor of bifocals was intelligent. The second new rule is **symmetry** (Sm), which allows us to interchange terms on either side of the identity sign in either an identity statement or the negation of one. For example, we can by Sm move inferentially from the truth of "a = b" to the truth of "b = a" and from the truth of "~x = y" to the truth of "~y = x." The rule Sm is reasonable since the identity relation is symmetrical. The last new rule is **identity** (Id), which allows us to introduce on any subsequent line of a proof (regardless of previous lines) an identity statement with the same individual constant or individual variable flanking both sides of the identity sign. Thus, we may, in virtue of Id, introduce on a line of proof something like "a = a" or "x = x." The rule Id is valid since the identity relation is obviously reflexive.

DISCUSSION OF KEY CONCEPTS

I. Predicates and Quantifiers

A. Helpful Reminders

1. A translation into the language of PL, like a translation into the language of SL, is always relative to a scheme of abbreviation. So, always remember to provide such a scheme, if one is not already provided for you, for any translation you make.

2. The truth conditions of a statement are the general circumstances in which the statement is true. Keep in mind the truth conditions of universal and particular statements when rendering English-language generalizations into the language of PL. Remember that a proposed PL-language statement is a correct translation of an English-language statement only if the truth conditions of each statement are the same. That is why universal generalizations are translated using the universal quantifier and the arrow and particular generalizations are translated using the existential quantifier and the dot.

3. Statements of the form "Only A's are B's" are confusing to many people because the grammatical subject differs from the logical subject in such statements. For example, consider the statement "Only adults are voters." In this case, the grammatical subject is "adults," and the logical subject is "voters." It would be incorrect to translate this statement (using obvious abbreviations) as "(x)(Ax → Vx)," because this says that all adults are voters, which is false since adults who commit felonies are not allowed to vote. The correct translation is "(x)(Vx → Ax)," meaning "All voters are adults" or "One is a voter only if one is an adult," which is true. Since voters are the first things about which "all" is said in these alternative English versions of this statement, it follows that "voters" is the logical subject.

B. Commonly Asked Questions

1. What steps should you take when trying to recast an English statement as a formula in the language of PL?

You should first determine the overall form of the statement. If it is an atomic statement, then it should be translated as such. If it is a statement having a truth-functional operator as its main operator (what is sometimes called a molecular statement), then you should apply the translation techniques developed for statement logic. If the statement you are translating is a generalization, then you should translate it according to the way in which the four traditionally recognized kinds of categorical statements are rendered into the language of PL. Once you have recognized the overall form of the statement and know what is the overall form of the translation, you should then look for the various parts of the statement (the simpler component statements and the logical subject and predicate terms) and translate them accordingly. It may help to write out the statement's complete translation into logicese before constructing the statement's final translation into the language of PL.

2. How do you know when to use a universal quantifier and when to use an existential quantifier in translating an English statement into the language of PL?

Any statement that says something about all the members of a domain (or universe) should be translated as a statement containing a universal quantifier. Any statement that says something about only some instead of all the members of a domain should be translated as a statement containing an existential quantifier.

Traditional **A** and **E** categorical statements make claims about all the members of a domain and are thus translated using a universal quantifier. Traditional **I** and **O** categorical statements make claims that, when true, may only be true for some of the members of a domain and are thus translated using an existential quantifier. Usually, but not always, the occurrence in a statement of a word like "all," "every," "each," "any," "always," "only," "no," "none," and "never" (or a longer word or expression containing one of these words) indicates that the statement should be translated using a universal quantifier. Typically, the occurrence of a word or expression like "some," "somebody," "somewhere," "someplace," "sometimes," "there is," "there are," and "at least one" indicates that the statement should be translated using an existential quantifier. Be careful when an English statement uses only the indefinite article ("a" or "an") to signify quantity. Such a statement can be, depending on its content, either a universal or a particular generalization.

C. Exercises

Translate the following statements into the language of PL using the given scheme of translation.

Cx: x is a cat
Dx: x is a dog
Mx: x is a mammal
e: Felix
f: Fido

1. No cats are dogs.
2. No noncats are dogs.
3. If Felix is a cat, then Fido is a dog.
4. All cats and dogs are mammals.
5. Some dogs are not cats.
6. If something is a dog, then everything is a cat.
7. If no nonmammals are cats, then something is a mammal.
8. Some mammals are not either cats or dogs.
9. Only mammals are cats.
10. If Felix is a cat, then only nondogs are nonmammals.

II. Demonstrating Invalidity

A. Helpful Reminders

1. The finite universe method for demonstrating invalidity utilizes the abbreviated truth table method from SL. To use this method of showing invalidity, first choose a finite universe with just a few members, then replace all universally quantified statements in the argument with equivalent conjunctive statements and all existentially quantified statements in the argument with equivalent disjunctive statements. You then apply the abbreviated truth table method to the resulting argument to show that it is possible for the conclusion to be false even when all the premises are true.

2. When interpreted to be about the members of a finite universe, a universal statement is equivalent to a conjunction, while a particular statement is equivalent

to a disjunction. What a universal statement asserts is said to be true of everything in the universe, and what a particular statement asserts is said to be true of at least one thing in the universe. Therefore, in a universe with just *a* and *b*, for example, what a universal statement asserts is true of *a* and true of *b*, and what a particular statement asserts is true of *a* or true of *b*. When interpreting a universal or particular statement in relation to a finite universe, you obtain each of the conjuncts or disjuncts by removing the quantifier and uniformly replacing all occurrences of the free variable with each of the individual constants that name the items in the finite universe.

B. Commonly Asked Questions

1. Why does the finite universe method work to demonstrate invalidity in PL?

If a PL argument is valid, then, regardless of what universe the argument's generalizations are interpreted to be about, it should not be possible for the conclusion to be false if all the premises are true. So, if you can find a real or imaginary universe (domain) in which to interpret the argument in a way that makes all the premises true and the conclusion false, then you have shown the argument to be invalid. The finite universe method involves just this sort of interpretation, and that is why it works (when it does work) to demonstrate invalidity in PL.

2. How do I know what size of finite universe to choose?

Unfortunately, there is no rule that you can follow that will always tell you in every case exactly how many things there must be in the finite universe you choose. (However, an invalid argument constructed of statements whose predicates are all one-place can always be shown to be invalid by considering a universe with 2^n members, where n is the number of predicates, but the interpretation relative to such a universe might well be too unwieldy.) Fortunately, though, most of the arguments that you are likely to encounter can be shown to be invalid by considering a universe with no more than three members. So, first try small finite universes of one, two, and three members. If none of these allow you to demonstrate invalidity, try increasingly larger finite universes until you find one that works.

C. Exercises

Use the finite universe method to show that the following arguments are invalid.

1. $(\exists x)(Px \bullet Gx)$ $\therefore (y)(Py \bullet Gy)$

2. $\sim(x)(Px \rightarrow Gx)$ $\therefore (x)(Px \rightarrow Gx)$

3. $(\exists x)(Fx \vee Gx)$ $\therefore (\exists x)(Fx \bullet Gx)$

4. $(x)(\sim Mx \vee \sim Nx)$ $\therefore (x)(\sim Mx \bullet \sim Nx)$

5. $\sim(x)\sim(Fx \leftrightarrow Gx)$ $\therefore \sim(\exists x)(Fx \leftrightarrow Gx)$

III. Constructing Proofs

A. Helpful Reminders

1. The rules UI, EI, UG, and EG are all implicational inference rules and thus cannot be applied to only part of a line. So, when you apply one of these rules to a line of proof, make sure that you are dealing with a generalization and not a molecular statement. Note that only a single application of any one of these rules can be made at one time. You cannot, for instance, remove two quantifiers by UI or add two quantifiers by EG on a single line of proof. Quantifiers must be removed by successive applications of UI or EI and added by successive applications of UG or EG.

2. UG and EI are the only rules that are apt to give you any trouble. Just remember always to do EI before UI, and never do UG on a variable that is free in a line obtained by EI.

3. The use of the rule UG mirrors the kind of reasoning often used in mathematical proofs. For example, a proof in geometry may involve inferring that all triangles have a certain property P from the fact that an arbitrary triangle has P. The mathematician typically begins such a proof by "picking an arbitrary triangle" and then using geometrical facts to show that the triangle has the property P. As long as the triangle chosen is arbitrary, which means that nothing is assumed about the figure other than the fact that it is a triangle, the mathematician can legitimately infer that all triangles have the property P. If, however, the mathematician's conclusion rests on the assumption that the triangle chosen is, for instance, an equilateral triangle, then the conclusion may not be true for all triangles. For a similar reason, when you use UG to infer a universal statement, you must make sure that the line you apply UG to does not rest on premises that make the free variable on that line not arbitrary.

B. Commonly Asked Questions

1. What basic strategy should one follow to construct a proof in PL?

Most proofs in PL are constructed in the same manner. You first remove existential quantifiers from lines by EI and universal quantifiers from lines by UI. You then keep applying the inference rules of statement logic to the quantifier-free lines until you reach a line that can become the conclusion with the addition of one or more quantifiers. The final lines of the proof then involve adding the necessary quantifiers to the outside of a formula by UG and/or EG so as to obtain the desired conclusion.

2. Why does the order in which one removes quantifiers, either from a single line or from different lines in a proof, matter?

Quantifiers are always removed from a formula from the left to the right and are always added to a formula from the right to the left. To do otherwise would be to apply (incorrectly) the implicational inference rules to just part of a line. Existential quantifiers are removed from lines before universal quantifiers are removed from other lines so as to avoid problems with the restrictions placed on the rules EI and UG.

C. Exercises

(a) Annotate the following proofs:

    1. 1. $(x)(Fx \rightarrow Gx)$ $\therefore Fc \rightarrow Gc$
       2. $Fc \rightarrow Gc$

2. 1. $(x)(Fx \rightarrow Gx)$
   2. $(\exists y)Fy$ $\therefore (\exists x)Fx$
   3. Fy
   4. $Fy \rightarrow Gy$
   5. Gy
   6. $(\exists x)Gx$

3. 1. $(\exists z)Az \rightarrow (y)Fy$
   2. $\sim(y)Fy$ $\therefore \sim(\exists z)Az$
   3. $\sim(\exists z)Az$

4. 1. $(\exists y)Gy$
   2. $(x)(\sim Gx \vee \sim Mx)$ $\therefore (\exists y)\sim My$
   3. Gy
   4. $\sim Gy \vee \sim My$
   5. $\sim\sim Gy$
   6. $\sim My$
   7. $(\exists y)\sim My$

5. 1. $(x)(Mx \rightarrow Nx)$
   2. $(w)(Nw \rightarrow Ow)$
   3. $(z)\sim Oz$ $\therefore (x)\sim Mx$
   4. $Nx \rightarrow Ox$
   5. $\sim Ox$
   6. $Mx \rightarrow Nx$
   7. $\sim Nx$
   8. $\sim Mx$
   9. $(x)\sim Mx$

(b) Construct proofs for each of the following valid arguments:

1. 1. $(x)(Bx \rightarrow Cx)$
   2. $(y)By$ $\therefore (z)Cz$

2. 1. $(x)Fx$
   2. $(x)Gx$ $\therefore (\exists x)(Gx \bullet Fx)$

3. 1. $(x)[Bx \rightarrow (\sim Ax \rightarrow Ca)]$
   2. $\sim Ab$ $\therefore Bb \rightarrow Ca$

4. 1. $\sim Pa$
   2. $(x)(y)[(Nx \vee Qy) \rightarrow (Pa \vee Pb)]$ $\therefore Na \rightarrow Pb$

5. 1. $(\exists z)(Mz \bullet Nz)$
   2. $(y)(Ny \rightarrow Py)$ $\therefore (\exists w)(Mw \bullet Pw)$

IV. Quantifier Negation, RAA, and CP

A. Helpful Reminders

1. The rule of quantifier negation (QN) is an equivalence rule of PL and can therefore be used on just part of a line. QN allows one to replace a negated quantifier with a quantified negation and to replace a quantified negation with a negated quantifier.

2. The rule QN can be a very helpful rule. Often, CP and RAA are used in tandem to minimize the length or complexity of a proof. However, the following proof was done in two fewer lines by using CP and QN without RAA.

1. $(x)Ax \lor (x)Bx$	$\therefore (x)(\sim Ax \rightarrow Bx)$
2. $\sim Ax$	Assume (CP)
3. $(\exists x)\sim Ax$	2, EG
4. $\sim(x)Ax$	3, QN
5. $(x)Bx$	1, 4, DS
6. Bx	5, UI
7. $\sim Ax \rightarrow Bx$	2-6, CP
8. $(x)(\sim Ax \rightarrow Bx)$	7, UG

Notice that UG is permissible on line 8 because the variable "x" in "$\sim Ax \rightarrow Bx$" does not occur within the scope of the assumption for CP (since "$\sim Ax$" is discharged at line 7).

B. Commonly Asked Questions

1. Do we really need the rule of quantifier negation?

Our proof system of PL is not made complete by the addition of QN to our set of rules, and there is no inference we can make using QN that we cannot make using the other rules. We therefore do not need the rule, but we nonetheless adopt the rule for the sake of convenience since some proofs are made shorter and easier by the use of the rule.

2. Why use the rule QN in a proof?

The rule QN allows you in effect to bring the negation sign from the outside to the inside of a formula or from the inside to the outside of a formula. It thus can enable you to obtain a universal or particular statement, or the negation of one, on a line of proof. QN is often used early in a proof to remove the negation sign from the outside of a formula to obtain a quantified statement. Doing so then enables one to remove a quantifier by a subsequent application of EI or UG.

C. Exercises

Construct proofs for each of the following valid arguments:

1. 1. $\sim(\exists x)\sim Mx$
   2. $(y)[(My \cdot Oy) \rightarrow Py]$ $\therefore (x)(Ox \rightarrow Px)$

2. 1. $(\exists y)Fy$
   2. $\sim(\exists z)(Fz \cdot \sim Hz)$
   3. $(z)[Fz \rightarrow (\sim Gz \rightarrow \sim Hz)]$ $\therefore (\exists y)Gy$

3. 1. $(v)(Fv \cdot {\sim}Gv)$ $\therefore {\sim}(\exists v)(Fv \rightarrow Gv)$

4. 1. $(w)(Bw \rightarrow {\sim}Cw)$ $\therefore {\sim}(\exists w)(Bw \cdot Cw)$

5. 1. $(y)[(My \cdot Ny) \rightarrow Oy]$
   2. ${\sim}(\exists y){\sim}Py$
   3. $(z)(Pz \rightarrow Mz)$ $\therefore {\sim}(\exists y)(Ny \cdot {\sim}Oy)$

V. The Logic of Relations: Symbolizations

A. Helpful Reminders

1. Note that the order in which different individual variables or constants occur in a polyadic predicate makes a difference to the meaning of the predicate. Note also that, when working with quantified relational statements, you cannot, in general, switch quantifiers around when the quantifiers are of different types. For example, the following two statements do not mean the same thing. Let "Lxy" be "x is larger than y."

   1. $(\exists x)(y)Lxy$
   2. $(y)(\exists x)Lxy$

Statement 1 says that something is larger than everything, but statement 2 says that everything is such that something is larger than it.

2. Note the distinctions between an asymmetrical and a nonsymmetrical relation, between an irreflexive and a nonreflexive relation, and between an intransitive and a nontransitive relation. These relations are all distinct.

B. Commonly Asked Questions

1. How can a relation be nonsymmetrical, nonreflexive, or nontransitive?
A relation that is symmetrical for some members of its domain and asymmetrical for other members of its domain is nonsymmetrical. A relation that is reflexive for some members of its domain and irreflexive for other members of its domain is nonreflexive. Similarly, a relation that is transitive for some members of its domain and intransitive for other members of its domain is nontransitive.

2. Can a relation exemplify more than one of the nine kinds of relations mentioned?
A particular relation can be an example of one or more of the nine kinds of relations. However, some combinations of traits are impossible. For instance, a relation cannot be both symmetrical and asymmetrical, both reflexive and nonreflexive, or both intransitive and nontransitive. Mathematicians often call a relation that is symmetrical, reflexive, and transitive an equivalence relation.

C. Exercises

Translate the following into the language of PL using the scheme of translation provided in the problem or in previous problems.

1. Keith knows some boring logic professors. (k: Keith; Kxy: x knows y; Bx: x is boring; Gx: x is a logic professor)

2. Every logic professor knows some student. (Sx: x is a student)
3. Keith does not know everything.
4. Rick does not pass every course he takes. (r: Rick; Pxy: x passes y; Txy: x takes y; Cx: x is a course)
5. No logic professor is both interesting and serious. (Ix: x is interesting; Rx: x is serious)
6. Rick takes every course that is neither difficult nor boring. (Dx: x is difficult)
7. If Keith is serious, then he takes every logic course. (Ox: x is a logic course)
8. There are no courses that Rick passes.
9. Keith doesn't like every logic professor. (Lxy: x likes y)
10. If Rick likes all logic courses, then some logic professor is not serious.

VI. The Logic of Relations: Proofs

A. Helpful Reminders

1. Be careful when removing or adding quantifiers from quantified statements containing polyadic predicates. The order in which you remove and add the various quantifiers is important to reaching the desired conclusion and avoiding problems because of the restrictions on the use of the inference rules.

2. Whenever you use the rules UG and EI, make sure that there is a one-to-one correspondence between occurrences of the relevant free variable in the statement function and occurrences of the variable bound by the quantifier. Whenever you use the rules UI and EG, you need only make sure that to each occurrence of the relevant free variable in the statement function (or the individual constant in the statement) there corresponds an occurrence of the variable bound by the quantifier.

B. Commonly Asked Questions

1. Why are there restrictions placed on the use of the inference rules of PL when these restrictions seem to make proofs more difficult, particularly when dealing with arguments containing relational predicates?

The restrictions on the rules are necessary, in spite of the fact that they complicate proof construction, in order to ensure that the inference rules are valid. If these restrictions were not placed on our inference rules, then we would be able to prove as valid certain invalid arguments.

2. How do you know what particular variables to use and in what order to introduce them when constructing a proof for an argument containing a polyadic predicate?

The primary dictates of the particular variables and the order in which they are introduced into a formula on a line of proof are the variables and their order in the conclusion. As a consequence, you may need to change the variables bound in the premises when instantiating them or change the variables free in an intermediate conclusion when universalizing. The order of the variables' introduction into the successive lines of a proof through instantiation and generalization is determined by the requirement not to violate any of the inference rules.

C. Exercises

Construct proofs for the following valid arguments. Use any of the rules you have available. Note that proofs 3, 4, and 5 may require some ingenuity because the variables are not always in the same order with respect to the same predicate letter. Be careful!

1. 1. $(z)(Pz \rightarrow Mz)$
   2. $(y)[(My \lor Ny) \rightarrow Oy]$ $\therefore \sim(\exists y)(Py \cdot \sim Oy)$

2. 1. $(\exists x)(y)Fxyx$ $\therefore \sim(x)(\exists y)\sim Fxyx$

3. 1. $\sim(y)(\exists x)\sim(Bxy \cdot Byx)$ $\therefore (\exists x)Bxx$

4. 1. $(x)(y)\sim Hxy$
   2. $(\exists y)(x)(Fx \rightarrow Hyx)$ $\therefore \sim(x)Fx$

5. 1. $(\exists x)(y)(\sim Axy \rightarrow Ayx)$ $\therefore \sim(x)(y)\sim Axy$

VII. Identity: Symbolizations

A. Helpful Reminders

1. Statements of everyday English can convey two different notions of identity. For example, statement S1 could mean either S2 or S3, depending on the context.

S1: The dime in my right hand is the same coin as the coin in my left hand.

S2: The dime in my right hand is similar to (or is the same kind as) the coin in my left hand.

S3: The dime in my right hand is the coin that is in my left hand.

If I had two numerically distinct dimes, one in each hand, S2 would be the correct meaning of S1 because S2 expresses qualitative identity. On the other hand, S3 would be a more accurate rendering of S1 if I were trying to convey that I was holding one dime with both hands. This is numerical identity, and this is what is meant by the identity sign, "=".

2. Not all statements in which "is" occurs are expressions of either qualitative or quantitative identity. For example, there is the "is" of existence, as when theists say, "God is," meaning that God exists. There is also the familiar "is" of predication, whose complement is either a predicate nominative or a predicate adjective used to attribute a property or an attribute to an individual. For example, the "is" in "Socrates is pale" is the "is" of predication, in which the property of paleness is attributed to the individual Socrates. In addition to these two uses of "is," there is also the "is" of class inclusion exemplified by claims like "A whale is a mammal." This statement is about all whales—as the indefinite article indicates—and says that the class of whales is included in the class of mammals.

B. Commonly Asked Questions

1. Why translate English statements containing the locution "There are at most" as universal instead of particular statements?

If we were to translate such English statements as particular statements, then the truth conditions of our translations would not correspond with the truth conditions of the statements translated. Such a statement as "There are at most three lawyers present" does not assert that there are any lawyers present; it only asserts that there are no more than three, if any, lawyers present. Since universal statements may be true without their logical subjects being true of anything, the truth conditions of appropriate universal statements can match the truth conditions of the English statements they translate.

2. Are all statements that contain the definite article "the" in the grammatical subject rendered into symbols as statements that contain the identity sign?

Not all statements that contain a phrase of the form "the so-and-so" as grammatical subject contain a definite description. For example, the statement "The large bullfrogs that inhabit the plains of western Africa are ferocious animals" has the same meaning as the statement "All large bullfrogs that inhabit the plains of western Africa are ferocious animals." The former statement thus does not actually contain a definite description and should not be translated using the identity sign. In addition, some statements that contain the phrase "the only" in the grammatical subject do not contain a disguised assertion of identity. For instance, the statement "The only people who eat tofu are vegetarians" has the same meaning as the statement "All people who eat tofu are vegetarians." The former statement is thus not translated as a statement containing the identity sign.

C. Exercises

Translate the following into the language of PL using the schemes of translation provided in each problem and previous ones. Use "Px" to translate "x is a person" whenever the context requires the addition of this predicate.

1. Only drunks were arrested. (Dx: x is a drunk; Ax: x was arrested)
2. Only George Bush upholds high moral standards in the White House. (b: George Bush; Wx: x upholds high moral standards in the White House)
3. The only person who really did well in the cattle futures market was Hillary Clinton. (h: Hillary Clinton; Cx: x really did well in the cattle futures market)
4. No one except George Bush asked for a tax refund. (Ax: x asked for a tax refund)
5. All drunks except Edith were happy. (e: Edith; Hx: x is happy)
6. Delbert Brewer is the tallest person. (d: Delbert Brewer; Txy: x is taller than y)
7. Mike Tyson is the strongest boxer. (m: Mike Tyson; Bx: x is a boxer; Sxy: x is stronger than y)
8. Nothing is greater than God. (Gxy: x is greater than y; g: God)
9. There is at most one Savior. (Sx: x is a Savior)
10. There are at least two Saviors.
11. There is at least one number. (Nx: x is a number)

12. There are at least two numbers.
13. There is exactly one number.
14. The author of *Waverly* was Scottish. (Wx: x wrote *Waverly*; Tx: x was Scottish)
15. The author of *Ivanhoe* was Sir Walter Scott. (Ix: x wrote *Ivanhoe*; s: Sir Walter Scott)

VIII. Identity: Proofs

A. *Helpful Reminders*

1. Leibniz' law (LL), sometimes referred to as the principle of substitutivity, allows you to replace one or more occurrences of an individual constant or individual variable in a statement with another individual constant or individual variable that refers to the same thing. LL allows you to replace only constants or free variables in a statement with other constants or variables that are not bound by a quantifier upon the substitution. Note that the statement into which the substitution is made can itself be an identity statement. Thus, from the truth of "a = b" and "b = c," one can infer by LL the truth of "a = c."

2. Note that LL allows you to substitute either one of the two terms (individual variables or constants) in an identity statement for the other in a statement containing the relevant term. Note also that the application of LL does not require you to replace all the occurrences of one term with the other term. It is perfectly permissible to replace some but not all the occurrences of a term with another term.

B. *Commonly Asked Questions*

1. Why do we have the rule of identity, since any statement with the same term on either side of the identity predicate is trivially true?

Statements such as "a = a" may be trivial truths, but there are arguments (for instance, many arguments that contain such an identity statement only in the conclusion) that cannot be proved valid without the rule of identity (Id) in our proof theory. Furthermore, using Id together with LL, we can reach as a conclusion any statement that can be inferred by applying just the rule of symmetry (Sm).

2. How does one use Id in a proof?

The rule Id is not applied to a previous line of proof, and so there is no line number to cite when justifying a conclusion reached by Id. The rule Id allows you to add on a line of proof, at any stage of a proof, any statement of the form n = n. To justify any line introduced into a proof by Id, you merely need to cite "Id" to the right of the line.

C. *Exercises*

Construct proofs to show that the following PL arguments are valid.

1. 1. (y)(z)(y = z → Ayz)
   2. (y)(z)(Azy → Bz)
   3. ~Ba   ∴ ~(a = b)

2. 1 $(\exists x)(\exists y)x = y \rightarrow (z)Mz$ $\therefore Mb$

3. 1. $(\exists x)(\exists y)x = y \rightarrow (z)(Fz \rightarrow Gz)$
   2. $b = c$ $\therefore Fb \rightarrow Gc$

4. 1. $(z)(z = a \rightarrow Gz)$ $\therefore Ga$

5. 1. $(x)(x = a \rightarrow Gx)$
   2. $a = b$ $\therefore (\exists w)Gw$

ANSWERS TO EXERCISES

Answers to Selected Exercises in the Text

Exercise 9.1
Part B

1. Whatever is a Zoroastrian fails to be a Moslem. For all x, if x is a Zoroastrian, then x is not a Moslem.
4. It is not the case that for all x, if x is a marsupial, then x is a kangaroo.
10. For some x, x is both mortal and human.
16. If only blue things are sky blue, then nothing else is sky blue; that is, every nonblue thing fails to be sky blue. Now, by Cont, for all x, if x is sky blue, then x is a blue thing.
22. All circles are perfect, and only circles are perfect. Thus, anything is a circle if and only if it is perfect. For all x, x is a circle if and only if x is perfect.

Part C

1. This is a statement about all things that are cats. So, for all x, if x is a cat, then x is an animal.
10. This means that there is no thing that is both right and wrong, or, for all x, if x is right, then x is not wrong.
19. If every x fails to be a ghost, then for all x, if x is a house, x fails to be haunted.

Part F

4. The "None but . . ." construction simply means "Only . . ." So, for all x, if x can vote, then x is a citizen.
10. For all x, if x is a fetus and x is neither human nor a moral agent, then x lacks a right to life.
19. Either for all x, x is not good, or there is some x such that x is evil. (Notice that the vee is the main connective.)
25. If there is someone who can play chess, then Kasparov can play chess. If there is an x such that x is a person and x can play chess, then Kasparov can play chess.

Exercise 9.2
Part A

1. Note that the premise and the conclusion contain different quantifiers. They must therefore be expanded differently.

Part B

1. The relative clause "who takes logic" adjectivally modifies the noun "students" and is thus translated as a predicate. For all x, if x is a student and x takes logic, then x is courageous.

Exercise 9.3
Part C

4. Whenever you universally generalize over some variable, ask yourself two questions: (1) Does that variable occur free in a line obtained by EI? (2) Does that variable occur free within the scope of an undischarged assumption? If the answer to either of these is yes, you used UG incorrectly. As you can see in the proof provided in the answers, the use of UG at line 6 is correct.
19. It is important here to remember Rule of Thumb 1: Use EI before UI.

Part D

7. Whenever your conclusion is a conjunction, work backward either to a logically equivalent negated disjunction or to each of the individual conjuncts.

Exercise 9.4
Part A

7. It almost goes without saying, but in almost all proofs Rule of Thumb 2 is applicable: Remove quantifiers and then use the inference rules of SL.

Part B

1. Your conclusion is a universally quantified conditional, so consider Rule of Thumb 4 and try CP.
4. Since your conclusion is a particular statement, consider Rule of Thumb 5 and try a proof by RAA.

Part D

7.   1. For some x, x is both a reprobate and boring.
      2. For some x, x is both highly moral and humorous.
      3. If for some x, x is a reprobate, then for all x, if x is humorous, then, if x is highly moral, then x is fascinating.
   So, 4. For some x, x is both highly moral and fascinating.

   Rule of Thumb 5 can be very helpful; however, if you use it on this proof and try RAA, you may end up needing more than twenty lines to complete the proof.

Exercise 9.5
Part B

> 7. (x)[Dx → (y)(Hy → ~Wxy)]
> 10. (x)[(Ox • Px) → (y)[(Oy • Wy) → ~Rxy]]
> 19. (x)(Sx → ~(y)(z)[(Py • Dz) → Hxyz])

Exercise 9.6
Part B

> 10. Think of Rule of Thumb 4 and make two assumptions to set up CP. UG will be used twice, but that should not present any problems.

Exercise 9.7
Part A

> 4. It is not the case that there is an x such that x is not identical to x.
> 10. There is an x and there is a y such that x is a person and y is a person and x invented the airplane and y invented the airplane and x is not identical to y.

Part B

> 7. There is an x such that x is a person and x shot Abraham Lincoln and, for all y, if y is a person and y shot Abraham Lincoln, then x is identical to y.
> 10. Kierkegaard is a Dane and is gloomy, and, for all x, if x is a Dane and x is not identical to Kierkegaard, then x is not gloomy.

Exercise 9.8
Part A

> 4. Note in the proof provided in the answers the application of Sm to line 2 before the application of MP to lines 1 and 4.

Answers to Supplemental Exercises

I

> 1. (x)(Cx → ~Dx)
> 2. (x)(~Cx → ~Dx)
> 3. Ce → Df
> 4. (x)[(Cx ∨ Dx) → Mx]
> 5. (∃x)(Dx • ~Cx)
> 6. (∃x)Dx → (x)Cx
> 7. (x)(~Mx → ~Cx) → (∃x)Mx
> 8. (∃x)[Mx • ~(Cx ∨ Dx)]
> 9. (x)(Cx → Mx)
> 10. Ce → (x)(~Mx → ~Dx)

II

1.

Pa	Pb	Ga	Gb	(Pa • Ga) ∨ (Pb • Gb)	∴ (Pa • Ga) • (Pb • Gb)
T	F	T	T	T T T T F F T	T T T F F F T

The assignment of "T" to Ga, Gb, and Pa and "F" to Pb makes the premise true and the conclusion false.

2.

Pa	Pb	Ga	Gb	~[(Pa→Ga) • (Pb→Gb)]	∴(Pa→Ga) • (Pb→Gb)
T	T	F	T	T T FF F T T T	T FF F T T T

The assignment of "T" to Pa, Pb, and Gb and "F" to Ga makes the premise true and the conclusion false.

3.

Fa	Fb	Ga	Gb	(Fa ∨ Ga) ∨ (Fb ∨ Gb)	∴ (Fa • Ga) ∨ (Fb • Gb)
F	F	T	T	F T T T F T T	F F T F F F T

The assignment of "T" to Ga and Gb and "F" to Fa and Fb makes the premise true and the conclusion false.

4.

Ma	Mb	Na	Nb	(~Ma ∨ ~Na) • (~Mb ∨ ~Nb)
F	F	T	T	TF TFT T TF TFT

∴ (~Ma • ~Na) • (~Mb • ~Nb)

TF FF T F TF FFT

The assignment of "T" to Na and Nb and "F" to Ma and Mb makes the premise true and the conclusion false.

5.

Fa	Fb	Ga	Gb	~[~(Fa ↔ Ga) • ~(Fb ↔ Gb)]
T	T	T	T	TF TT T FF TT T

∴ ~(Fa ↔ Ga) ∨ (Fb ↔ Gb)

FT T T T T T T

The assignment of "T" to Fa, Fb, Ga, and Gb makes the premise true and the conclusion false.

III(a)

1. 1. (x)(Fx → Gx)   ∴ Fc → Gc
    2. Fc → Gc   1, UI

2. 1. (x)(Fx → Gx)
    2. (∃y)Fy   ∴ (∃x)Fx
    3. Fy   2, EI
    4. Fy → Gy   1, UI
    5. Gy   3, 4, MP
    6. (∃x)Gx   5, EG

3. 1. $(\exists z)Az \rightarrow (y)Fy$
   2. $\sim(y)Fy$ $\therefore \sim(\exists z)Az$
   3. $\sim(\exists z)Az$ 1, 2, MT

4. 1. $(\exists y)Gy$
   2. $(x)(\sim Gx \lor \sim Mx)$ $\therefore (\exists y)\sim My$
   3. Gy 1, EI
   4. $\sim Gy \lor \sim My$ 2, UI
   5. $\sim\sim Gy$ 3, DN
   6. $\sim My$ 4, 5, DS
   7. $(\exists y)\sim My$ 6, EG

5. 1. $(x)(Mx \rightarrow Nx)$
   2. $(w)(Nw \rightarrow Ow)$
   3. $(z)\sim Oz$ $\therefore (x)\sim Mx$
   4. $Nx \rightarrow Ox$ 2, UI
   5. $\sim Ox$ 3, UI
   6. $Mx \rightarrow Nx$ 1, UI
   7. $\sim Nx$ 4, 5, MT
   8. $\sim Mx$ 6, 7, MT
   9. $(x)\sim Mx$ 8, UG

III(b)

1. 1. $(x)(Bx \rightarrow Cx)$
   2. $(y)By$ $\therefore (z)Cz$
   3. $By \rightarrow Cy$ 1, UI
   4. By 2, UI
   5. Cy 3, 4, MP
   6. $(z)Cz$ 5, UG

2. 1. $(x)Fx$
   2. $(x)Gx$ $\therefore (\exists x)(Gx \bullet Fx)$
   3. Gx 2, UI
   4. Fx 1, UI
   5. $Gx \bullet Fx$ 3, 4, Conj
   6. $(\exists x)(Gx \bullet Fx)$ 5, EG

3. 1. $(x)[Bx \rightarrow (\sim Ax \rightarrow Ca)]$
   2. $\sim Ab$ $\therefore Bb \rightarrow Ca$
   $\lceil$ 3. Bb Assume
   | 4. $Bb \rightarrow (\sim Ab \rightarrow Ca)$ 1, UI
   | 5. $\sim Ab \rightarrow Ca$ 3, 4, MP
   $\lfloor$ 6. Ca 2, 5, MP
   7. $Bb \rightarrow Ca$ 3-6, CP

4.   1. ~Pa
      2. (x)(y)[(Nx ∨ Qy) → (Pa ∨ Pb)]   ∴ Na → Pb
      3. (y)[(Na ∨ Qy) → (Pa ∨ Pb)]   2, UI
      4. (Na ∨ Qy) → (Pa ∨ Pb)   3, UI
      5. Na   Assume
      6. Na ∨ Qy   5, Add
      7. Pa ∨ Pb   4, 6, MP
      8. Pb   1, 7, DS
      9. Na → Pb   5-8, CP

5.   1. (∃z)(Mz • Nz)
      2. (y)(Ny → Py)   ∴ (∃w)(Mw • Pw)
      3. My • Ny   1, EI
      4. Ny → Py   2, UI
      5. My   3, Simp
      6. Ny   3, Simp
      7. Py   4, 6, MP
      8. My • Py   5, 7, Conj
      9. (∃w)(Mw • Pw)   8, EG

IV

1.   1. ~(∃x)~Mx
      2. (y)[(My • Oy) → Py]   ∴ (x)(Ox → Px)
      3. (x)~~Mx   1, QN
      4. (x)Mx   3, DN
      5. (Mx • Ox) → Px   2, UI
      6. Mx → (Ox → Px)   5, Exp
      7. Mx   4, UI
      8. Ox → Px   6, 7, MP
      9. (x)(Ox → Px)   8, UG

2.   1. (∃y)Fy
      2. ~(∃z)(Fz • ~Hz)
      3. (z)[Fz → (~Gz → ~Hz)]   ∴ (∃y)Gy
      4. Fy   1, EI
      5. (z)~(Fz • ~Hz)   2, QN
      6. ~(Fy • ~Hy)   5, UI
      7. ~Fy ∨ ~~Hy   6, DeM
      8. ~~Fy   4, DN
      9. ~~Hy   7, 8, DS
    10. Fy → (~Gy → ~Hy)   3, UI
    11. ~Gy → ~Hy   4, 10, MP
    12. ~~Gy   9, 11, MT
    13. Gy   12, DN
    14. (∃y)Gy   13, EG

3. 1. (v)(Fv • ~Gv)   ∴ ~(∃v)(Fv → Gv)
   2. (v)(~~Fv • ~Gv)   1, DN
   3. (v)~(~Fv ∨ Gv)   2, DeM
   4. (v)~(Fv → Gv)   3, MI
   5. ~(∃v)(Fv → Gv)   4, QN

4. 1. (w)(Bw → ~Cw)   ∴ ~(∃w)(Bw • Cw)
   2. (w)(~Bw ∨ ~Cw)   1, MI
   3. (w)~(Bw • Cw)   2, DeM
   4. ~(∃w)(Bw • Cw)   3, QN

5. 1. (y)[(My • Ny) → Oy]
   2. ~(∃y)~Py
   3. (z)(Pz → Mz)   ∴ ~(∃y)(Ny • ~Oy)
   4. (My • Ny) → Oy   1, UI
   5. (y)~~Py   2, QN
   6. ~~Py   5, UI
   7. Py → My   3, UI
   8. Py   6, DN
   9. My   7, 8, MP
   10. My → (Ny → Oy)   4, Ex
   11. Ny → Oy   9, 10, MP
   12. ~Ny ∨ Oy   11, MI
   13. ~Ny ∨ ~~Oy   12, DN
   14. ~(Ny • ~Oy)   13, DeM
   15. (y)~(Ny • ~Oy)   14, UG
   16. ~(∃y)(Ny • ~Oy)   15, QN

V

1. (∃x)[(Gx • Bx) • Kkx]
2. (x)[Gx → (∃y)(Sy • Kxy)]
3. ~(x)Kkx
4. ~(x)[(Cx • Trx) → Prx]
5. (x)[Gx → ~(Ix • Rx)]
6. (x)([Cx • (~Dx • ~Bx)] → Trx)
7. Rk → (x)(Ox → Tkx)
8. ~(∃x)(Cx • Prx)
9. ~(x)(Gx → Lkx)
10. (x)(Ox → Lrx) → (∃y)(Gy • ~Ry)

VI

1. 1. $(z)(Pz \rightarrow Mz)$
    2. $(y)[(My \lor Ny) \rightarrow Oy]$ $\therefore \sim(\exists y)(Py \cdot \sim Oy)$
    ⎡ 3. $(\exists y)(Py \cdot \sim Oy)$ Assume
    | 4. $Py \cdot \sim Oy$ 3, EI
    | 5. $Py \rightarrow My$ 1, UI
    | 6. $(My \lor Ny) \rightarrow Oy$ 2, UI
    | 7. Py 4, Simp
    | 8. My 5, 7, MP
    | 9. $My \lor Ny$ 8, Add
    | 10. Oy 6, 9, MP
    | 11. $\sim Oy$ 4, Simp
    ⎣ 12. $Oy \cdot \sim Oy$ 10, 11, Conj
    13. $\sim(\exists y)(Py \cdot \sim Oy)$ 3-12, RAA

2. 1. $(\exists x)(y)Fxyx$ $\therefore \sim(x)(\exists y)\sim Fxyx$
    ⎡ 2. $(x)(\exists y)\sim Fxyx$ Assume
    | 3. $(y)Fxyx$ 1, EI
    | 4. $(\exists y)\sim Fxyx$ 2, UI
    | 5. $\sim(y)Fxyx$ 4, QN
    ⎣ 6. $(y)Fxyx \cdot \sim(y)Fxyx$ 3, 5, Conj
    7. $\sim(x)(\exists y)\sim Fxyx$ 2-6, RAA

3. 1. $\sim(y)(\exists x)\sim(Bxy \cdot Byx)$ $\therefore (\exists x)Bxx$
    2. $(\exists y)\sim(\exists x)\sim(Bxy \cdot Byx)$ 1, QN
    3. $\sim(\exists x)\sim(Bxy \cdot Byx)$ 2, EI
    4. $(x)\sim\sim(Bxy \cdot Byx)$ 3, QN
    5. $(x)(Bxy \cdot Byx)$ 4, DN
    6. $Byy \cdot Byy$ 5, UI
    7. Byy 6, Re
    8. $(\exists x)Bxx$ 7, EG

4. 1. $(x)(y)\sim Hxy$
    2. $(\exists y)(x)(Fx \rightarrow Hyx)$ $\therefore \sim(x)Fx$
    3. $(x)(Fx \rightarrow Hzx)$ 2, EI
    4. $Fx \rightarrow Hzx$ 3, UI
    5. $(y)\sim Hzy$ 1, UI
    6. $\sim Hzx$ 5, UI
    7. $\sim Fx$ 4, 6, MT
    8. $(\exists x)\sim Fx$ 7, EG
    9. $\sim(x)Fx$ 8, QN

5. 1. $(\exists x)(y)(\sim Axy \rightarrow Ayx)$ $\therefore \sim(x)(y)\sim Axy$
    2. $(y)(\sim Axy \rightarrow Ayx)$ 1, EI
    3. $\sim Axx \rightarrow Axx$ 2, UI
    4. $\sim\sim Axx \lor Axx$ 3, MI
    5. $\sim\sim Axx \lor \sim\sim Axx$ 4, DN
    6. $\sim\sim Axx$ 5, Re

```
        7. (∃y)~~Axy              6, EG
        8. ~(y)~Axy               7, QN
        9. (∃x)~(y)~Axy           8, EG
       10. ~(x)(y)~Axy            9, QN
```

VII

```
    1.  (x)(Ax → Dx)
    2.  Wb • (x)(Wx → x = b)
    3.  (Ph • Ch) • (x)[(Px • Cx) → x = h]
    4.  (Ab • Pb) • (x)[(Px • ~x = b) → ~Ax]
        Alternatively:  (Pb • Ab) • (x)[(Px • Ax) → x = b]
    5.  (De • ~He) • (x)[(Dx • ~x = e) → Hx]
    6.  Pd • (x)[(Px • ~x = d) → Tdx]
    7.  Bm • (x)[(Bx • ~x = m) → Smx]
    8.  ~(∃x)Gxg
    9.  (x)(y)[(Sx • Sy) → x = y]
   10.  (∃x)(∃y)[(Sx • Sy) • ~x = y]
   11.  (∃x)Nx
   12.  (∃x)(∃y)[(Nx • Ny) • ~x = y]
   13.  (∃x)[Nx • (y)(Ny → x = y)]
   14.  (∃x)([Wx • (y)(Wy → x = y)] • Tx)
   15.  (∃x)([Ix • (y)(Iy → x = y)] • x = s)
        Alternatively:  Is • (y)(Iy → y = s)
```

VIII

```
    1.  1.  (y)(z)(y = z → Ayz)
        2.  (y)(z)(Azy → Bz)
        3.  ~Ba                   ∴ ~a = b
        4.  (z)(Azb → Bz)         2, UI
        5.  Aab → Ba              4, UI
        6.  ~Aab                  3, 5, MT
        7.  (z)(a = z → Aaz)      1, UI
        8.  a = b → Aab           7, UI
        9.  ~a = b                6, 8, MT

    2.  1.  (∃x)(∃y)x = y → (z)Mz    ∴ Mb
        2.  a = a                    Id
        3.  (∃y)a = y                2, EG
        4.  (∃x)(∃y)x = y            3, EG
        5.  (z)Mz                    1, 4, MP
        6.  Mb                       5, UI
```

3. 1. $(\exists x)(\exists y)x = y \rightarrow (z)(Fz \rightarrow Gz)$
   2. $b = c$ $\therefore Fb \rightarrow Gc$
   3. $(\exists y)b = y$ 2, EG
   4. $(\exists x)(\exists y)x = y$ 3, EG
   5. $(z)(Fz \rightarrow Gz)$ 1, 4, MP
   6. $Fb \rightarrow Gb$ 5, UI
   7. $Fb \rightarrow Gc$ 2, 6, LL

4. 1. $(z)(z = a \rightarrow Gz)$ $\therefore Ga$
   2. $a = a \rightarrow Ga$ 1, UI
   3. $a = a$ Id
   4. Ga 2, 3, MP

5. 1. $(x)(x = a \rightarrow Gx)$
   2. $a = b$ $\therefore (\exists w)Gw$
   3. $b = a \rightarrow Gb$ 1, UI
   4. $b = a$ 2, Sm
   5. Gb 3, 4, MP
   6. $(\exists w)Gw$ 5, EG

FOR FURTHER CONSIDERATION

With the addition of the account of identity to PL, the result is a formal theory of logic that some logicians consider to be the only account of logical form needed to analyze the validity or invalidity of any argument. These logicians, in other words, consider logic just to be predicate logic with identity.[*] Other logicians disagree and contend that there are still some intuitively valid or invalid inferences that standard predicate logic with identity cannot adequately analyze. After all, even some inferences involving identity seem problematic. Consider the following argument:

Harry desires to marry Tina. Tina is the male transvestite in Apartment 2. So, Harry desires to marry the male transvestite in Apartment 2. (h: Harry; t: Tina; Mxy: x desires to marry y; m: the male transvestite in Apartment 2)

The argument seems to be invalid, for Harry might not know that Tina is a transvestite and Harry might not want to marry a transvestite. However, by using the scheme of abbreviation provided (which treats the definite description "the male transvestite in Apartment 2" as a name), we can give an apparently valid symbolization and a simple proof of this argument:

   1. Mrt
   2. $t = m$ $\therefore$ Mrm
   3. Mrm   1, 2, LL

---

[*]See, for instance, W. V. O. Quine, *Philosophy of Logic,* 2nd ed. (Cambridge, Mass.: Harvard University Press, 1986), pp. 1–109ff.

What has gone wrong? Have we mistranslated the argument? Is Leibniz' law flawed, or is the argument valid after all? Is there something unusual about the relation "x desires to marry y" that makes the context a special one? There are other such idioms (such as "knows that," "believes that," and "wonders whether") that create contexts wherein the unrestricted substitution of terms having the same reference is suspect. These contexts have been called "referentially opaque" and have given rise to some classical problems of interpretation.

CHAPTER 10

Induction

Chapter 10, we return to the subject of inductive logic, that area of logic that is concerned with tests for the strength and weakness of arguments. The focus is on the most common types of inductive arguments and the general considerations that determine inductive strength for each type of argument.

CHAPTER HIGHLIGHTS

A **strong** argument is such that it is likely (although not certain or necessary) that if its premises are all true, then its conclusion is also true. A **weak** argument is such that it is *not* likely that if its premises are all true, then its conclusion is also true. A **cogent** argument is an argument that is strong and has premises all of which are true. An **uncogent** argument is an invalid argument that is not cogent (and is thus either a weak argument or a strong argument with at least one false premise). A sound argument cannot have a false conclusion, but a cogent argument, regardless of how strong it is, can have a false conclusion. Every argument that has a valid form is a valid argument, but, in general, an argument's inductive strength is not determined by its form alone. An argument may have the form of a strong argument and yet fail to be strong, because evidence that makes the conclusion less likely has been omitted. A person who gives such an argument can be said to have committed the **fallacy of incomplete evidence**. Whereas the validity of arguments is an all-or-nothing phenomenon, the strength of arguments comes in degrees. Thus, if two arguments are strong, one of them may be stronger than the other.

It is sometimes claimed that valid arguments will always proceed from the general to the specific and that strong arguments will always proceed from the specific to the general. Even though there are strong arguments that have premises about particular things and a general conclusion about kinds of things, there are many strong arguments that don't follow this pattern. Likewise, there are many valid arguments that don't have a generalization as a premise and a conclusion about a particular thing.

In the present context, we can say that a **"properly constructed"** argument is one that (a) has the form of an argument that can be cogent and (b) avoids the fallacy of incomplete evidence. There are several different kinds of arguments that are sometimes strong. A statistical syllogism, an argument from authority, an induction by enumeration, and an argument from analogy are all sometimes strong.

A **statistical syllogism** has the form "_____ percent of As are Bs. *c* is an A. So, *c* is a B." In any argument of this form, the letter "*c*" is replaced by a singular term and "A" and "B" are replaced by class terms. The blank in such an argument is replaced by a numeral between "50" and "100" (exclusive) or by certain words or phrases such as "many," "most," or "the vast majority of."

Arguments from authority have the form "R is a reliable authority regarding S. R sincerely asserts that S. So, S." In any argument of this form, "R" gets replaced by the name of a reliable source of information, and "S" gets replaced by a statement. In general, the more reliable the authority cited and the greater the consensus among authorities regarding the truth of the conclusion, the stronger the argument. A fallacious appeal to unreliable authority has a different form from an argument from authority and is thus a different kind of argument. An argument from authority can fail to be strong when an arguer commits the fallacy of incomplete evidence by overlooking the fact that an authority at least as reliable as the authority cited denies the conclusion. One can avoid committing this fallacy by finding out what a number of distinct reliable authorities have to say about the subject or what authorities who have a special expertise in the subject have to say. An argument from authority can also fail to be cogent when one misquotes or misrepresents the words of the authority cited, thus making one of the premises of the argument false, or when the authority cited does not base a judgment on solid evidence.

An **induction by enumeration** occurs in arguments of the form "_____ percent of a sample of A is B. So, approximately _____ percent of A are B." In any argument of this form, the blank is replaced by a numeral from "0" to "100" (inclusive), "A" is replaced by a class term, and "B" is replaced by either a predicate expression or a class term. In this kind of argument, a certain percentage of a sample of individuals from a population is observed to have a certain property or to be included within a certain class. From this, it is inferred that approximately the same percentage of individuals in the entire population has the property or is included within the class.

The fallacy of incomplete evidence arises in connection with these arguments when the sample is too small or is biased. To avoid such errors in sampling, one needs to take a sample that is representative of the population as a whole. A representative sample is random, of appropriate size, and not distorted due to psychological factors. A sample is **random** if and only if each member of the population has an equal chance of being included within the sample. When it is known that the population exhibits a high degree of uniformity, the randomness of a sample is especially easy to obtain. However, bias can always creep into a sample, sometimes in very subtle ways, and researchers use elaborate methods to avoid biased samples. The appropriateness of the sample size will depend upon the size and uniformity of the population and on the acceptable degree of sampling error. The **sampling error** is the extent to which the percentage of the sample having some feature differs from the percentage of the entire population having that feature. Oddly enough, it is not always true that the larger the population, the larger the sample needs to be. While the margin of error can always be reduced by increasing the size of the sample, reducing the sampling error may not be worth the cost (in time, effort, and/or money), depending on the purposes of the researchers and the availability of resources. Samples may also fail to be representative because of distortion due to psychological factors. The nature of the questions asked on a survey, for example, may render it likely that people will not respond truthfully.

John Stuart Mill proposed five methods to use in reaching conclusions about causes and effects. These methods are the method of agreement, the method of difference, the joint method, the method of concomitant variation, and the method of residues. Unfortunately, the word "cause" is often used ambiguously. By a cause, one may mean an event whose presence is sufficient for some other event to occur, an event whose presence is necessary for some other event to occur, or an event whose presence is neither sufficient nor necessary for some other event to occur but that serves as a triggering event that leads to the occurrence of the other event. Mill's **method of agreement** involves finding a factor that is always present whenever the effect is present. The **method of difference** involves finding a factor that is always followed by the effect and is thus always absent whenever the effect is absent. The **joint method** (of agreement and difference) involves finding a factor that is present when and only when the effect is present. The **method of concomitant variation** is applied when an investigator is searching for a factor whose quantitative changes vary in proportion with quantitative changes in the effect. If most of the effects associated with a particular phenomenon have been accounted for with respect to most of the known causes of that phenomenon, then, according to the **method of residues**, the remaining causes of the phenomenon are responsible for the remaining effects. However, to reason that a certain factor is a cause merely because it conforms to the principles of Mill's methods is not to give a valid argument. Furthermore, to use Mill's method's effectively, we often must rely upon our background knowledge to sort out, from all the various factors associated with an effect, only those factors that may be causally relevant.

Scientific reasoning, in essence, involves describing a phenomenon, formulating hypotheses to explain the phenomenon, and testing these hypotheses for accuracy. In testing a scientific hypothesis, a researcher investigates the empirical consequences the theory would have if it were true, provided that a complex of background theory and assumptions is taken for granted. If what is implied by a scientific hypothesis turns out to be false, the hypothesis is then rejected unless the truth of background theories and/or assumptions is called into question. When a specific implication of a scientific hypothesis is found to be true in a particular case, the hypothesis is said to have a **confirming instance**. If a scientific hypothesis has an overwhelming number or an extraordinary variety of confirming instances, then the hypothesis is often accepted. A good scientific hypothesis is one that (a) is logically consistent with established theory, (b) has explanatory power in that known facts can be inferred from it (including, of course, those facts the hypothesis is supposed to explain), (c) is testable in that it has empirical consequences that can be determined to be true or false, and (d) is the simplest acceptable hypothesis.

Arguments from analogy are arguments of the form "A is similar to B in relevant respects. B has property P. So, A has property P." In any argument of this form, "A" and "B" will be replaced by terms designating particular objects, persons, events, or situations (or types or kinds of such things), and "P" will be replaced by a predicate expression. In evaluating the strength of an argument from analogy, we must determine the extent to which the similarity among the items brought into the analogy provides a reasonable basis for drawing the conclusion. To achieve this end, it usually helps to ask three questions about an argument from analogy: (1) What are the relevant respects in which the items in the analogy are said to be similar? The more respects that are relevant to the possession of the property in question, the stronger is the argument. (2) Are the items in the analogy dissimilar in relevant respects? The more differences between the items in the analogy, the less likely the conclusion will be true, provided that the differences are relevant to a thing's not possessing the property in question. (3) Are there other items that could be brought into the analogy, and, if so, do they or do they not also have the property in question? If there are other items that are similar in the same respects and also have the property in question, the argument is strengthened. If there are other items that are similar in the same respects but do not have the property in question, the argument is weakened. Arguments from analogy are often employed in legal and moral reasoning. Even if we are unable to come finally to a definitive pronouncement regarding the strength of an argument from analogy, the analysis of the argument may still have yielded valuable insights into the nature of the issues the argument addresses.

DISCUSSION OF KEY CONCEPTS

I. Inductive and Deductive Logic: Contrasts and Clarifications

A. Helpful Reminders

1. It is important to keep in mind the nature of strong and weak, and cogent and uncogent, arguments. Even though a review of the crucial distinctions and key definitions occurs in the first part of section 10.1 of *The Power of Logic*, it may be of benefit to you to reread parts of the discussion in Chapter 1 of that text at this time.

2. As a consequence of the definition of inductive strength presented in Chapters 1 and 10 of *The Power of Logic*, an invalid argument will be strong when its corresponding conditional is probably (although not necessarily) true, and an invalid argument will be weak when its corresponding conditional is not likely to be true. (The notion of an argument's corresponding conditional was introduced in Chapter 7.)

3. Note that the strength of an argument is not determined merely by its form, unlike the validity of an argument, which is determined by its form. A weak argument that commits the fallacy of incomplete evidence can have the same form as a strong argument.

B. Commonly Asked Questions

1. What is the relationship between inductive strength and validity?

Valid arguments are neither strong nor weak, for any argument that is either strong or weak is invalid. Furthermore, all invalid arguments are either strong or weak. Valid arguments satisfy a certain rigorous standard for the logical merit of an argument, and, while strong arguments fail to meet this standard, they do nonetheless meet another standard for the logical and practical value of an argument.

2. How generally do you evaluate an argument for its inductive strength?

In very general terms, one evaluates an argument for its inductive strength by determining whether it is a properly constructed argument. In order to determine whether an argument is properly constructed, one must determine whether the argument (1) has the proper form for an argument that may be strong and (2) does not commit the fallacy of incomplete evidence. Weak arguments do not have the form of strong ones and/or fail to take into consideration all the relevant information.

C. Exercises

Indicate whether the following statements are true or false. Justify your answer.

1. Any sound argument is also a cogent argument.
2. Any argument that is not cogent is uncogent.
3. A cogent argument has premises that are all true.
4. The terms "strong" and "weak" are like the terms "valid" and "invalid" in that all arguments are either strong or weak, there being no middle ground.
5. If an argument is not valid, then it is either strong or weak.

II. Arguments from Authority and Induction by Enumeration

A. Helpful Reminders

1. Note that, given the notion of a "properly constructed" argument, any weak argument that has the same form as a strong argument is weak because it commits the fallacy of incomplete evidence. Thus, a weak argument that does not commit the fallacy of incomplete evidence is an argument that does not actually have the same form as a strong argument. This is why arguments that constitute a fallacious appeal to unreliable authority actually have a different form from strong arguments from authority, for the former are weak appeals to authority that do not commit the fallacy of incomplete evidence. Of course, anyone who makes a fallacious appeal to unreliable authority seldom, if ever, presents an argument that is explicitly of the form "R is an authority whose reliability in regard to S can reasonably be doubted. R sincerely asserts that S. So, S." Indeed, the fallacious appeal may not be recognized as such, because the unreliability of the authority cited is not apparent to the audience. (Remember from Chapter 4 that an informal fallacy is a faulty argument not because of its explicit form but because of its content.) Therefore, fallacious appeals to unreliable authority have at least an implicit form that is distinct from the form of a strong argument from authority. So, generalizing, we can say that weak arguments that do not commit the fallacy of incomplete evidence have a form that is at least implicitly distinct from the form of a similar strong argument.

2. In order for an induction by enumeration to be a strong argument, the sample (the set of all cases that have been examined) must be representative of the entire population of things from which the sample is drawn. A speaker or writer who presents an induction by enumeration that is weak because the sample is unrepresentative due to bias is sometimes said to commit the fallacy of biased sampling. A speaker or writer who gives an induction by enumeration that is weak because the sample is unrepresentative due to small sample size is sometimes said to commit the fallacy of hasty generalization.

B. Commonly Asked Questions

1. Is a weak argument from authority always a case of an appeal to unreliable authority?

A weak argument from authority that does not commit the fallacy of incomplete evidence is always an example of an appeal to unreliable authority (and is thus at least implicitly of a form different from that of a strong argument from authority). However, some weak arguments from authority do have the same form as a strong argument from authority and are thus not cases of an appeal to unreliable authority. Such arguments are weak only because they commit the fallacy of incomplete evidence by omitting authoritative testimony that makes the conclusion less likely.

2. How large must the sample size be for an induction by enumeration to be a strong argument?

There is no easy answer to this question. The requisite size of the sample is determined by a number of factors: the size of the population, the manner in which the features of the sample are distributed in the population, the nature of the conclusion, and the arguer's willingness to risk accepting a conclusion that is false or rejecting a conclusion that is true. For the details, consult a good textbook on statistics.

C. Exercises

Identify each of the following arguments as either a statistical syllogism, an argument from authority, an appeal to unreliable authority, or an induction by enumeration.

1. Most Americans are overweight. Joe is an American. So, Joe is overweight.
2. According to some physicists, psychology is not a scientific discipline. Therefore, psychology is not a scientific discipline.
3. Sixty-five percent of Japanese live in Tokyo. Akihiko is Japanese. Thus, Akihiko lives in Tokyo.
4. All the artificial Christmas trees they have at the local Wal-Mart look totally unnatural. Thus, all artificial Christmas trees probably look unnatural.
5. Out of a thousand Americans surveyed in a recent poll, 51 percent said they preferred Coke over Pepsi. Therefore, about 51 percent of all Americans prefer Coke over Pepsi.
6. The vast majority of Roman Catholics and religious fundamentalists in this country believe that abortion is immoral. Thus, the vast majority of people in this country believe that abortion is immoral.
7. Everyone in our party of two hundred became very ill after eating food at Long John Silver's. Thus, people probably should avoid the place, at least at this time, because everyone who eats there will get sick.
8. Since noted herpetologist Joseph Collins says that Texas toads do not occur in Kansas, we can be sure that Texas toads do not occur in Kansas.
9. Although the umpire's back was turned and he did not see the player on first base try to steal second base, the umpire called the player "out." Therefore, the ball must have been thrown to second base before the player got there.
10. The word "truculent" means savage because that is one of the meanings of the word given by the *Oxford English Dictionary*.

III. Mill's Methods and Scientific Reasoning

A. Helpful Reminders

1. It is somewhat easy to confuse Mill's method of agreement with Mill's method of difference. According to the method of agreement, factor F (which is sometimes present and sometimes absent) is a possible cause of an effect E (which is sometimes present and sometimes absent) if the conditional "If E is present, then F is present" is always true. According to the method of difference, factor F is a possible

cause of effect E if the conditional "If F is present, then E is present" is always true. Hence, according to Mill's joint method, recurring factor F is a possible cause of recurring effect E if the biconditional "F is present if and only if E is present" is always true.

2. Note the distinction between saying that a scientific hypothesis is testable and saying that a scientific hypothesis has explanatory power. A scientific hypothesis is in general testable if, by assuming that the hypothesis is true, an investigator can draw conclusions about past observations and make predictions about what will or would happen under certain specifiable circumstances. A scientific hypothesis has explanatory power when it is testable and when what can be inferred from it, if the hypothesis should be true, about past events corresponds with the facts, and the predictions it makes possible about what will or would happen are all true. A scientific hypothesis that allows false statements about past and future phenomena to be deduced from the assumption of its truth is testable without having explanatory power. Thus, a scientific hypothesis can be testable but lack explanatory power.

B. Commonly Asked Questions

1. What is another example of the use of Mill's method of residues?

As another example of the application of the method of residues, consider the case of a veterinarian who wishes to determine the weight of an animal and proceeds as follows. She first weighs an empty cage and then puts the animal in the cage and weighs the cage and the animal together. Knowing how the one effect (the reading on the scale caused by the empty cage) contributes to the total effect (the reading on the scale caused by the cage with the animal in it), she deduces that the remaining causal factor (the animal itself) is responsible for the remaining component effect (that portion of the reading on the scale caused by the animal).

2. What is meant by calling a hypothesis "unscientific"?

What is often meant by saying that a hypothesis is unscientific is that it is not, even in principle, verifiable or is unable to account for the known facts or, in some cases, that it runs contrary to well-established scientific theory.

3. If a new scientific hypothesis must be consistent with current scientific theory that is well established, then how does scientific theory ever change?

In general, good scientific explanations are explanations that do not involve compromising well-established scientific theory. Such theory has been put to the test, and hence there is much empirical evidence that supports it. The forfeiture of such theory often requires that alternative explanations be given for the vast array of phenomena the theory explains, and this may be difficult to accomplish. Thus, in attempting to explain a previously unexplained phenomenon, scientists tend at least initially to propose hypotheses that conform to the existing theoretical framework. However, sometimes an adequate explanation requires bold hypotheses that cannot be accommodated within current scientific theory. Such scientific hypotheses can get accepted and thereby force a change in scientific theory if the new hypotheses can successfully account for the unexplained phenomenon without sacrificing explanations for phenomena the old theory could explain.

C. Exercises

The following chart presents the relationships among the presence and absence of factors A, B, and C and effects X, Y, and Z that have obtained in eight cases. (When a letter occurs by itself, with no tilde attached, this indicates the *presence* of the factor or the effect. When a tilde is attached to a letter, this indicates the *absence* of the factor or the effect.) Answer the questions that follow.

Case #	Factors	Effects
1	A, ~B, C	X, ~Y, Z
2	A, B, ~C	X, Y, ~Z
3	~A, B, C	~X, ~Y, Z
4	~A, ~B, C	~X, Y, Z
5	A, ~B, ~C	X, Y, ~Z
6	~A, B, C	~X, ~Y, Z
7	~A, ~B, ~C	~X, ~Y, Z
8	A, B, C	X, Y, Z

1. What factors may be a cause of effect X, according to Mill's method of agreement?
2. What factors may be a cause of effect X, according to Mill's method of difference?
3. What factors may be a cause of effect X, according to Mill's joint method?
4. What factors may be a cause of effect Y, according to Mill's method of agreement?
5. What factors may be a cause of effect Y, according to Mill's method of difference?
6. What factors may be a cause of effect Y, according to Mill's joint method?
7. What factors may be a cause of effect Z, according to Mill's method of agreement?
8. What factors may be a cause of effect Z, according to Mill's method of difference?
9. What factors may be a cause of effect Z, according to Mill's joint method?

IV. Arguments from Analogy

A. Helpful Reminders

1. An argument from analogy is also sometimes called an argument by analogy or an analogical argument. An arguer who gives an argument from analogy notes a similarity between two (or more) items in a number of respects and draws a conclusion about one item in the analogy on the basis of the similarity. Thus, in an analogical argument, a conclusion is always inferred from the analogy made. However, not every comparison between two or more things will be a component of an argument, for there are nonargumentative uses of analogies. An analogy can occur as part of a description or an explanation of some object or event, and analogies are often used to illustrate difficult or unusual concepts. Speakers and writers often find it useful to compare that which is unfamiliar to that which is familiar in order to convey to an audience the idea of the former. Critics of a particular position or a theory often will compare that position or theory with another one that is clearly absurd for the pur-

pose of ridicule. So, be careful. Just because a speaker or writer draws an analogy in the course of presenting an argument does not necessarily mean that an analogical argument has been offered.

2. Of all the possible questions that can be asked about an analogical argument as a means of assessing its strength, the question of whether the analogy drawn is relevant to establishing the truth of the conclusion is the most important question. In a sense, the three questions that you should ask about arguments from analogy amount to that particular question of relevancy. The more properties the items in the analogy have in common and the less important the dissimilarities between those items are (and the more items there are that are likewise similar and also have the property in question), the greater the likelihood, in general, that there is some basis for drawing the conclusion from the analogy. When there is a basis for drawing the conclusion, the similarities among the items in the analogy are relevant. Analogies are very easy to construct, but for some of them there is no reasonable basis for reaching a meaningful conclusion just from the noted similarities displayed by the items in the analogy. In fact, any two items can be said to be analogous in an infinite number of ways. For example, both the moon and the letter "A" are similar in that neither one of them is the planet Mars, neither one of them is the number 1, neither one of them is the number 2, neither one of them is the number 3, and so on.

B. Commonly Asked Questions

1. What specific steps should one take when asked to evaluate the strength of an argument from analogy?

You should first make sure that you understand the argument in terms of the proper form of an argument from analogy. It may well help to rewrite the argument so that it is an instance of that proper form. If you cannot put the argument into the proper form, then the argument either is defective or relies on information that is being assumed but not explicitly stated. Once you have interpreted the argument in light of the form such arguments are supposed to take, you should then proceed to evaluate the argument by asking the three questions pertaining to arguments from analogy. You should thus inquire about the extent of both the relevant similarities among the items brought into the analogy and the relevant differences between the item the conclusion is about and the other items the premises are about. You should also ask yourself whether other items relevantly similar to the items referred to in the premises likewise have the property mentioned in the conclusion.

2. What determines which similarities and differences among things are relevant when assessing the inductive strength of an argument from analogy?

The similarities among the items involved in the analogy that increase the likelihood that the conclusion is true are relevant. The differences between the item mentioned in the conclusion and the other items brought into the analogy are relevant when they decrease the likelihood that the conclusion is true. The factors that determine which features are relevant and which are not provide a basis for drawing the conclusion. What exactly these factors are in every case is, unfortunately, not easy to specify. When an argument from analogy occurs in science (or in one of the technical arts such as medicine), there is often a theoretical background that provides the basis for reaching the conclusion from the analogy cited. A researcher may, for example, note a similarity between HIV and BIV (a virus that infects cattle) and infer that the same sort of agent that blocks replication of the latter will also block replication of the former. The basis for such an inference may be provided by a theoretical account of the kind of virus of which both HIV and BIV are instances. The similarities between HIV and BIV are thus relevant to drawing the conclusion in virtue of the background theory. When there is no basis for reaching a certain conclusion from a particular analogy, the similarities noted in the argument from that analogy lack the needed relevancy, and the conclusion is most likely little more than a guess.

C. Exercises

For each of the following passages, determine whether an argument from analogy is or is not present.

1. Stars appear to twinkle because the light from distant stars is distorted as it passes through the upper atmosphere in a manner much like the way in which sunlight is distorted when it passes through water.
2. It is sometimes claimed that mathematicians bring certain entities into existence by their definitions. However, this makes no more sense than to say that cartographers bring mountains and oceans into existence by their labeling of regions on a map.
3. Both species and the organisms that make them up come into existence at a particular time, flourish for a time, and then go out of existence. Both species and organisms are composed of parts that are integrated into a functioning whole. Since a particular organism is clearly an individual, a particular species also must be an individual and therefore not a kind.
4. The relation between the intension of a term and the extension of a term is much like the relation between a picture of a thing and the thing depicted. For every picture there does not always exist in reality the thing depicted, but everything that exists in reality can be depicted. Furthermore, pictures that are identical depict the same thing, but one and the same thing can be depicted by pictures that are different.
5. The Venus flytrap is an insectivorous plant that grows traps that snap shut like bear traps and have toothlike projections to imprison insects like the bars of a cage.

ANSWERS TO EXERCISES

Answers to Selected Exercises in the Text

Exercise 10.1
Part A

1. True. A cogent argument is a strong argument with premises that are all true.
4. True. A strong argument with premises that are all true is a cogent argument.
7. True. A weak argument is one that is not strong and is thus an uncogent argument.
10. False. Valid arguments are neither strong nor weak.

13. True. Weak arguments, as well as strong arguments, are always invalid arguments.
16. False. An argument from analogy, for instance, can be strong and yet not proceed from the specific to the general.
19. False. A valid argument with a false premise is an unsound argument, not an uncogent argument. An uncogent argument is always an invalid argument.

Answers to Supplemental Exercises

I

1. False. A sound argument is valid and is thus neither strong nor weak and therefore neither cogent nor uncogent.
2. False. A valid but unsound argument, for instance, is neither cogent nor uncogent.
3. True. A cogent argument is, by definition, a strong argument all the premises of which are true.
4. False. The strength of arguments, unlike the validity and invalidity of arguments, varies in degrees from those arguments that are very strong and moderately strong to those that are weak and very weak.
5. True. Any argument that is not valid is invalid and is thus either strong or weak.

II

1. statistical syllogism
2. appeal to unreliable authority (Physics and psychology are two distinct disciplines.)
3. statistical syllogism
4. induction by enumeration
5. induction by enumeration
6. induction by enumeration (In addition, this is also a case of biased sampling.)
7. induction by enumeration
8. argument from authority
9. appeal to unreliable authority (Although the umpire has the authority to call the player out, the umpire in this case is not a cognitive authority on whether such a call is legitimate.)
10. argument from authority

III

1. Only factor A is a possible cause of effect X, according to the method of agreement.
2. Only factor A is a possible cause of effect X, according to the method of difference.
3. Only factor A is a possible cause of effect X, according to the joint method.
4. No factor is a possible cause of effect Y, according to the method of agreement.

5. No factor is a possible cause of effect Y, according to the method of difference.
6. No factor is a possible cause of effect Y, according to the joint method.
7. No factor is a possible cause of effect Z, according to the method of agreement.
8. Only factor C is a possible cause of effect Z, according to the method of difference.
9. No factor is a possible cause of effect Z, according to the joint method.

IV

1. This is not an argument from analogy.
2. What is stated explicitly in this passage is not an argument from analogy.
3. This is an argument from analogy.
4. This is not an argument from analogy.
5. This is not an argument from analogy.

FOR FURTHER CONSIDERATION

All arguments are either valid or invalid, but some invalid arguments are still worthwhile and are therefore strong while other invalid arguments are worthless and are therefore weak. There are thus in effect two standards for the logical value of an argument. The discussion of what constitutes a valid argument goes smoothly, since the features that fix the validity of an argument are purely formal and are clearly recognized and understood. Unfortunately, the discussion of what determines the strength of an argument turns ugly. We are informed that, in order to determine an argument's inductive strength, we may need to check the background of the authority cited to ensure that the source is reliable or determine whether relevant information has been left out and whether the arguer's ignorance of such information is excusable. What, though, does all this have to do with the *logical* nature of an argument? All these things seem to be extralogical considerations that are only relevant to our judgment about the believability of statements, the practical significance of arguments, or the culpability of one who gives us a bad argument. The discussion of inductive logic thus seems to lead us into a vast gray area that seems to be outside the direct province of logicians.

Let us suggest here a radical proposal. Perhaps inductive logic is a myth. Perhaps the distinction between deductive logic and what has been termed "inductive logic" is not based, in the final analysis, on a purely logical distinction. Arguments in the real world are often imprecisely stated and typically occur in the context of other relevant information that is being taken for granted. Some or all of this extra information may not be explicitly stated. You have to be aware of any roughness in the way an argument is stated and must often take into consideration this background information in order to reconstruct an argument in an accurate way and to assess its validity or its alleged strength. It may be that so-called strong arguments are actually enthymemes and that, if statements detailing the relevant background beliefs and assumptions are added as premises and the conclusions in some cases modified slightly, such arguments are actually valid arguments. Thus, it may be that the arguments that are the concern of what has been known as inductive logic are either invalid arguments or valid arguments whose validity is concealed by the manner in which they are stated.

If the arguments that are the concern of inductive logic are actually enthymemes, then the difficulty posed by the fact that two arguments can have the same form and yet differ in "strength" can be resolved. (Remember that in inductive logic, in contrast with deductive logic, there are no argument forms all instances of which are strong arguments.) Consider the two statistical syllogisms presented in section 10.1 of *The Power of Logic*:

4. Ninety-five percent of women over 30 years of age cannot run the mile in under 5 minutes. Rebekah is a woman over 30 years of age. Hence, Rebekah cannot run the mile in under 5 minutes.

5. Eighty percent of women over 30 who are world-class marathoners can run the mile in under 5 minutes. Rebekah is a woman over 30 who is a world-class marathoner. Therefore, Rebekah can run the mile in under 5 minutes.

Arguments 4 and 5 apparently have the same form, but their conclusions are inconsistent even though their premises are not. So strength, unlike validity, is not determined just by form. Nevertheless, there is a hidden assumption involved in each of these arguments. The conclusion of argument 4 will be warranted, given the nature of statistical inference, only if it is assumed that Rebekah is a typical member of the class of women over age 30 (i.e., that Rebekah has the same chance as any other woman over age 30 of being in the class of people who cannot run the mile in under five minutes). For the same reason, the plausibility of argument 5 rests on the assumption that Rebekah is a typical member of the class of world-class marathoners (i.e., that Rebekah has the same chance as any other world-class marathoner of being in the class of people who can run the mile in under 5 minutes). These two assumptions are incompatible (given the premises in the two arguments), and any complete reconstruction of these arguments will contain these assumptions as premises (together with at least one other premise left out of the original as well as a restatement of the conclusion). So, when fully reconstructed, these two arguments are actually of two different forms. The apparent situation of two arguments with the same form being of different "strength" can perhaps always be accounted for in this manner when the arguments are fully reconstructed.*

How, though, can the notion of there being arguments that vary in their degree of strength be accounted for if all arguments are just valid or invalid (and sound or unsound)? In some strong or weak arguments (particularly arguments that at least implicitly are about probabilities), it is plausible to take the uncertainty of the

---

*The following argument may perhaps represent a complete reconstruction of argument 4:

Ninety-five percent of the population of women over 30 years of age possess the property of not being able to run the mile in under 5 minutes. Rebekah is a typical member of the population of women over 30 years of age. An individual who is a typical member of a population a certain percentage of the members of which possess a particular property has that percentage chance of possessing that property. So, Rebekah has a 95 percent chance of possessing the property of not being able to run the mile in under 5 minutes.

conclusion as being an implicit part of what is stated by the conclusion. The conclusion of such arguments can be restated so as to make the relative degree of certainty explicit. The fact that a certain statement has a particular degree of certitude may then follow from the premises, given certain relevant background information about probabilities. The apparent degree of strength can also be explained by the fact that the unstated premises of strong or weak arguments are believable to varying degrees. If the premises of an argument constitute the basis for believing the conclusion, then any doubt about any one of the premises will, in general, translate into doubt about the conclusion. On this interpretation, strong arguments are valid arguments whose premises can all be held to a relatively high degree of belief, and weak arguments are arguments that are either invalid or valid with premises that can be held to only a relatively low degree of belief. Because the strength and weakness of arguments turns out to be a function of the believability of their premises, it is no wonder that discussions of inductive logic seem to stray from the primary concern of logic.

If our proposal for a "unified field theory" for logic turns out to be tenable, then it will mean that there is essentially only one notion of evidential support or entailment. It will also mean that relatively uniform methods for the evaluation of all arguments are at least theoretically possible. Should this latter possibility be fully realized, it would have the happy consequence of freeing logicians from prying into the personal lives of those who present arguments and those on whose reliability the plausibility of arguments rests.

CHAPTER 11

Probability

The precise determination of the inductive strength of arguments requires the assessment of the probabilities of statements. The present chapter begins with a discussion of three proposals for assigning probabilities to simple statements and then presents some of the basic laws of probability theory. The chapter ends with a discussion of Bayes' theorem, an important mathematical result that we can use to calculate the extent to which the evidence makes hypotheses more or less likely.

CHAPTER HIGHLIGHTS

The probability (P) of an event or of a statement's being true is a number between zero and one. The closer a probability value is to one, the greater is the likelihood of what is assigned that value; the closer a probability value is to zero, the smaller is the likelihood of what is assigned that value. Before we can assign a probability to a compound statement, we must assign a probability to each of its simpler component statements. There are three general strategies that have been proposed to assign probabilities to single events or statements. These three proposed methods are characterized as three theories of probability in section 11.1 of *The Power of Logic*.

According to the **classical theory**, the probability of an event or of a statement being true is calculated as the proportion of the number of possible outcomes that are favorable (i.e., that correspond to the event occurring or make the statement true) to the total number of possible outcomes. Thus, if "P(s)" denotes the probability of the event s or of the statement s being true, and f is the number of favorable outcomes, and n is the total number of possible outcomes, then we have $P(s) = f/n$. However, the technique of counting the numbers of possible outcomes and determining the relevant fraction can be applied to determine a probability only if it is reasonable to make two important assumptions. It must be assumed that (1) every possible outcome is equally likely and (2) all possible outcomes are considered and thus counted. Assumption (1) is known as the **principle of indifference**. Unfortunately, it is not always the case that every possible outcome is equally probable, and sometimes it is difficult or impossible to take into consideration every possible outcome. This method of calculating probabilities is therefore not applicable in every case.

To determine the probability of an event or of a statement's being true according to the **relative frequency theory**, one observes a number of outcomes and keeps track of the number of times the event occurs or the statement is true. The probability is calculated as the proportion of the number of favorable outcomes observed to the total number of outcomes observed. Thus, if f_0 is the number of observed favorable outcomes, and n_0 is the total number of outcomes observed, then we have, as the probability of s, $P(s) = f_0 / n_0$. This strategy of determining probabilities is also not always applicable since it is not always possible to find an appropriate sample of cases among which the observed frequency of favorable outcomes can be used to calculate a probability.

According to the **subjectivist theory** of probability, the probability of an event or statement being true is a person's level of confidence, or degree of belief, that the event will occur or that the statement is true. That degree of belief will be reflected in the odds the person assigns to a bet on the event's occurrence or the statement's truth. These odds represent the probability that the event will occur (or the statement is true) divided by the probability that the event will not occur (or the statement is false). Thus, if a person lays x-to-y odds on s occurring or being true, then the person assigns s the probability determined by the formula, $P(s) = x / (x + y)$. The subjectivist theory may be difficult to apply since people do not always agree on what probability to assign to a particular event or statement.

Regardless of the method or methods employed, once probabilities have been assigned to individual events or statements, the probabilities of compound statements or of complexes of events or statements can be determined according to the laws of probability. The basic laws of probability theory can thus be stated as rules that govern the probabilities associated with various kinds of compound statements, as follows:

Rule 1: If p is a tautology, then $P(p) = 1$. That is, the probability of any tautology is one.

Rule 2: If p is a contradiction, then $P(p) = 0$. That is, the probability of any contradiction is zero.

Rule 3: If p and q are mutually exclusive statements, then $P(p/q) = P(p) + P(q)$. That is, the probability of a disjunction of mutually exclusive statements is equal to the sum of the probabilities of each statement. This rule is the **restricted disjunction rule**. Two statements are **mutually exclusive** if they cannot both be true.

Rule 4: If p is a statement and $\sim p$ is its negation, then $P(\sim p) = 1 - P(p)$. That is, the probability of the negation of a statement is equal to one minus the probability of the statement. This rule is the **negation rule**. A complex of statements is **jointly exhaustive** if it must be the case that at least one of the statements in the complex is true. Since a statement and its negation are jointly exhaustive, the probability of a disjunction of a statement and its negation is one. Since a statement and its negation are mutually exclusive, the probability of a disjunction of a statement and its negation is, by the restricted disjunction rule, equal to the sum of the probability of the statement and the probability of its negation. Thus, the subtraction from one of the probability of a statement will yield the probability of the statement's negation.

Rule 5: If p and q are statements, then $P(p \lor q) = P(p) + P(q) - P(p \bullet q)$. That is, the probability of any disjunction of statements is equal to the sum of the probabilities of each disjunct minus the probability of a conjunction of the statements. This is the **general disjunction rule**. When the statements in the disjunction are mutually exclusive, the probability of the conjunction is zero, and in such a case the general disjunction rule yields the restricted disjunction rule. In addition, since "p → q" is equivalent to "~p ∨ q" (see Chapter 7), and therefore P($p → q$) is equal to P($\sim p ∨ q$), the general disjunction rule and the negation rule allow us to determine the probability of a material conditional. (Unfortunately, statements about conditional probabilities typically do not involve the material conditional.)

Rule 6: If p and q are statements, then P(q/p) = P($p • q$) / P(p). That is, the conditional probability that one statement is true, given the truth of a second statement, is equal to the probability of a conjunction of both statements divided by the probability of the second statement. This is the **conditional rule**.

Rule 7: If p and q are statements, then P($p • q$) = P(p) × P(q/p). That is, the probability of a conjunction is equal to the probability of the left conjunct multiplied by the conditional probability that the right conjunct is true given the truth of the left conjunct. This is the **general conjunction rule**, and it can be derived immediately from the conditional rule.

Rule 8: If p and q are independent statements, then P(p • q) = P(p) × P(q). That is, the probability of a conjunction of independent statements is equal to the product of the probabilities of each conjunct. This is the **restricted conjunction rule**. Two statements are **independent** if the probability of either one does not affect the probability of the other. If p and q are independent, then P(p/q) = P(p) and P(q/p) = P(q). Notice that, in virtue of the restricted conjunction rule, a conjunction of independent statements each one of which is highly probable (or has a probability greater than one-half) may not itself be highly probable (or may itself have a probability less than one half).

Bayes' theorem is an important mathematical theorem that enables us to discover the degree to which a given hypothesis is supported by certain evidence. In order to apply Bayes' theorem, we need to know (1) the **prior** or **antecedent** probability of the hypothesis, P(h), which is the probability of the hypothesis independent of the evidence, (2) the conditional probability of the evidence given that the hypothesis is true, P(e/h), and (3) the conditional probability of the evidence given that the hypothesis is not true, P($e/\sim h$). Of course, the probability that the hypothesis is not true, P($\sim h$), is equal to 1 − P(h) by the negation rule. The evidence e is a statement that summarizes the latest observational evidence. We normally can appeal to background information to determine the probability of the hypothesis h without taking into consideration the evidence e. In light of these considerations, Bayes' theorem can be represented by the following equation.

$$P(h \ / \ e) = \frac{[P(h) \times P(e/h)]}{\{[P(h) \times P(e/h)] + [P(\sim h) \times P(e/\sim h)]\}}$$

Note that, as you would expect due to the negation rule, P(h / e) + P($\sim h / e$) = 1, or, in other words, P($\sim h / e$) = 1 − P(h / e).

Even in cases where we are unable to determine precise numerical values for the three probabilities needed to apply Bayes' theorem, namely, P(h), P(e/h), and P($e/\sim h$), the theorem still may yield useful information about the relationship between the hypothesis and the evidence. In some cases, knowledge of just the relative values of the three probabilities is sufficient to determine whether, according to the theorem, the hypothesis is made more or less likely by the evidence. Typically, this is possible when we have good reasons to believe that the hypothesis is, antecedently, more likely true than false and that the evidence is more likely to obtain given the truth of the hypothesis rather than its falsity. Sometimes, an appreciation of Bayes' theorem can inspire the participants in a philosophical dispute to focus on an assessment of the relative values of the probabilities involved in an application of the theorem and thereby provide structure to a rational dialogue and help motivate strategies of argumentation.

Bayes' theorem can also be generalized to cover cases in which the evidence is being used to assess the probability of more than one hypothesis. Thus, if, for instance, h_1, h_2, and h_3 are three mutually exclusive and jointly exhaustive hypotheses, then Bayes' theorem can also be represented by the following equation.

$$P(h_1/e) = \frac{[P(h_1) \times P(e/h_1)]}{\{[P(h_1) \times P(e/h_1)] + [P(h_2) \times P(e/h_2)] + [P(h_3) \times P(e/h_3)]\}}$$

In a similar fashion, we can extend Bayes' theorem to accommodate any number of mutually exclusive and jointly exhaustive hypotheses by adding the relevant products to the denominator. To apply Bayes' theorem, we must assign values to all the conditional probabilities mentioned in the denominator and to the prior probabilities of at least all but one of the hypotheses. (If we have values for the prior probabilities of all but one of the hypotheses, we can calculate the prior probability of the remaining hypothesis by subtracting the values for all the other hypotheses from one.)

DISCUSSION OF KEY CONCEPTS

I. Three Theories of Probability

A. Helpful Reminders

1. The classical approach to determining probabilities involves counting the number of favorable outcomes and the total number of possible outcomes and then expressing the probability as a ratio of the former number to the latter number. The numbers of possible outcomes must be determined in order to apply this method, and various theorems in probability theory have been deduced that enable one to calculate the relevant numbers easily. If all the possible outcomes are not equally likely, then the classical approach of just counting the numbers of possible outcomes cannot be applied. That is why knowledge of just the numbers of possible outcomes is not always sufficient to determine a probability value. As a consequence, just because, for instance, there being an earthquake tomorrow or there not being an earthquake tomorrow are the two possibilities does not mean that the probability of an earthquake tomorrow is one half.

2. According to the relative frequency idea of probability, the more probable an event the greater the number of times the event should occur in a series of actual outcomes. So, if the probability of an event is x/y, then by the relative frequency

theory you should expect the event to occur x times for every y observed outcomes. This means that, for example, on the hypothesis that the probability of drawing a diamond from a standard deck of playing cards is $1/4$, you should expect, on average, to draw a diamond once out of every four draws from the deck.

2. The subjective probability of an event or of a statement is a person's degree of belief instead of a ratio of possible outcomes or a relative frequency. This degree of belief is reflected in the specific odds the person gives *on* an event's occurrence or a statement's truth. It is also reflected in the odds the person gives *against* an event's occurrence or a statement's truth. The odds on an event reflect the relative degree to which a person believes the event will occur in relation to the degree to which the person believes the event will not occur. Conversely, the odds against an event reflect the relative strength of the latter belief in comparison to the former belief. Any rational person will give x-to-y odds on an event's occurrence if and only if he or she gives y-to-x odds against the event's occurrence.

B. Commonly Asked Questions

1. Given that both the classical theory and the relative frequency theory determine a probability value as a ratio of the number of favorable outcomes versus the total number of outcomes, what really is the difference between the two approaches?

The determination of a probability value on the classical approach results in what is sometimes called the a priori probability of an event or a statement. Such a probability value is not the result of any actual empirical investigation into the matter but reflects only considerations about what is possible. In contrast, the determination of a probability value as an observed relative frequency involves a researcher observing a sample or making a series of observations and noting the number of times an event actually occurs or a statement is true in order to calculate its relative abundance in the sample.

2. Why is it that if someone gives x-to-y odds on some event, then the probability of that event happening is $x/(x+y)$?

A rational person believes that an event either will or will not occur to the maximum extent possible (namely, 1). The acceptance of x-to-y odds on an event means that, for each x units of belief that the event will occur, there are y units of belief that the event will not occur. Thus, by proportioning 1 in an x/y ratio, which requires the division of 1 into $x+y$ units of belief, we obtain $x/(x+y)$ as the subjective probability that the event will occur and $y/(x+y)$ as the subjective probability that the event will not occur.

C. Exercises

For each of the following passages, indicate whether a probability is being determined by (a) the classical theory, (b) the relative frequency theory, or (c) the subjectivist theory.

1. Since there are 52 cards in a standard deck of playing cards, and half of them are black cards, the probability of drawing a black card from a standard deck is $1/2$.
2. Since two of the balls in the box are red, and three of the balls in the box are blue, the probability of drawing a red ball from the box is $2/3$.

3. Out of a thousand automobiles that were observed to pass by a certain spot along the highway, 451 of them were not passenger cars. Thus, 0.451 is the probability that an automobile that is not a passenger car will pass by that spot.
4. There are six sides on a die, and every side is just as likely to come up. Hence, the probability that a two will be thrown on a die is $1/6$.
5. One hundred hybrid *Althea* seeds were planted, and 37 of the seeds yielded plants with blue flowers, while 63 yielded plants with white flowers. Hence, your chance of obtaining a plant with blue flowers by planting one of these hybrid seeds is $37/100$.
6. Tom considers it three times more likely that Bill and Susan will eventually marry than that they will not marry. So, as far as Tom is concerned, the probability of Bill and Susan getting married is $3/4$.
7. Since a person has ten toes, and each toe is equally vulnerable, knowing only that one of the animal-keeper's toes was bitten off by a giant lizard means that the probability that the keeper's left big toe was the one bitten off is $1/10$.
8. Billy believes he is twice as likely to fail the next test than he is not to fail it. So, Billy considers the probability of his failing the next test to be $2/3$.
9. Jian gives 3-to-2 odds that China will invade Taiwan in the next decade. Jian therefore considers the probability that China will invade Taiwan to be $3/5$ and the probability that China will not invade Taiwan to be $2/5$.
10. Out of the ten Tokay geckos born in the collection, only four lived beyond 20 years of age. The probability of a Tokay gecko living beyond 20 years is therefore $4/10$.

II. The Rules of Probability

A. Helpful Reminders

1. When using the laws of probability to figure out a probability value, make sure that you understand the situation adequately and that you apply the appropriate formula. Note that the restricted disjunction rule (Rule 3) applies only to disjunctions with mutually exclusive disjuncts and that the restricted conjunction rule (Rule 8) applies only to conjunctions with independent conjuncts. (Note that, if two statements are independent, then they must be mutually exclusive.) You will usually apply the general disjunction and general conjunction rules (Rules 5 and 7) only when you do not know that you are dealing with mutually exclusive disjuncts or independent conjuncts. Note that the conditional rule (Rule 6) does not give you the probability of a material conditional, and thus a conditional probability is not the probability of such a conditional. Note also that you can always use the negation rule (Rule 4) to figure out the probability of a statement when you have the probability of its negation.

2. A tautology must be true and thus has a probability of 1, and a contradiction cannot be true and thus has a probability of 0. Thus, Rules 1 and 2 are entirely reasonable. The probability of a statement and the probability of its negation must sum to 1, and this consideration alone leads to Rule 4. The plausibility of Rules 3, 5, 6, and 7 can actually be shown with a kind of Venn diagram. The set of all possible outcomes that may be observed in connection with certain events is called the sample

space (S), and each possible outcome is called a sample point. Each event is associated with a particular subset of the sample space that contains all and only those outcomes that correspond to (are favorable to) the event. If we are considering the two events A and B, the general situation can be depicted in the following diagram:

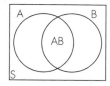

The A-circle represents the subset of S corresponding to event A, and the B-circle represents the subset of S corresponding to event B. The region AB represents the set of all and only those sample points that correspond to both event A and event B. To determine the probability of any particular region (event) in S, you sum the probabilities assigned to the sample points in that region (which just amounts to counting the number of sample points in the region and dividing by the total number of sample points in S if all sample points are equally probable). If A and B are mutually exclusive events, then region AB is empty, and you determine the probability that either A or B will occur by summing the probabilities assigned to all the sample points that are either in A or in B. If A and B are not mutually exclusive events, then you determine the probability that either A or B will occur by summing the probabilities assigned to all the sample points in A and to all those in B and then subtracting the probabilities assigned to the sample points in region AB (since these latter probabilities have been added twice). Thus, Rules 3 and 5 (the disjunction rules) make sense. The probability that an outcome is favorable to B given that it is favorable to A amounts to the probability that any sample point in A is also in B. The conditional probability (B/A) is therefore given by the ratio of the sum of the probabilities assigned to the points in AB to the sum of the probabilities assigned to the points in A. Furthermore, if you already know this ratio, which is P(B/A), and the probability of A, then by multiplying the two values you thereby determine the probability that an outcome is favorable to both A and B. Rules 6 and 7 thus make sense.

B. Commonly Asked Questions

1. How does one know if events or statements are independent?

Two events will be independent if the occurrence or nonoccurrence of one has no effect on the occurrence or nonoccurrence of the other, and two statements will be independent if the truth or falsity of one has no effect on the truth or the falsity of the other. Usually, a consideration of the nature of the events or the statements is sufficient to determine if they are independent. Note that, if you know that two events or statements p and q are such that $P(q/p) = P(q)$ and $P(p/q) = P(p)$, then you can conclude that p and q are independent.

2. Since we need to know $P(p \cdot q)$ in order to determine $P(q/p)$ by Rule 6, and we can determine $P(q/p)$ by Rule 7 only if we know $P(p \cdot q)$, how do we use these rules?

You will use Rule 6 to calculate a conditional probability when you already know the probability of the relevant conjunction or can determine the latter probability independently of Rule 7. You will use Rule 7 to calculate the probability of a conjunction when you already know the relevant conditional probability or can determine the latter probability independently of Rule 6. The conditional rule is generally applied when you know or have determined the probability that a single outcome will be favorable to two events or make two statements true. In contrast, the restricted conjunction rule and the general conjunction rule are most often applied when you need to calculate the probability that two (distinct or not necessarily distinct) events will occur in series.

C. Exercises

Use the rules of probability and the given information to answer the following questions.

1. If a single die is rolled, what is the probability of getting a one?
2. If a single die is rolled, what is the probability of getting either a one or a three?
3. If two dice are rolled, what is the probability of getting a pair of ones ("snake eyes")?
4. If a single card is drawn from a standard deck of playing cards, what is the probability that the card drawn is both a three and a red card?
5. If a single card is drawn from a standard deck of playing cards, what is the probability that the card drawn is either a red card or a face card (i.e., a jack, king, or queen)?
6. If a single card is drawn from a standard deck of playing cards, what is the probability that the card drawn either is a black card or is not a ten?
7. If two cards are drawn successively from a standard deck of playing cards, and the first card drawn is not replaced before the second card is drawn, what is the probability that one black card and one red card will be drawn (not necessarily in that order)?
8. If a fair coin is tossed four times, what is the probability that not every toss will be heads?
9. On average, only one-half of the students who take Statistics 1 pass the course, while four out of every five students who take Statistics 2 succeed in passing. Assuming that passing Statistics 1 is a prerequisite for taking (and thus for passing) Statistics 2, what is the probability that a student who has never taken Statistics 1 and intends to take both statistics classes will end up passing Statistics 2?
10. The germination rate of a certain hybrid seed is 97%, and one out of every three seeds that does germinate will yield a plant with blue flowers. What is the probability that sowing a seed of this hybrid will result in a plant with blue flowers?

III. Bayes' Theorem

A. Helpful Reminders

1. What Bayes' theorem gives us is the conditional probability that the hypothesis under consideration is true given the addition information provided by the evidence obtained. Note that to apply the theorem one needs values for the prior

(antecedent) probabilities that the hypotheses, or the hypothesis and its negation, are true, and for the conditional probabilities that the evidence would obtain given the truth of each hypotheses, or the hypothesis and its negation. Do not confuse the prior probability of a hypothesis with a conditional probability. The prior probability of a hypothesis is the probability that the hypothesis is true in the absence of the additional information provided by the evidence obtained (i.e., the probability that the hypothesis is true if one does not have knowledge of the evidence obtained).

2. The equations given for Bayes' theorem may look complicated, but their plausibility can be shown given some relatively simple considerations. An understanding of the plausibility of the theorem is important since it will make easier remembering the equations and applying them correctly. Consider the most general (and most complicated) equation given for the theorem. We have the evidence e together with the mutually exclusive and jointly exhaustive hypotheses h_1, h_2, and h_3. If any one of the hypotheses could be true, then the hypotheses partition the sample space S into the three regions H_1, H_2, and H_3, respectively. Given that the evidence is compatible with the truth of each hypothesis, some sample points in each of these regions are contained in the set E of all sample points corresponding to the evidence. There is thus a partition of E into the regions E_1, E_2, and E_3 where H_1, H_2, and H_3, respectively, intersect E. The interrelations between these regions are depicted in the following diagram.

If we are determining a value for $P(h_1/e)$, then we want to know what the probability is that an outcome corresponding to the evidence e also corresponds to the hypothesis h_1. This conditional probability is given by the ratio of the sum of the probabilities assigned to the sample points in E_1 to the sum of the probabilities assigned to all the sample points in E. (If every sample point is equally likely, then this ratio is just the number of sample points in E_1 divided by the total number of sample points in E.) Since $E = E_1 + E_2 + E_3$ and each region of E is mutually exclusive, we have the following:

1. $P(H_1/E) = P(E_1)/[P(E_1) + P(E_2) + P(E_3)]$

Since, according to our definitions, $P(H_1/E)$ is just $P(h_1/e)$ and $P(E_1) = P(h_1 \bullet e)$, $P(E_2) = P(h_2 \bullet e)$, and $P(E_3) = P(h_3 \bullet e)$, we can obtain from equation 1, by applying the general conditional rule—i.e., $P(p \bullet q) = [P(p) \times P(q/p)]$—the following equation:

2. $P(h_1 / e) = \dfrac{P(h_1) \times P(e/h_1)}{\{[P(h_1) \times P(e/h_1)] + [P(h_2) \times P(e/h_2)] + [P(h_3) \times P(e/h_3)]\}}$

Equation 2 is just the more general equation for Bayes' theorem. The theorem is thus entirely plausible.

B. Commonly Asked Questions

1. Does one need to know how Bayes' theorem is derived in order to understand and apply the theorem?

It is not necessary to know how Bayes' theorem is derived from a formula for a certain conditional probability in order to understand and apply the theorem. Nevertheless, knowing from what considerations Bayes' theorem is a consequence may well contribute to an understanding of the theorem. Furthermore, in order to apply the theorem correctly, one needs to understand what the theorem enables one to calculate and what information is required to make the calculation.

2. How does Bayes' theorem tell us anything about the probability of the hypothesis given the evidence, when one does not have exact probability values to "plug into" one of the equations?

When the prior probability of the hypothesis and the conditional probability of the evidence given the hypothesis are not at odds, then Bayes' theorem will tell us that the conditional probability of the hypothesis given the evidence will follow suit, even if we only know the relative values of the probabilities involved. More specifically, if we know only that the hypothesis is highly probable even in the absence of the evidence, and the evidence is made more likely by the truth of the hypothesis, then Bayes' theorem will assure us that the hypothesis is made more likely by the evidence. Similarly, Bayes' theorem will assure us that the evidence makes the hypothesis less likely when we know only that the prior probability of the hypothesis is low and the evidence is made less likely by the truth of the hypothesis. Only when the probabilities are at odds will we need specific values for all the probabilities involved in order to reach a conclusion by appealing to one of the equations. The power of Bayes' theorem is that it enables us to take into account the different effects of the various factors quantitatively and to come to a specific conclusion when the evidence obtained runs contrary to the prior probabilities.

C. Exercises

Use Bayes' theorem, together with the information provided, to solve the following problems. (You may use decimal numbers and round to the nearest hundredth.)

1. Only 10 percent of all the concrete used in construction projects is a high-strength concrete made of a special mixture of ingredients. A concrete slab made of the high-strength concrete has a 90 percent chance of withstanding the pressure put on it. In contrast, a concrete slab not made of the high-strength concrete has only a 15 percent chance of withstanding the pressure put on it. Given that a particular slab of concrete has been observed to withstand the pressure put on it, what is the probability that it is made of the high-strength concrete?

2. A community consists of 95 percent knights and 5 percent knaves. A knight answers a question truthfully 99 percent of the time, and a knave answers a question truthfully 90 percent of the time. A person in the community is chosen at random and asked whether he is a knight or a knave. What is the probability that the person chosen is a knight given that he responds to the question by saying he is a knave?

3. A legislative body consists of 45 percent Democrats and 55 percent Republicans. If 10 percent of the Democrats and 75 percent of the Republicans are conservatives, what is the probability that a conservative legislator is a Republican?

4. Tom owns both a sedan and a van. He drives to and from work in the sedan three-fourths of the time and drives to and from work in the van one-fourth of the time. When he drives the sedan, he arrives home from work by six o'clock 75 percent of the time. When he drives the van, he arrives home from work by six o'clock 60 percent of the time. If Tom arrived home from work today by six o'clock, what is the probability that he drove the sedan?

5. A newly established fishing pond is stocked with 40 percent catfish, 50 percent crappie, and 10 percent bass. A catfish will take a live worm 25 percent of the time, a crappie 45 percent of the time, and a bass 55 percent of the time. An inexperienced angler catches a fish he cannot identify. What is the probability that the fish is a crappie given that a live worm was used as bait?

ANSWERS TO EXERCISES

Answers to Selected Exercises in the Text

Exercise 11.1
Part A

   3. 1/2
   5. 1/2
   8. 4/52 = 1/3
  10. 13/52 = 1/4

Part B

1. Of course, even if the coin is fair and the actual probability of getting heads corresponds to what you obtain using the classical theory, you cannot really expect the coin to come up heads exactly 500 times in 1000 tosses.

Part D

1. According to the classical theory, you should expect a six to come up on the die about 16 times in 100 rolls. The classical theory seems not to be applicable in this case (although we cannot really prove that it is not) since the possible outcomes of rolling the die do not appear to be all equally likely.

Exercise 11.2
Part B

8. $13/52 \times 25/51 = 25/204$
9. $4/51$
10. $26/51$

Part C

8. $3/10 + 3/5 - (3/10 \times 9/10) = 63/100$
9. $9/10$
11. $3/10$
14. $9/10 + 3/10 - (9/10 \times 3/10) = 93/100$

Part D

1. Given that the premises are all true, the conclusion is thus two-thirds likely to be true.

Answers to Supplemental Exercises

I

1. (a)   2. (a)   3. (b)   4. (a)   5. (b)   6. (c)   7. (a)   8. (c)   9. (c)   10. (b)

II

1. $1/6$
2. $1/6 + 1/6 = 1/3$
3. $1/6 \times 1/6 = 1/36$
4. $1/13 \times 1/2 = 1/26$
5. $1/2 + 12/52 - 6/52 = 8/13$
6. $1/2 + (1 - 4/52) - 24/26 = 1/2$
7. $[1/2 \times 26/51] + [1/2 \times 26/51]$
   $= 26/51$
8. $1 - 1/16 = 15/16$
9. $1/2 \times 4/5 = 2/5$
10. $97/100 \times 1/3 = 97/300$

III

1. $(0.1 \times 0.9) / [(0.1 \times 0.9) + (0.9 \times 0.15)] = 0.4$
2. $(0.95 \times 0.01) / [(0.95 \times 0.01) + (0.05 \times 0.9)] = 0.17$
3. $(0.55 \times 0.75) / [(0.55 \times 0.75) + (0.45 \times 0.1)] = 0.90$
4. $(0.75 \times 0.75) / [(0.75 \times 0.75) + (0.25 \times 0.6)] = 0.79$
5. $(0.5 \times 0.45) / [(0.5 \times 0.45) + (0.4 \times 0.25) + (0.1 \times 0.55)] = 0.59$

FOR FURTHER CONSIDERATION

The classical approach to determining a probability just by counting the numbers of possible outcomes is severely limited. It cannot be used in cases where the principle of indifference is not satisfied or the outcomes cannot all be taken into consideration by counting them. Many stochastic (probabilistic) processes that are of interest to scientists result in outcomes that vary continuously (or at least can be considered to vary continuously) over a certain range of values. The rate of growth of a bacterial colony under various conditions or the concentration of products given the concentration of reagents, for example, may assume virtually any value within a range determined by certain parameters. In cases where the sample space is not a finite set, discrete probability theory is generally not applicable. Nevertheless, calculus can be used to determine the "density" of (rather than the number of) possible outcomes and the probabilities over various intervals in a manner that is reminiscent of the way probabilities are determined in discrete cases.

Calculus is also needed in order to state precisely the idea of a probability as a relative frequency. Technically speaking, the fraction that represents the frequency with which an event has been observed to occur in the sample is only an estimate of the probability of the event, regardless of the size of the sample. That estimate, though, tends to reflect more accurately the actual probability of the event the larger the sample. As the sample size becomes larger, the observed frequency of an event on average gets closer and closer to one certain value; the relative frequency theorist interprets the probability of the event to be just that value. Certain concepts introduced in calculus are required to give an exact specification of this interpretation of probability.

The subjective probability of an event or of a statement's truth is indeed reflected in the odds that a person attributes to the event's occurrence or the statement's truth. However, the really important issue for the subjective probability theorist is just how such a theorist can identify the odds a person places on, and the probability he attributes to, an event or statement. In order to see how a person's betting behavior can be used to determine these odds and probability, we need to introduce the notion of the expected value of a bet. The expected value of a bet is the average net value of the bet (i.e., the average net gain or loss that would accrue to the individual if he were to make the same bet over and over again). To calculate the expected value of a bet on an event, (1) subtract the amount the person wagered from the amount the person would receive if he won the bet, and multiply this difference by the probability that the event will occur; (2) multiply the amount wagered (the amount lost) by the probability that the event will not occur; and (3) subtract the latter product from the former product. We normally anticipate that people always will make those bets, on or against the occurrence of an event, that will maximize their expected values. When a person does not care which one of two particular bets to make, the person takes the expected value of each bet to be the same.

Now consider the case in which a person is indifferent to wagering a certain amount to bet on the truth of some statement to gain a certain amount and wagering the same amount to bet against the truth of the same statement to gain a different amount. Lets say that the first bet (B_1) involves wagering an amount w in order to gain an amount g_1 in a bet on the truth of the statement a, which has a probability of $P(a)$. The second bet (B_2) involves wagering the same amount w in order to gain an amount g_2 in a bet on the falsity of statement a, the negation of a having a probability of $1 - P(a)$. Since the person is indifferent to making either bet, the expected value of B_1 must equal the expected value of B_2. We thus have the following equation.

$$[(g_1 - w) \times P(a)] - [w \times (1 - P(a))] = [(g_2 - w) \times (1 - P(a))] - (w \times P(a))$$

The above equation can be solved algebraically for P(a). The following sequence of lines represents such a solution. (Multiplication signs have been omitted to save writing.)

$$g_1 P(a) - wP(a) - w + wP(a) = g_2 - g_2 P(a) - w + wP(a) - wP(a)$$
$$g_1 P(a) - w = g_2 - g_2 P(a) - w$$
$$g_1 P(a) = g_2 - g_2 P(a)$$
$$g_1 P(a) + g_2 P(a) = g_2$$
$$P(a)(g_1 + g_2) = g_2$$
$$P(a) = g_2 / (g_1 + g_2)$$

Thus, the probability the person assigns to the statement a is equal to the fraction $g_2 / (g_1 + g_2)$. As a consequence, the person attributes g_2-to-g_1 odds on the statement's truth. This case suggests a general strategy for calculating the odds someone lays on a statement's truth and the probability the person assigns to the statement. Find the amounts g_1 and g_2 such that a person is indifferent to losing a certain amount in a bet on the statement in order to gain g_1 (if the statement is true) and to losing the same amount in a bet against the same statement in order to gain g_2 (if the statement is false). Determine the odds the person gives to the statement's truth as the ratio of the gross amount gained if he bets against the statement and wins to the gross amount gained if he bets on the statement and wins. The probability that the person attributes to the statement is then determined according to the standard formula for figuring the probability from the odds.